DATA SCIENCE AND ANALYTICS

(WITH PYTHON, R AND SPSS PROGRAMMING)

V.K. JAIN

BE(E), M.TECH, FIE, FIETE
CHARTERED AND CONSULTANT ENGINEER
VISITING FACULTY

KHANNA BOOK PUBLISHING CO. (P) LTD.

Publisher of Engineering and Computer Books

4C/4344, Ansari Road, Darya Ganj, New Delhi-110002
Phone: 011-23244447-48 **Mobile:** +91-9910909320
E-mail: contact@khannabooks.com, sales@khannapublishers.com
Website: www.khannabooks.com

Dear Readers,

To prevent the piracy, this book is secured with HIGH SECURITY HOLOGRAM on the front title cover. In case you don't find the hologram on the front cover title, please write us to at contact@khannabooks.com or whatsapp us at +91-99109 09320 and avail special gift voucher for yourself.

Specimen of Hologram on front Cover title:

Moreover, there is a SPECIAL DISCOUNT COUPON for you with EVERY HOLOGRAM.

How to avail this SPECIAL DISCOUNT:

Step 1: Scratch the hologram
Step 2: Under the scratch area, your "coupon code" is available
Step 3: Logon to www.khannabooks.com
Step 4: Use your "coupon code" in the shopping cart and get your copy at a special discount
Step 5: Enjoy your reading!

Price: ₹ 425.00

ISBN: 978-93-86173-67-6

Data Science & Analytics
by Er. V.K. Jain

First Edition: 2018
Reprint: 2025

To view complete list of books,
Please scan the QR Code:

KPH

Published by:
Khanna Book Publishing Co. (P) Ltd.
CIN: U22110DL1998PTC095547

Visit us at: **www.khannabooks.com**
Write us at: **contact@khannabooks.com**

Printed in Bharat.

PREFACE

"Every day,we create 2.5 quintillion bytes of data so much that 90% of the data in the world today has been created in the last two years alone.

The ability to take data, to be able to understand it, to process it, to extract value from it, to visualize it, to communicate it's going to be a at the professional level

As an area of expertise and field, data science is defined as a "concept to unify statistics, data analysis and their related methods" in order to "understand and analyze actual phenomena" with data. It employs techniques and theories drawn from many fields within the broad areas of mathematics, statistics, information science, and computer science, in particular from the subdomains of machine learning, classification, cluster analysis, data mining, databases, and visualization.

Turing award winner Jim Gray imagined data science as a "fourth paradigm" of science (empirical, theoretical, computational and now data-driven) and asserted that "everything about science is changing because of the impact of information technology" and the data deluge.

When Harvard Business Review called it "The Sexiest Job of the 21st Century", the term became a buzzword, and is now often applied to business analytics, or even arbitrary use of data, or used as a sexed-up term for statistics. While many university programs now offer a data science degree, there exists no consensus on a definition or curriculum contents.

Big data is a broad term for data sets so large or complex that traditional data processing applications are inadequate. Challenges include analysis, capture, data curation, search, sharing, storage, transfer, visualization, querying and information privacy. The term often refers simply to the use of predictive analytics or certain other advanced methods to extract value from data, and seldom to a particular size of data set. Accuracy in big data may lead to more confident decision making, and better decisions can result in greater operational efficiency, cost reduction and reduced risk. Big Data and its driving force Hadoop is occupying entire media more than any other single subject. The Hadoop platform provides sufficient coverage in getting mass public opinion in unprecedented manner over a very wide canvas in Zettabyte range 1021.

The overall goal of the book is to provide a broad understanding of big data, data science and analytics in an integrated manner.

While composing this book my intention was not to introduce a collection of new techniques and protocols, but rather to selectively present techniques from those currently available in the public domain.

Computer science has the greatest drawback of non- standardization of the stuff, not only of its software but in courseware also. A vast amount of curriculum exists at different levels of various Universities. As such I have tried to include all desired courseware from the syllabi for different levels.

The various facades of computer science are changing its attributes with such a fast speed that its very difficult to keep track of latest development and its a great task to get aware with the latest happenings in the field. Therefore in presenting the state-of-the art text ware, immense help had been sought by the author from various literature forms who in turn expresses his gratitude to the authors of the works from where information has been derived.

I am to acknowledge with great sense of gratitude to Mrs. Heera Jain and Anurag Jain Director NICT (Vikas Marg Branch) and my publishers especially Mukul Seth for the great help provided in Manu scripting and in preparation of the figures etc.

Er. V.K. Jain

CONTENTS

Chapter 1

INTRODUCTION TO DATA SCIENCE

☞ Learning Objectives and Outcomes

In this unit we will learn about

- ☞ Introduction to core concepts and technologies
- ☞ Familiarity with terminology related with Data Science
- ☞ Dealing with Data science process,
- ☞ Getting acquainted with various popular Data science toolkits
- ☞ Types of data dealt with in Data Science
- ☞ Familiarity with example applications

1.1 DATA SCIENCE

Data science, also known as *data-driven science*, is an interdisciplinary field of scientific methods, processes, and systems to extract knowledge or insights from data in various forms, either structured or unstructured,[1][2] similar to data mining. We shall learn about data mining in short in this unit itself. In fact it is emerging as convergence of various knowledge domains for effective utilisations of various analysis methods for better output of experts in their activities (vide Figure 1.1).

Convergence of various knowledge domains	
Math and Theory	• Statistics, Linear Algebra, Optimization, Time Series, etc.
Applied Algorithms	• Machine Learning, Data Structures, Parallel Algorithms, etc.
Engineering and Technologies	• Storage and computing platforms, statistical tools, etc.
Domain Expertise	• Text, Finance, Images, Economies etc.
Art	• Visualization, Infographics
Best practices and hacks	• Handle missed values in data, transform and represent data, etc.

Fig. 1.1: Data science as convergence of various knowledge domains

As such Data Science is one of the recent fields combining *big data, unstructured data* and *combination of statistics* and *analytics* and *business intelligence*. It is a new field that has emerged within the field of Data Management providing understanding of correlation between structured and unstructured data. More accurately, Data Science is the discipline of using quantitative methods from **statistics** and **mathematics** along with **technology** (computers and software) to develop algorithms designed to discover patterns, predict outcomes, and find optimal solutions to complex problems. Nowadays, data scientists are in great demand as they can transform unstructured data into actionable insights, helpful for businesses.

Data science is blossoming as "concept to unify statistics, data analysis and their related methods" in order to "understand and analyze actual phenomena" with big data.[3]. In its extended canvas (i.e. while dealing with Big. data), data science employs techniques and theories drawn from many fields within the broad areas of mathematics, statistics, information science, and computer science, in particular from the sub-domains of *machine learning, classification, cluster analysis, data lakes data mining and warehousing, databases,* and *visualization* (vide Figure 1.2).We shall learn about dimensions of Big data in this unit very shortly.

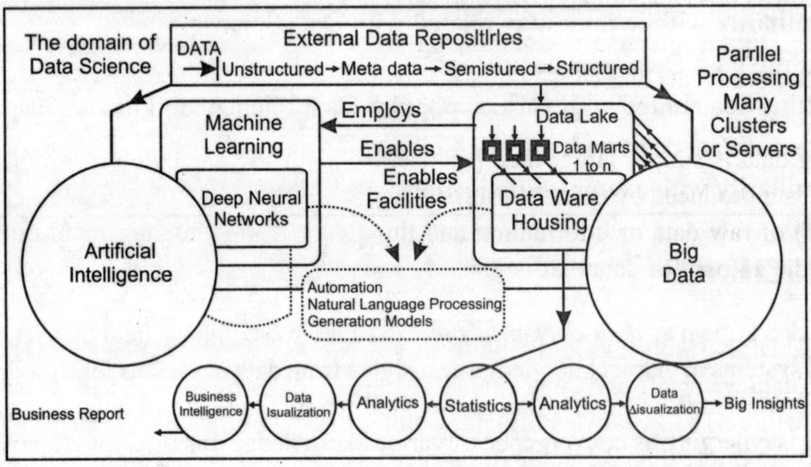

Fig. 1.2: Broad Canvas of Data Science Dealing with Big Data

Turing award winner Jim Gray imagined data science as a "fourth paradigm" of science (empirical, theoretical, computational and now data-driven) and asserted that "everything about science is changing because of the impact of information technology" and the data deluge.[4][5]

1.2 TERMINOLOGY RELATED WITH DATA SCIENCE

1.2.1 Big Data

As per Oxford English Dictionary , the definition of Big Data is "data of a very large size, typically to the extent that its manipulation and management present significant logistical challenges." Actually Big data is a term applied to data sets whose size or type is beyond the ability of traditional relational databases to capture, manage, and process the data with low-latency.

Big data usually includes data sets with sizes beyond the ability of commonly used software tools to capture, curate, manage, and process data within a tolerable elapsed time. For reader's convenience and as memory refresher, I am giving the numeric details of decimal number system below:

1000 (10^3) kB 1 kilobyte

1000 (10^6) MB 1 megabyte

1000 (10^9) GB 1 gigabyte

1000 (10^{12}) TB 1 terabyte

1000 (10^{15}) PB 1 petabyte

1000 (10^{18}) EB 1 exabyte

1000 (10^{21}) ZB 1 zettabyte

1000 (10^{24}) YB 1 yottabyte

Actually 1 KB = 1024 = 2^8 .We have to enhance each of above by this magnitude. A processor with a 64-bit address bus can address 16 exbibytes of memory, which is over 18 exabytes.

As per IDC, Digital universe is doubling in size every two years, and by 2020 the digital universe – the data we create and copy annually – will reach 44 zettabytes, or 44 trillion gigabytes. Between 2013

Because big data is simply larger than life itself, it can offer a detailed rendition of the user. The amount of data produced by users has surpassed the petabyte (10^{15}) level; it has clocked many zettabytes (10^{21}) of raw data or information and this figure is growing at a rapid range. In some years to come, the amount of data that is globally stored is expected to clock the yottabyte (10^{24}) level.

As per IDC, Digital universe is doubling in size every two years, and by 2020 the digital universe i.e. the data we create and copy annually will reach 44 zettabytes, or 44 trillion gigabytes. By 2025, there will be 163 zettabytes of data. Compare it with the human capacity of the human brain that is only not more than 2.5 petabytes as per IBM.

1.2.2 Business Intelligence (BI)

Business Intelligence is the technology which uses the transformed and loaded historical data to get or create the reports. It is a set of methodologies, process, theories that transform raw data into useful information to help companies make better decisions

BI is a process for analyzing data and presenting actionable information to help executives, managers and other corporate end users make informed business decisions and thus help in decision making. Common functions of business intelligence technologies include reporting, online analytical processing, analytics, data mining, process mining, complex event processing, business performance management, benchmarking, text mining, predictive analytics and prescriptive analytics.

Business intelligence can be used by enterprises to support a wide range of business decisions - ranging from operational to strategic. Basic operating decisions include product positioning or pricing. Strategic business decisions involve priorities, goals and directions at the broadest level. Often BI applications use data gathered from a data warehouse (DW) or from a data mart.

1.2.3 Data Analytics

Data analytics and **analytics**, by contrast, are general terms used to describe the field and a comprehensive collection of associated methods. All these terms tend to be used for the application of analytic methods to data that large organizations generate or have available ("big data").We shall learn in detail about application of data science in big data in unit 6 of this book.

Data analysts collect, process and perform statistical analyses of data. Their skills may not be as advanced as data scientists (e.g. they may not be able to create new algorithms), but their goals are the same – to discover how data can be used to answer questions and solve problems.

1.2.3.1 Difference between Big Data & Business Intelligence

The difference between Big Data & Business Intelligence is synonymous to fishing in the sea versus fishing in the lake. ... If you try to understand your business data that is structured and not of huge volume or variety or velocity then you make use of typical business intelligence tools & technologies.

Big Data collectively refers to the act of generating, capturing and usually processing enormous amounts of data on a continuing basis. Unlike business Intelligence, which encompasses only commercial activities, its domain is larger. The data is collected in data lakes and refined in data ware housing through data mining techniques. Refinement is done department wise first in datamarts and then in ware housing.

Business Intelligence collectively refers to software and systems that import data streams of any size and use them to generate informational displays that point towards specific decisions.

Big data is the technology which collects transforms the huge data which is in a unstructured manner. It takes help from Artificial intelligence techniques which demands unusually high rate processing of data. Figure 1.1 is an effort by author to mitigate differences.

1.2.4 Data Wrangling

The process of conversion of data, often through the use of scripting languages, to make it easier to work with is known as data *Wrangling* or *data munging*. If you have 900,000 birthYear values of the format yyyy-mm-dd and 100,000 of the format mm/dd/yyyy and you write a Perl script to convert the latter to look like the former so that you can use them all together, you're doing data wrangling. Discussions of data science often bemoan the high percentage of time that practitioners must spend doing data wrangling; the discussions then recommend the hiring of data engineers to address this

Data engineers build massive reservoirs for big data. They develop, construct, test and maintain architectures such as databases and large-scale data processing systems. Once continuous pipelines are installed to – and from – these huge "pools" of filtered information, data scientists can pull relevant data sets for their analyses.

1.2.5 Algorithm

A series of repeatable steps for carrying out a certain type of task with data. As with data structures, people studying computer science learn about different algorithms and their suitability for various tasks. Specific data structures often play a role in how certain algorithms get implemented.

1.2.6 Machine Learning

Analytics in which computers "learn" from data to produce models or rules that apply to those data and to other similar data. Predictive modelling techniques such as neural nets, classification and regression trees (decision trees), naive Bayes, k-nearest neighbour, and support vector machines are generally included. One characteristic of these techniques is that the form of the resulting model is flexible, and adapts to the data. Statistical modelling methods that have highly structured model forms, such as linear regression, logistic regression and discriminant analysis are generally not considered part of machine learning. Unsupervised learning methods such as association rules and clustering are also considered part of machine learning.

1.2.7 Web Analytics

Statistical or machine learning methods applied to web data such as page views, hits, clicks, and conversions (sales), generally with a view to learning what web presentations are most effective in achieving the organizational goal (usually sales). This goal might be to sell products and services on a site, to serve and sell advertising space, to purchase advertising on other sites, or to collect contact information. Key challenges in web analytics are the volume and constant flow of data, and the navigational complexity and sometimes lengthy gaps that precede users' relevant web decisions.

1.3 METHODS OF DATA REPOSITORY

Data repository is a somewhat general term used to refer to a destination designated for data storage.A data repository refers to an enterprise data storage entity (or sometimes entities) into which data has been specifically partitioned for an analytical or reporting purpose.

Data repositories may assume several different shapes like:

1. Data lakes ,
2. Data Marts
3. Data Ware Housing
4. Big Data and Hadoop and similar frameworks.

1.3.1 Data Lake

A data lake is a storage repository that holds a vast amount of raw data in its native format until it is needed and refined elsewhere. Data lake shares a data environment that comprises multiple repositories and capitalizes on big data technologies. It provides data to an organization for a variety of analytics processes.

A data lake is a storage repository that holds an enormous amount of raw or refined data in native format until it is accessed. The term data lake is usually associated with Hadoop-oriented object storage in which an organization's data is loaded into the Hadoop platform and then business analytics and data-mining tools are applied to the data where it resides on the Hadoop cluster.

To enable operations managers to become more data-driven, the corporates set up a Hadoop data lake environment that also includes HBase, Hive, the Spark processing engine, the Kafka message queueing system and a mix of other technologies. But the data lake platform also includes HBase; Hadoop's companion NoSQL database; the Hive SQL-on-Hadoop software; and various other Apache open source technologies such as Pig, Sqoop, Oozie and Zookeeper.

The data lake blends the historical data with new info — for example, sensor data transmitted via cellular networks from cars, which Allstate uses to monitor mileage, driving and braking speeds, hours spent on the road and other metrics for auto insurance customers who can qualify for premium discounts if they're deemed to be safe drivers.

The data lake concept takes Hadoop deployments to their extreme, creating a potentially limitless reservoir for disparate collections of structured, semi-structured and unstructured data generated by transaction systems, social networks, server logs, sensors and other sources.

However, data lakes can also be used effectively without incorporating Hadoop depending on the needs and goals of the organization. The term data lake is increasingly being used to describe any large data pool in which the schema and data requirements are not defined until the data is queried.

Pentaho CTO James Dixon has generally been credited with coining the term "data lake". He describes a data mart (a subset of a data warehouse) as akin to a bottle of water…"cleansed, packaged and structured for easy consumption" while a data lake is more like a body of water in its natural state. Data flows from the streams (the source systems) to the lake. Users have access to the lake to examine, take samples or dive in. The data lake allows an organization to shift its focus from centralized control to a shared model to respond to the changing dynamics of information management. This enables quick segregation of data into the data lake, thereby reducing the overhead time.

Characteristics of Data Lake:

1. All data is loaded from source systems. No data is turned away.
2. Data is stored at the leaf level in an untransformed or nearly untransformed state.
3. Data is transformed and schema is applied to fulfil the needs of analysis.

1.3.2 Data Warehouse

Data warehousing is the process of constructing and using a data warehouse. A data warehouse is constructed by integrating data from multiple heterogeneous sources that support analytical reporting, structured and/or ad hoc queries, and decision making. Data warehousing involves data cleaning, data integration, and data consolidations. A core component of business intelligence, the data warehouse is a central repository of integrated data from one or more disparate sources, and it's used for reporting and data analysis. It is hierarchical database that stores data in files or folders, a data lake uses a flat architecture to store data.

Wikipedia, defines Data Warehouses as: "central repositories of integrated data from one or more disparate sources. They store current and historical data and are used for creating trending reports for senior management reporting such as annual and quarterly comparisons."

This is a very high level definition that describes the purpose of a data warehouse but doesn't explain how the purpose is achieved.

When the board makes a strategic decision on its future, or a call center agent reviews a customer's profile—the data is typically being sourced from a data warehouse.

The term "Data Warehouse" was first coined by Bill Inmon in 1990. According to Inmon, a data warehouse is a subject oriented, integrated, time-variant, and non-volatile collection of data. This data helps analysts to take informed decisions in an organization.

An operational database undergoes frequent changes on a daily basis on account of the transactions that take place. Suppose a business executive wants to analyze previous feedback on any data such as a product, a supplier, or any consumer data, then the executive will have no data available to analyze because the previous data has been updated due to transactions.

A data warehouses provides us generalized and consolidated data in multidimensional view. Along with generalized and consolidated view of data, a data warehouses also provides us Online Analytical Processing (OLAP) tools. These tools help us in interactive and effective analysis of data in a multidimensional space. This analysis results in data generalization and data mining.

Data mining functions such as association, clustering, classification, prediction can be integrated with OLAP operations to enhance the interactive mining of knowledge at multiple level of abstraction. That's why data warehouse has now become an important platform for data analysis and online analytical processing.

1.3.2.1 Understanding a Data Warehouse

1. A data warehouse is a database, which is kept separate from the organization's operational database.
2. There is no frequent updating done in a data warehouse.
3. It possesses consolidated historical data, which helps the organization to analyze its business.
4. A data warehouse helps executives to organize, understand, and use their data to take strategic decisions.
5. Data warehouse systems help in the integration of diversity of application systems.
6. A data warehouse system helps in consolidated historical data analysis

1.3.2.2 Data Warehouse Models

From the perspective of data warehouse architecture, we have the following data warehouse models–

1. Virtual Warehouse
2. Data mart
3. Enterprise Warehouse

1. **Virtual Warehouse:** The view over an operational data warehouse is known as a virtual warehouse. It is easy to build a virtual warehouse. Building a virtual warehouse requires excess capacity on operational database servers.
2. **Data Mart:** Data mart contains a subset of organization-wide data. This subset of data is valuable to specific groups of an organization.

   In other words, we can claim that data marts contain data specific to a particular group. For example, the marketing data mart may contain data related to items, customers, and sales. Data marts are confined to subjects.

   Points to remember about Data Marts

   1. Window-based or Unix/Linux-based servers are used to implement data marts. They are implemented on low-cost servers.
   2. The implementation data mart cycles is measured in short periods of time, i.e., in weeks rather than months or years.
   3. The life cycle of a data mart may be complex in long run, if its planning and design are not organization-wide.
   4. Data marts are small in size.
   5. Data marts are customized by department.
   6. The source of a data mart is departmentally structured data warehouse.
   7. Data mart are flexible.
3. **Enterprise Warehouse:** An enterprise warehouse collects all the information and the subjects spanning an entire organization
   1. It provides us enterprise-wide data integration.
   2. The data is integrated from operational systems and external information providers.
   3. This information can vary from a few gigabytes to hundreds of gigabytes, terabytes or beyond.

1.3.2.3 Process Flow in Data Warehouse

There are four major processes that contribute to a data warehouse –

1. Extract and load the data.
2. Cleaning and transforming the data.
3. Backup and archive the data.
4. Managing queries and directing them to the appropriate data sources.

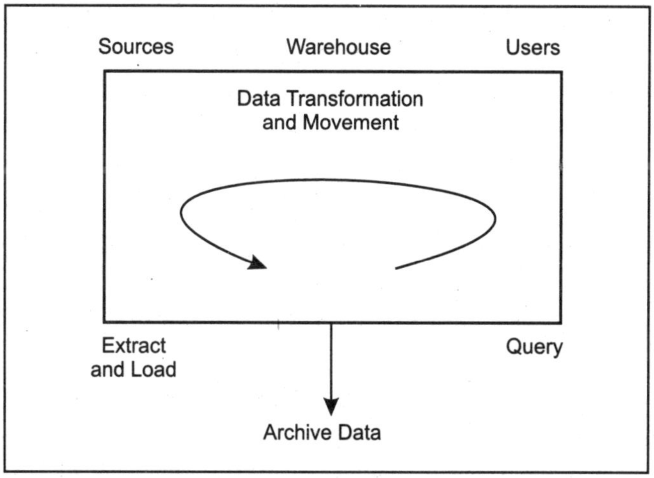

Fig. 1.3: Processes in Data Warehouse

1.3.2.4 Functions of Data Warehouse Tools and Utilities

The following are the functions of data warehouse tools and utilities –

1. **Data Extraction**—Involves gathering data from multiple heterogeneous sources.
2. **Data Cleaning**—Involves finding and correcting the errors in data.
3. **Data Transformation**—Involves converting the data from legacy format to warehouse format.
4. **Data Loading**—Involves sorting, summarizing, consolidating, checking integrity, and building indices and partitions.
5. **Refreshing**—Involves updating from data sources to warehouse.

> **Note:** Data cleaning and data transformation are important steps in improving the quality of data and data mining results.

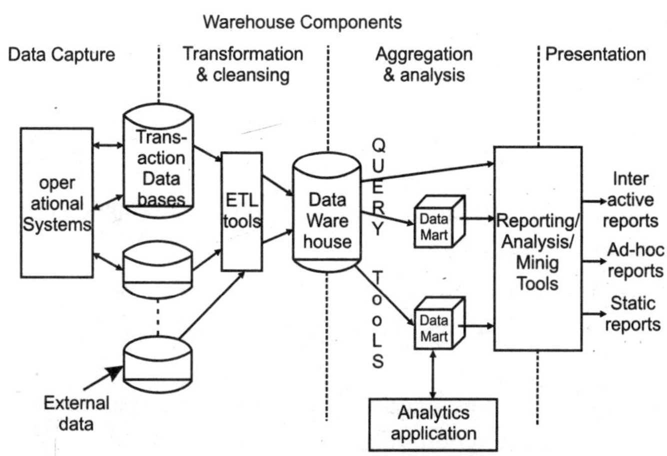

Fig. 1.4: Functions of Data Ware Housing

(*a*) **Extract and Load Process:** Data extraction takes data from the source systems. Data load takes the extracted data and loads it into the data warehouse.

Note: Before loading the data into the data warehouse, the information extracted from the external sources must be reconstructed.

(*b*) **Controlling the Process:** Controlling the process involves determining when to start data extraction and the consistency check on data. Controlling process ensures that the tools, the logic modules, and the programs are executed in correct sequence and at correct time.

(*c*) **When to Initiate Extract:** Data needs to be in a consistent state when it is extracted, i.e., the data warehouse should represent a single, consistent version of the information to the user.

For example, in a customer profiling data warehouse in telecommunication sector, it is illogical to merge the list of customers at 8 pm on Wednesday from a customer database with the customer subscription events up to 8 pm on Tuesday. This would mean that we are finding the customers for whom there are no associated subscriptions.

(*d*) **Loading the Data:** After extracting the data, it is loaded into a temporary data store where it is cleaned up and made consistent.

Note: Consistency checks are executed only when all the data sources have been loaded into the temporary data store.

(*e*) **Clean and Transform Process:** Once the data is extracted and loaded into the temporary data store, it is time to perform Cleaning and Transforming. Here is the list of steps involved in Cleaning and Transforming –

1. Clean and transform the loaded data into a structure
2. Partition the data
3. Aggregation

(*f*) **Clean and Transform the Loaded Data into a Structure:** Cleaning and transforming the loaded data helps speed up the queries. It can be done by making the data consistent :

1. within itself.
2. with other data within the same data source.
3. with the data in other source systems.
4. with the existing data present in the warehouse.

Transforming involves converting the source data into a structure. Structuring the data increases the query performance and decreases the operational cost. The data contained in a data warehouse must be transformed to support performance requirements and control the ongoing operational costs.

(*g*) **Partition the Data:** It will optimize the hardware performance and simplify the management of data warehouse. Here we partition each fact table into multiple separate partitions.

(*h*) **Aggregation:** Aggregation is required to speed up common queries. Aggregation relies on the fact that most common queries will analyze a subset or an aggregation of the detailed data.

(*i*) **Backup and Archive the Data:** In order to recover the data in the event of data loss, software failure, or hardware failure, it is necessary to keep regular back ups. Archiving involves removing the old data from the system in a format that allow it to be quickly restored whenever required.

For example, in a retail sales analysis data warehouse, it may be required to keep data for 3 years with the latest 6 months data being kept online. In such as scenario, there is often a requirement to be able to do month-on-month comparisons for this year and last year. In this case, we require some data to be restored from the archive.

(*j*) **Query Management Process**

This process performs the following functions –

1. Manages the queries.
2. Helps speed up the execution time of queris.
3. Directs the queries to their most effective data sources.
4. Ensures that all the system sources are used in the most effective way.
5. Monitors actual query profiles.

The information generated in this process is used by the warehouse management process to determine which aggregations to generate. This process does not generally operate during the regular load of information into data warehouse.

1.4 PERSONNEL INVOLVED WITH DATA SCIENCE

1.4.1 Data Scientist

"A data scientist is someone who is better at statistics than any software engineer and better at software engineering than any statistician." Data science" is often used to define a (new) profession whose practitioners are capable in many or all the above areas; one often sees the term "*data scientist*" in job postings. While "statistician" typically implies familiarity with research methods and the collection of data for studies, "*data scientist*" implies the ability to work with large volumes of data generated not by studies, but by ongoing organizational processes. Due to the complexity of dealing with large datasets and data flows, most of the day-to-day work of a data scientist lies in data pipeline challenges - storing relevant data, getting it into appropriate form for analysis, and managing the real-time implementation of models.

(*a*) **Data Scientist Responsibilities**

On any given day, a data scientist may be required to:

1. Conduct undirected research and frame open-ended industry questions
2. Extract huge volumes of data from multiple internal and external sources
3. Employ sophisticated analytics programs, machine learning and statistical methods to prepare data for use in predictive and prescriptive modeling
4. Thoroughly clean and prune data to discard irrelevant information
5. Explore and examine data from a variety of angles to determine hidden weaknesses,

trends and/or opportunities

6. Devise data-driven solutions to the most pressing challenges
7. Invent new algorithms to solve problems and build new tools to automate work
8. Communicate predictions and findings to management and IT departments through effective data visualizations and reports
9. Recommend cost-effective changes to existing procedures and strategies
10. Every company will have a different take on job tasks. Some treat their data scientists as glorified data analysts or combine their duties with data engineers; others need top-level analytics experts skilled in intense machine learning and data visualizations.

As data scientists achieve new levels of experience or change jobs, their responsibilities invariably change. For example, a person working alone in a mid-size company may spend a good portion of the day in data cleaning and munging. A high-level employee in a business that offers data-based services may be asked to structure big data projects or create new products.

(*b*) Technical Skills Required

- Math (e.g. linear algebra, calculus and probability)
- Statistics (e.g. hypothesis testing and summary statistics)
- Machine learning tools and techniques (e.g. k-nearest neighbors, random forests, ensemble methods, etc.)
- Software engineering skills (e.g. distributed computing, algorithms and data structures)

  Data mining
- Data cleaning and munging
- Data visualization (e.g. ggplot and d3.js) and reporting techniques
- Unstructured data techniques
- R and/or SAS languages
- SQL databases and database querying languages
- Python (most common), C/C++ Java, Perl
- Big data platforms like Hadoop, Hive & Pig
- Cloud tools like Amazon S3

(*c*) Business Skills Required

- **Analytic Problem-Solving:** Approaching high-level challenges with a clear eye on what is important; employing the right approach/methods to make the maximum use of time and human resources.
- **Effective Communication:** Detailing your techniques and discoveries to technical and non-technical audiences in a language they can understand.
- **Intellectual Curiosity:** Exploring new territories and finding creative and unusual ways to solve problems.
- **Industry Knowledge:** Understanding the way your chosen industry functions and how data are collected, analyzed and utilized.

1.4.2 Data Analyst

Data analysts collect, process and perform statistical analyses of data. Their skills may not be as advanced as data scientists (e.g. they may not be able to create new algorithms), but their goals are the same – to discover how data can be used to answer questions and solve problems.

1. Data Analyst Responsibilities

Depending on their level of expertise, data analysts may:

1. Work with IT teams, management and/or data scientists to determine organizational goals
2. Mine data from primary and secondary sources
3. Clean and prune data to discard irrelevant information
4. Analyze and interpret results using standard statistical tools and techniques
5. Pinpoint trends, correlations and patterns in complicated data sets
6. Identify new opportunities for process improvement
7. Provide concise data reports and clear data visualizations for management
8. Design, create and maintain relational databases and data systems
9. Triage code problems and data-related issues
10. Data analysts are sometimes called "junior data scientists" or "data scientists in training." Instead of being free to create their own big data projects, they may be limited to tackling specific business tasks using existing tools, systems and data sets.

2. Technical Skills

- Statistical methods and packages (e.g. SPSS)
- R and/or SAS languages
- Data warehousing and business intelligence platforms
- SQL databases and database querying languages
- Programming (e.g. XML, Javascript or ETL frameworks)
- Database design
- Data mining
- Data cleaning and munging
- Data visualization and reporting techniques
- Working knowledge of Hadoop & MapReduce
- Machine learning techniques
- This is a sample list and subject to change.

3. Business Skills

- **Analytic Problem-Solving:** Employing best practices to analyze large amounts of data while maintaining intense attention to detail.
- **Effective Communication:** Using reports and presentations to explain complex technical ideas and methods to an audience of laymen.
- **Creative Thinking:** Questioning established business practices and brainstorming new approaches to data analysis.

- **Industry Knowledge:** Understanding what drives your chosen industry and how data can contribute to the success of a company/organization strategy

4. Data Science vs. Data Analysis

It's very important to know that data science and Data analysis are little similar but, there so many differences between them. Let's check out the differences

Data Science	Data Analysis
Providing strategic actionable insights into the world	Providing operational observations into issues
Mathematical, technical and strategic knowledge are mandatory	Data analysis and visualization skills required
Deal with big data	Not necessarily deal with big data

1.4.3 Data Engineer

A specialist in data wrangling. "Data engineers are the ones that take the messy data... and build the infrastructure for real, tangible analysis. They run ETL software, marry data sets, enrich and clean all that data that companies have been storing for years."

1. Data Engineer Responsibilities

In his/her role as a hardcore builder, a data engineer may be required to:

1. Design, construct, install, test and maintain highly scalable data management systems
2. Ensure systems meet business requirements and industry practices
3. Build high-performance algorithms, prototypes, predictive models and proof of concepts
4. Research opportunities for data acquisition and new uses for existing data
5. Develop data set processes for data modelling, mining and production
6. Integrate new data management technologies and software engineering tools into existing structures
7. Create custom software components (e.g. specialized UDFs) and analytics applications
8. Employ a variety of languages and tools (e.g. scripting languages) to marry systems together
9. Install and update disaster recovery procedures
10. Recommend ways to improve data reliability, efficiency and quality
11. Collaborate with data architects, modellers and IT team members on project goals
12. Data engineers may work closely with data architects (to determine what data management systems are appropriate) and data scientists (to determine which data are needed for analysis). They often wrestle with problems associated with database integration and messy, unstructured data sets. Their ultimate aim is to provide clean, usable data to whomever may require it.

2. **Desired Technical Skills**

   A bachelor's degree in computer science, software/computer engineering, applied math, physics, statistics or a related field and a lot of real-world skills to qualify for most entry-level positions and additionally:

   1. Statistical analysis and modelling
   2. Database architectures
   3. Hadoop-based technologies (e.g. MapReduce, Hive and Pig)
   4. SQL-based technologies (e.g. PostgreSQL and MySQL)
   5. NoSQL technologies (e.g. Cassandra and MongoDB)
   6. Data modelling tools (e.g. ERWin, Enterprise Architect and Visio)
   7. Python, C/C++ Java, Perl
   8. MatLab, SAS, R
   9. Data warehousing solutions
   10. Predictive modelling, NLP and text analysis
   11. Machine learning
   12. Data mining
   13. UNIX, Linux, Solaris and MS Windows

   Since new data management technologies are appearing every day, this list is subject to change.

3. **Expected Business Skills**

   1. **Creative Problem-Solving:** Approaching data organization challenges with a clear eye on what is important; employing the right approach/methods to make the maximum use of time and human resources.
   2. **Effective Collaboration:** Carefully listening to management, data scientists and data architects to establish their needs.
   3. **Intellectual Curiosity:** Exploring new territories and finding creative and unusual ways to solve data management problems.
   4. **Industry Knowledge:** Understanding the way your chosen industry functions and how data can be collected, analyzed and utilized; maintaining flexibility in the face of big data developments.

1.4.4 Data Architect

Data architects create blueprints for data management systems. After assessing a company's potential data sources (internal and external), architects design a plan to integrate, centralize, protect and maintain them. This allows employees to access critical information in the right place, at the right time.

1. **Data Architect Responsibilities**

   A data architect may be required to:

1. Collaborate with IT teams and management to devise a data strategy that addresses industry requirements
2. Build an inventory of data needed to implement the architecture
3. Research new opportunities for data acquisition
4. Identify and evaluate current data management technologies
5. Create a fluid, end-to-end vision for how data will flow through an organization
6. Develop data models for database structures
7. Design, document, construct and deploy database architectures and applications (e.g. large relational databases)
8. Integrate technical functionality (e.g. scalability, security, performance, data recovery, reliability, etc.)
9. Implement measures to ensure data accuracy and accessibility
10. Constantly monitor, refine and report on the performance of data management systems
11. Meld new systems with existing warehouse structures
12. Produce and enforce database development standards
13. Maintain a corporate repository of all data architecture artifacts and procedures

One shouldn't get surprised to hear that this is a difficult job. Some companies need data architects who are ninjas in data modelling techniques; others want experts in data warehousing, ETL tools, SQL databases or data administration. Most data architects are senior-level employees with plenty of years in business intelligence under their belts.

To become a data architect, you should start with a bachelor's degree in computer science, computer engineering or a related field. Coursework should include coverage of data management, programming, big data developments, systems analysis and technology architectures. For senior positions, a master's degree is usually preferred.

The key aspect of your employment application will be experience. Top employers expect job candidates to have spent at least five years dealing with application architecture, network management and performance management, if not more.

2. Technical Skills Required

1. Application server software (e.g. Oracle)
2. Database management system software (e.g. Microsoft SQL Server)
3. User interface and query software (e.g. IBM DB2)
4. Enterprise application integration software (e.g. XML)
5. Development environment software
6. Backup/archival software
7. Agile methodologies and ERP implementation
8. Predictive modeling, NLP and text analysis
9. Data modeling tools (e.g. ERWin, Enterprise Architect and Visio)
10. Data mining

11. UML
12. ETL tools
13. Python, C/C++ Java, Perl
14. UNIX, Linux, Solaris and MS Windows
15. Hadoop and NoSQL databases
16. Machine learning
17. Data visualization

As always, this list is subject to changes in technology.

3. **Expected Business Skills**
    1. Analytical Problem-Solving: Approaching high-level data challenges with a clear eye on what is important; employing the right approach/methods to make the maximum use of time and human resources.
    2. Effective Communication: Carefully listening to management, data analysts and relevant staff to come up with the best data design; explaining complex concepts to non-technical colleagues.
    3. Expert Management: Effectively directing and advising a team of data modelers, data engineers, database administrators and junior architects.
    4. Industry Knowledge: Understanding the way your chosen industry functions and how data are collected, analyzed and utilized; maintaining flexibility in the face of big data developments.
    5. Data Scientist
    6. Data scientists are big data wranglers. They take an enormous mass of messy data points (unstructured and structured) and use their formidable skills in math, statistics and programming to clean, massage and organize them. Then they apply all their analytic powers – industry knowledge, contextual understanding, scepticism of existing assumptions – to uncover hidden solutions to business challenges.

1.5 TYPES OF DATA

Thus Data and Big Data includes huge volume, high velocity, and extensible variety of data. The data in it will be of three types.

1. Unstructured data : Word, PDF, Text, Media Logs.
2. Semi Structured data : XML data.
3. Meta Data :Data about data
4. Structured data : Relational data.

1.5.1 Unstructured Big Data

Any data with unknown form or the structure is classified as unstructured data. In addition to the size being huge, un-structured data poses multiple challenges in terms of its processing for deriving value out of it. Typical example of unstructured data is, a heterogeneous data source containing a combination of simple text files, images, videos etc. Now a day organizations have wealth of data available with them but unfortunately they don't know how to derive value out of it since this data is in its raw form or unstructured format.

Any data that can be stored, accessed and processed in the form of fixed format is termed as a 'structured' data. Over the period of time, talent in computer science have achieved greater success in developing techniques for working with such kind of data (where the format is well known in advance) and also deriving value out of it. However, now days, we are foreseeing issues when size of such data grows to a huge extent, typical sizes are being in the rage of multiple zettabyte.

An 'Employee' table in a database is an example of Structured Data

Employee_ID	Employee_Name	Gender	Department	Salary_in_lacs
2365	Rajsh Kulkarni	Male	Finance	650000
3398	Pratibha Joshi	Female	Admin	650000
7465	Shushil Roy	Male	Admin	500000
7500	Shubhojit Das	Male	Finance	500000
7699	Priya Sane	Female	Finance	550000

1.5.2 Semi-structured data

Semi-structured data can contain both the forms of data. We can see semi-structured data as a strcutured in form but it is actually not defined with e.g. a table definition in relational DBMS. Example of semi-structured data is a data represented in XML file.

Personal data stored in a XML file

<rec><name>Amitabh Bajaj</name><sex>Male</sex><age>45</age></rec>

<rec><name>Jyotsna Agarwal</name><sex>Female</sex><age>41</age></rec>

<rec><name>Anurag Jain</name><sex>Male</sex><age>39</age></rec>

<rec><name>Subrato Roy</name><sex>Male</sex><age>26</age></rec>

<rec><name>Jeremiah J.</name><sex>Male</sex><age>35</age></rec>

Web pages are generated in scripting of HTML which is also an example of **Semi-structured data.**

1.5.3 Meta Data

Metadata is defined as the data providing information about one or more aspects of the data; it is used to summarize basic information about data which can make tracking and working with specific data easier.[

There are three main types of metadata:

- **Descriptive metadata** describes a resource for purposes such as discovery and identification. It can include elements such as title, abstract, author, and keywords.

- **Structural metadata** indicates how compound objects are put together, for example, how pages are ordered to form chapters.
- **Administrative metadata** provides information to help manage a resource, such as when and how it was created, file type and other technical information, and who can access it. There are several subsets of administrative data; two that are sometimes listed as separate metadata types are:
  1. Rights management metadata, which deals with intellectual property rights, and
  2. Preservation metadata, which contains information needed to archive and preserve a resource.

Metadata Repository

Metadata repository is an integral part of a data warehouse system. It contains the following metadata –

- **Business metadata** – It contains the data ownership information, business definition, and changing policies.
- **Operational metadata** – It includes currency of data and data lineage. Currency of data refers to the data being active, archived, or purged. Lineage of data means history of data migrated and transformation applied on it.
- **Data for mapping from operational environment to data warehouse** – It metadata includes source databases and their contents, data extraction, data partition, cleaning, transformation rules, data refresh and purging rules.
- **The algorithms for summarization** – It includes dimension algorithms, data on granularity, aggregation, summarizing, etc.

1.5.4 Structured

Any data that can be stored, accessed and processed in the form of fixed format is termed as a 'structured' data. Over the period of time, talent in computer science have achieved greater success in developing techniques for working with such kind of data (where the format is well known in advance) and also deriving value out of it. However, now days, we are foreseeing issues when size of such data grows to a huge extent, typical sizes are being in the zettabyte. rage of multiple

An 'Employee' table in a database is an example of Structured Data

Employee_ID	Employee_Name	Gender	Department	Salary_in_lacs
2365	Rajsh Kulkarni	Male	Finance	650000
3398	Pratibha Joshi	Female	Admin	650000
7465	Shushil Roy	Male	Admin	500000
7500	Shubhojit Das	Male	Finance	500000
7699	Priya Sane	Female	Finance	550000

1.6 THE DATA SCIENCE PROCESS (DSP)

DSP is an agile, iterative data science methodology to deliver predictive analytics solutions and intelligent applications efficiently. DSP helps improve team collaboration and learning. It contains a distillation of the best practices and structures from Microsoft and others in the industry that facilitate the successful implementation of data science initiatives. The goal is to help companies fully realize the benefits of their analytics program.

We provide a generic description of the process here that can be implemented with a variety of tools. A more detailed description of the project tasks and roles involved in the lifecycle of the process is provided in additional linked topics.

The process may involve 7 clear cut steps for data analysis as shown in Figure 1.5 :

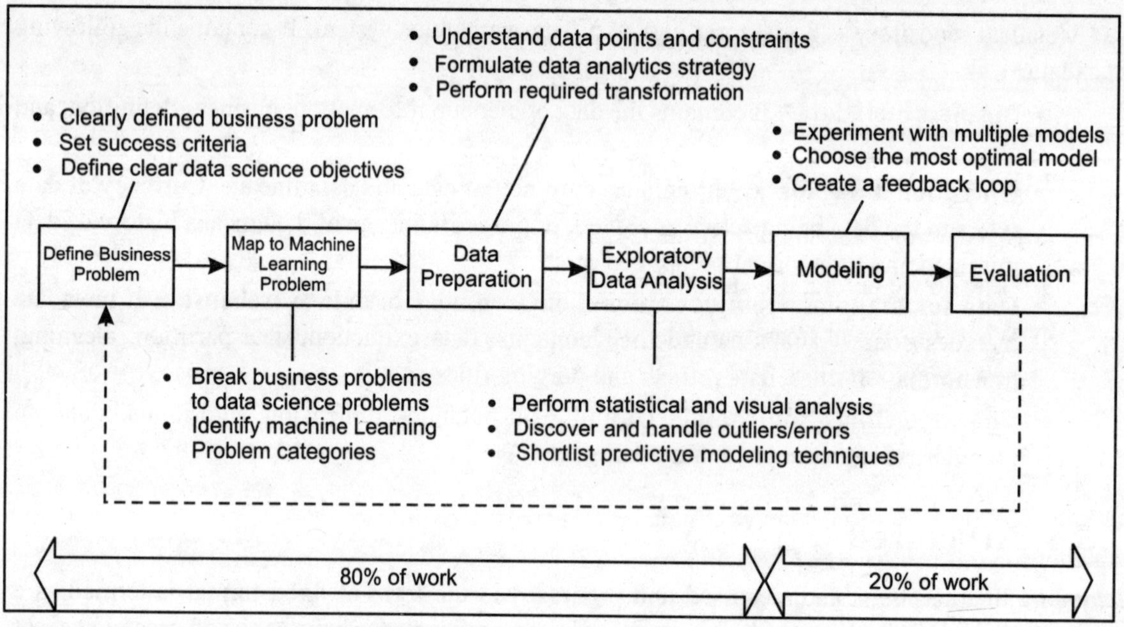

Fig. 1.5: Seven steps of the Data Science Process (DSP)

Step 1: Frame or define the (business) problem

Step 2: Collect the raw data needed for your problem (and map it to machine learning in case of Big data

Step 3: Data Preparation for process the data for analysis

Step 4: Explore the data (Exploratory Data Analysis (EDA)

Step 5: Perform in-depth analysis (Modelling) and producing prescriptive Business Insights

Step 6: Evaluation

Step 7: Visualisation and Communication of Results of the Analyse

Step 1: Frame or define the (business) problem [7]

The first thing you have to do before you solve a problem is to define exactly what it is. You need to be able to translate data questions into something actionable.

You'll often get ambiguous inputs from the people who have problems. You'll have to develop the intuition to turn scarce inputs into actionable outputs–and to ask the questions that nobody else is asking.

Say you're solving a problem for the VP Sales of your company. You should start by understanding their goals and the underlying why behind their data questions. Before you can start thinking of solutions, you'll want to work with them to clearly define the problem.

A great way to do this is to ask the right questions.

You should then figure out what the sales process looks like, and who the customers are. You need as much context as possible for your numbers to become insights.

You should ask questions like the following:

1. Who are the customers?
2. Why are they buying our product?
3. How do we predict if a customer is going to buy our product?
4. What is different from segments who are performing well and those that are performing below expectations?
5. How much money will we lose if we don't actively sell the product to these groups?

In response to your questions, the VP Sales might reveal that they want to understand why certain segments of customers have bought less than expected. Their end goal might be to determine whether to continue to invest in these segments, or de-prioritize them. You'll want to tailor your analysis to that problem, and unearth insights that can support either conclusion.

It's important that at the end of this stage, you have all of the information and context you need to solve this problem.

Step 2: Collect the raw data needed for your problem (and map it to machine learning in case of Big data

Once you've defined the problem, you'll need data to give you the insights needed to turn the problem around with a solution. This part of the process involves thinking through what data you'll need and finding ways to get that data, whether it's querying internal databases, or purchasing external datasets.

You might find out that your company stores all of their sales data in a CRM or a customer relationship management software platform. You can export the CRM data in a CSV file for further analysis. In case of big data, you have to adopt Machine Learning Process.

Step 3: Data Preparation for process the data for analysis

Now that you have all of the raw data, you'll need to process it before you can do any analysis. Oftentimes, data can be quite messy, especially if it hasn't been well-maintained. You'll see errors that will corrupt your analysis: values set to null though they really are zero, duplicate values, and missing values. It's up to you to go through and check your data to make sure you'll get accurate insights.

You'll want to check for the following common errors:

1. Missing values, perhaps customers without an initial contact date
2. Corrupted values, such as invalid entries
3. Timezone differences, perhaps your database doesn't take into account the different timezones of your users
4. Date range errors, perhaps you'll have dates that makes no sense, such as data registered from before sales started
5. You'll need to look through aggregates of your file rows and columns and sample some test values to see if your values make sense. If you detect something that doesn't make sense, you'll need to remove that data or replace it with a default value. You'll need to use your intuition here: if a customer doesn't have an initial contact date, does it make sense to say that there was NO initial contact date? Or do you have to hunt down the VP Sales and ask if anybody has data on the customer's missing initial contact dates?

Once you're done working with those questions and cleaning your data, you'll be ready for Exploratory Data Analysis (EDA).

Step 4: Explore the data (Exploratory Data Analysis (EDA)

When your data is clean, you'll should start playing with it!

The difficulty here isn't coming up with ideas to test, it's coming up with ideas that are likely to turn into insights. You'll have a fixed deadline for your data science project (your VP Sales is probably waiting on your analysis eagerly!), so you'll have to prioritize your questions. '

You'll have to look at some of the most interesting patterns that can help explain why sales are reduced for this group. You might notice that they don't tend to be very active on social media, with few of them having Twitter or Facebook accounts. You might also notice that most of them are older than your general audience. From that you can begin to trace patterns you can analyze more deeply.

Step 5: Perform in-depth analysis (Modelling) and producing prescriptive Business Insights

This step of the process is where you're going to have to apply your statistical, mathematical and technological knowledge and leverage all of the data science tools at your disposal to crunch the data and find every insight you can.

In this case, you might have to create a predictive model that compares your under performing group with your average customer. You might find out that the age and social media activity are significant factors in predicting who will buy the product.

If you'd asked a lot of the right questions while framing your problem, you might realize that the company has been concentrating heavily on social media marketing efforts, with messaging that is aimed at younger audiences. You would know that certain demographics prefer being reached by telephone rather than by social media. You begin to see how the way the product has been has been marketed is significantly affecting sales: maybe this problem group isn't a lost cause! A change in tactics from social media marketing to more in-person interactions could change everything for the better. This is something you'll have to flag to your VP Sales.

Step 6: Evaluation

You can now combine all of those qualitative insights with data from your quantitative analysis to craft a story that moves people to action.

It's important that the VP Sales understand why the insights you've uncovered are important. Ultimately, you've been called upon to create a solution throughout the data science process.

Step 7 : Visualisation and Communication of Results of the Analysis

Proper communication will mean the difference between action and inaction on your proposals.

You need to craft a compelling story here that ties your data with their knowledge. You start by explaining the reasons behind the underperformance of the older demographic. You tie that in with the answers your VP Sales gave you and the insights you've uncovered from the data. Then you move to concrete solutions that address the problem: we could shift some resources from social media to personal calls. You tie it all together into a narrative that solves the pain of your VP Sales: she now has clarity on how she can reclaim sales and hit her objectives.

Throughout the data science process, your day-to-day will vary significantly depending on where you are–and you will definitely receive tasks that fall outside of this standard process! You'll also often be juggling different projects all at once.

It's important to understand these steps if you want to systematically think about data science, and even more so if you're looking to start a career in data science.

1.5.7 Data Science Project's Lifecycle

The Team Data Science Process (TDSP) provides a lifecycle to structure the development of your data science projects. The lifecycle outlines the steps, from start to finish, that projects usually follow when they are executed.

If you are using another data science lifecycle, such as or your organization's own custom process, you can still use the task-based TDSP in the context of those development lifecycles. At a high level, these different methodologies have much in common.

This lifecycle has been designed for data science projects that ship as part of intelligent applications. These applications deploy machine learning or artificial intelligence models for predictive analytics. Exploratory data science projects or ad hoc analytics projects can also benefit from using this process. But in such cases some of the steps described may not be needed.+

CRISP-DM remains the top methodology for data mining projects.CRISP-DM was conceived around 1996.

The 6 high-level phases of CRISP-DM are still a good description for the analytics process, but the details and specifics need to be updated. CRISP-DM does not seem to be maintained and adapted to the challenges of Big Data and modern data science.

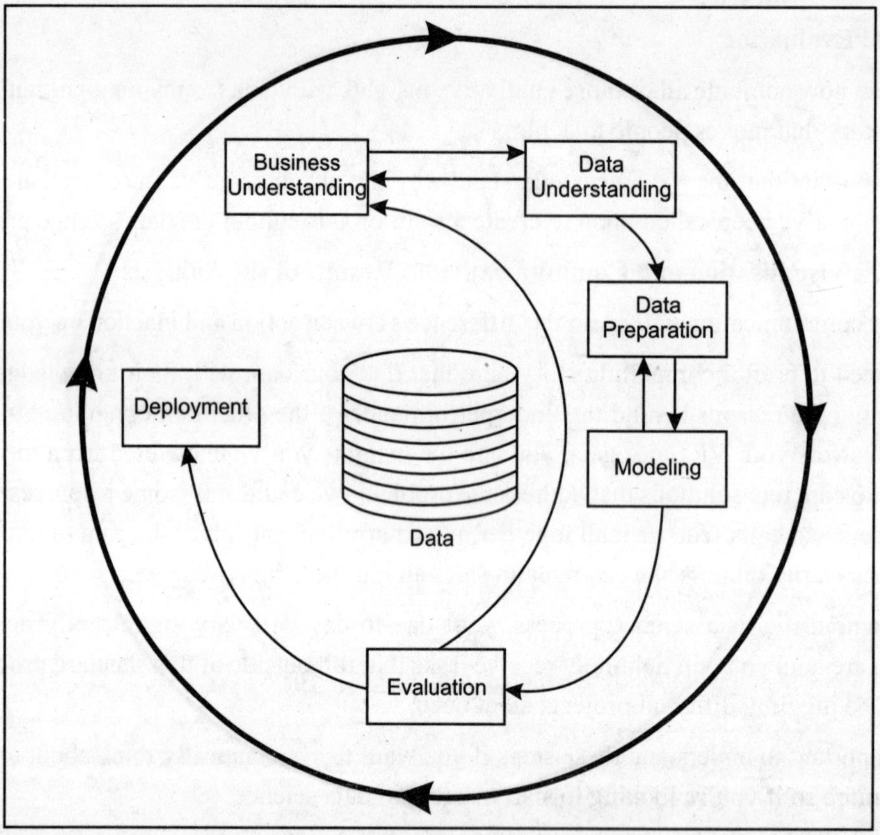

Fig. 1.6: The 6 high-level phases of CRISP-DM suggested for the Data Science Projects

The lifecycle outlines the major stages that projects typically execute, often iteratively:

- Business Understanding
- Data Acquisition and Understanding
- Modeling
- Deployment
- Customer Acceptance

Fig. 1.7 provides a visual representation of the Team Data Science Process lifecycle.

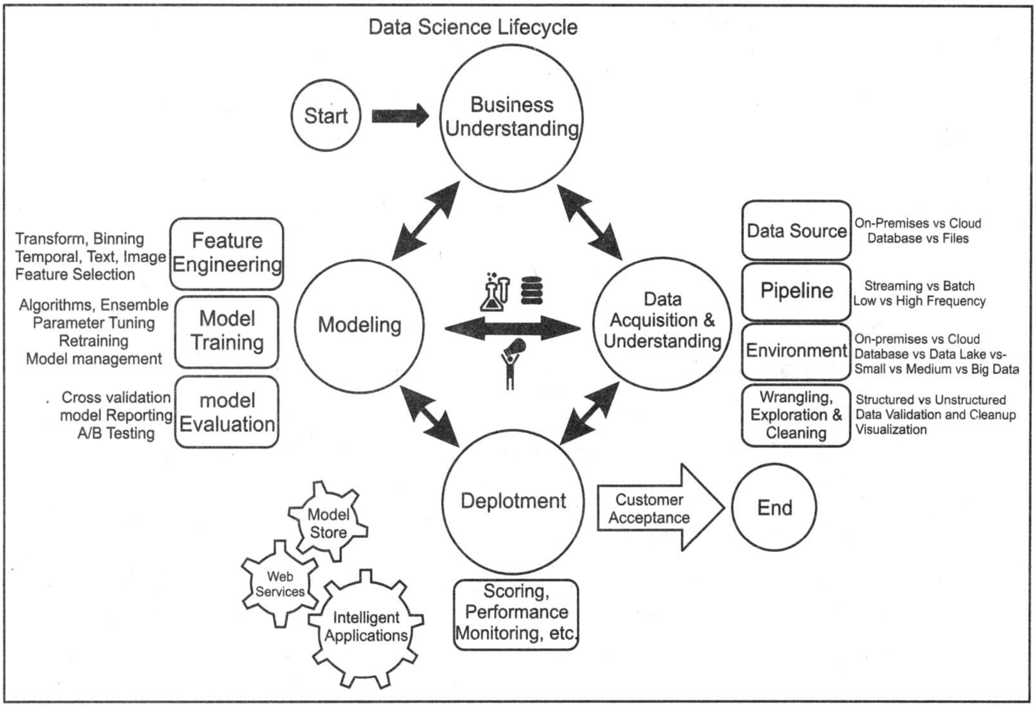

Fig. 1.7: Life Cycle of Data Science Process (Courtesy Microsoft Azure)

1.8 POPULAR DATA SCIENCE TOOLKITS

Tools are an important element of the data science field. The open source community has been contributing to the data science toolkit for years which has led to major advancements to the field. There has been debate in the data science community about the use of open source technology surpassing proprietary software offered by players such as IBM and Microsoft. In fact, many of the big enterprises have started to contribute to open source solutions so they can stay top of mind for users and the data science toolkit has increasingly become one dominated by open source tools.

Since there are a wide variety of open source tools available from data-mining platforms to programming languages, we put together a mix of technology that data scientists could add to their data science toolkit.

Naina Sethi of Spring Board[6] has described such tools in her article. Since there are a wide variety of open source tools available from data-mining platforms to programming languages, we put together a mix of technology that data scientists could add to their data science toolkit. All such tools listed here are free software.

1. **R Programming Language :** R is built by data Scientists for data scientist. R is a programming language used for data manipulation and graphics. Originating in 1995, this is a popular tool used among data scientists and analysts. It is the open source version of the S language widely used for research in statistics. According to data scientists, R is one of the easier languages to learn as there are numerous packages and guides available for users.

R has a steep learning curve and is generally built for stand alone systems. Although there are several packages to speed up the process.

If you are a beginner, I would strongly recommend downloading RStudio which is the de facto IDE for R.

Doing data analysis, building models, communicating results are the core strengths.

The major power of R is it's user community which offers extensive support and has developed the package base CRAN.

A few great packages for you to start exploring in R would be

1. ggplot2/ggvis – Data Visualization
2. dplyr (Data Munging and Wrangling)
3. data.table (Data Wrangling)
4. Caret: (Machine learning workbench)
5. reshape2: (Data Shaping)

We have used this language extensively in Unit 3.

2. **Python :** Python is another widely used language among data scientists, created by Dutch programmer Guido Van Rossem. It's a general-purpose programming language, focusing on readability and simplicity. If you are not a programmer but are looking to learn, this is a great language to start with. It's easier than other general-purpose languages and there are a number of tutorials available for non-programmers to learn. You can do all sorts of tasks such as sentiment analysis or time series analysis with Python, a very versatile general-purpose programming language. You can canvass open data sets and do things like sentiment analysis of Twitter accounts.

   Often the type of problem your solving has a bearing on the choice of language. If the nature of the problem at hand is to do thorough data analysis then I choose R, but If I need to write quick scripts to get things done, scrape the web then it is simpler to use Python.

   According to the data science survey conducted by O'Reilly almost 40% of the data scientists use Python to solve their problems. Python also has a great community of open source packages.

   The learning course about python is given in detail in unit 5 of this book.

3. **KNIME :** KNIME is a software company with headquarters in major tech hubs around the world. The company offers an open source analytics platform written in Java, used for data reporting, mining and predictive analysis. This base platform can be advanced with a suite of commercial extensions offered by the company, including collaboration, productivity and performance extensions.

4. **SQL :** Structured Query Language or SQL is a special-purpose programming language for data stored in relational databases. SQL is used for more basic data analysis and can perform tasks such as organizing and manipulating data or retrieving data from a database. Since SQL has been used by organizations for decades, there is a large SQL ecosystem in existence already which data scientists can tap into. Among data science tools, it ranks as one of the best at filtering and selecting through databases.

5. **Apache Hadoop and other Big data tools :** Apache Hadoop software library is a

framework, written in Java, for processing large and complex datasets. The base modules for the Apache Hadoop framework include Hadoop Common, Hadoop Distributed File System (HDFS), Hadoop Yarn and Hadoop MapReduce.

(*a*) **Apache Mahout:** Apache Mahout is an environment for building scalable machine learning algorithms. The algorithms are written on top of Hadoop. Mahout implements three major machine learning tasks: collaborative filtering, clustering and categorization.

(*b*) **Apache Spark:** Apache Spark is a cluster-computing framework for data analysis. It has been deployed in large organizations for its big data capabilities combined with speed and ease of use. It was originally developed at the University of California as Spark and later, the source code was donated to the Apache Foundation so that it could be free forever. It's often preferred to other big data tools due to its speed.

(*c*) **Impala:** Impala is the massive parallel processing (MPP) database for Apache Hadoop. It's used by data scientists and analysts allowing them to perform SQL queries for data stored in Apache Hadoop clusters.

(*d*) **Apache Storm:** Apache Storm is a computational platform for real-time analytics. It's often compared to Apache Spark and is known as a better streaming engine than Spark. It's written in the Clojure programming language and is known to be a simple, easy to use tool.

(*e*) **MongoDB:** MongoDB is a NoSQL database known for its scalability and high performance. It provides a powerful alternative to traditional databases and makes the integration of data in specific applications easier. It can be an integral part of the data science toolkit if you're looking to build large-scale web apps.

6. **D3 Data Science Tools :** D3 is a javascript library for building interactive data visualizations within your browser. It allows data scientists to create rich visualizations with a high level of customizability. It's a great addition to your data science toolkit if you're looking to dynamically express your data insights.

7. **Tensor Flow :** Tensor Flow is the product of Google's Brain Team coming together for the purpose of advancing machine learning. It's a software library for numerical computation and built for everyone from students and researchers to hackers and innovators. It allows programmers to access the power of deep learning without needing to understand some of the complicated principles behind it, and ranks as one of the data science tools that helps make deep learning accessible for thousands of companies. TensorFlow is an open-source software library for dataflow programming across a range of tasks. It is a symbolic math library, and also used for machine learning applications such as neural networks.

   TensorFlow was developed by the Google Brain team for internal Google use. It was released under the Apache 2.0 open source license on November 9, 2015.

   Keras is a deep learning library written in Python. It runs on TensorFlow allowing for fast experimentation. Keras was developed to make deep learning models easier and helping users treat their data intelligently in an efficient manner.

   We hope you've got some new data science tools for your data science toolkit in this article! Comment below if you can think of any more.

8. **Rstudio :** Rstudio integrates with R as an IDE (Integrated Developmet Environment) to provide further functionality. RStudio combines a source code editor, build automation tools and a debugger.

1.9 FAMILIARITY WITH EXAMPLE APPLICATIONS

1. **Airline Route Planning:** Airline Industry across the world is known to bear heavy losses. Except a few airline service providers, companies are struggling to maintain their occupancy ratio and operating profits. With high rise in air fuel prices and need to offer heavy discounts to customers has further made the situation worse. It wasn't for long when airlines companies started using data science to identify the strategic areas of improvements. Now using data science, the airline companies can:
   1. Predict flight delay
   2. Decide which class of airplanes to buy
   3. Whether to directly land at the destination, or take a halt in between (For example: A flight can have a direct route from New Delhi to New York. Alternatively, it can also choose to halt in any country.)
   4. Effectively drive customer loyalty programs

   Southwest Airlines, Alaska Airlines are among the top companies who've embraced data science to bring changes in their way of working.
2. **Fraud and Risk Detection:** One of the first applications of data science originated from Finance discipline. Companies were fed up of bad debts and losses every year. However, they had a lot of data which use to get collected during the initial paper work while sanctioning loans. They decided to bring in data science practices in order to rescue them out of losses. Over the years, banking companies learned to divide and conquer data via customer profiling, past expenditures and other essential variables to analyze the probabilities of risk and default. Moreover, it also helped them to push their banking products based on customer's purchasing power.
3. **Delivery logistics:** Who says data science has limited applications? Logistic companies like DHL, FedEx, UPS, Kuhne+Nagel have used data science to improve their operational efficiency. Using data science, these companies have discovered the best routes to ship, the best suited time to deliver, the best mode of transport to choose thus leading to cost efficiency, and many more to mention. Further more, the data that these companies generate using the GPS installed, provides them a lots of possibilities to explore using data science.
4. **Uber's Taxy Service:** Uber is a smartphone-app based taxi booking service which connects users who need to get somewhere with drivers willing to give them a ride. The service has been hugely controversial, due to regular taxi drivers claiming that it is destroying their livelihoods, and concerns over the lack of regulation of the company's drivers. This hasn't stopped it from also being hugely successful – since being launched to purely serve San Francisco in 2009, the service has been expanded to many major cities on every continent except for Antarctica.

The business is rooted firmly in Big Data and leveraging this data in a more effective way than traditional taxi firms have managed has played a huge part in its success.

Uber's entire business model is based on the very Big Data principle of crowd sourcing. Anyone with a car who is willing to help someone get to where they want to go can offer to help get them there. Uber holds a vast database of drivers in all of the cities it covers, so when a passenger asks for a ride, they can instantly match you with the most suitable drivers.

Fares are calculated automatically, using GPS, street data and the company's own algorithms which make adjustments based on the time that the journey is likely to take. This is a crucial difference from regular taxi services because customers are charged for the time the journey takes, not the distance covered.

These algorithms monitor traffic conditions and journey times in real-time, meaning prices can be adjusted as demand for rides changes, and traffic conditions mean journeys are likely to take longer. This encourages more drivers to get behind the wheel when they are needed – and stay at home when demand is low. The company has applied for a patent on this method of Big Data-informed pricing, which is calls "surge pricing".

UberPool allows users to find others near to them which, according to Uber's data, often make similar journeys at similar times, and offer to share a ride with them.Changing the way we book taxis is just a part of the grand plan though., it is claimed that the service will also cut the number of private, owner-operated automobiles on the roads of the world's most congested cities. In an interview last year he said that he thinks the car-pooling UberPool service will cut the traffic on London's streets by a third.

Uber's growth in the approximately 7 years of existence can be described by one word, "Phenomenal".But there's another way to define Uber, one that not many have given thought to. Uber is a Big Data company, on the likes of Google and Amazon. It not only uses existing data in its banks effectively for its business operations, but the process of gathering data – data from drivers, data about drivers, data of passengers, data about passengers, data of traffic systems around the world, transactional data – and analyzing all of it in real time, continues. Currently, UBER has more than 8 million users, 1 billion trips and near about 160,000+ people driving for across 66 countries.

5. **Price Comparison Websites:** At a basic level, these websites are being driven by lots and lots of data which is fetched using APIs and RSS Feeds. If you have ever used these websites, you would know, the convenience of comparing the price of a product from multiple vendors at one place. PriceGrabber, PriceRunner, Junglee, Shopzilla, DealTime are some examples of price comparison websites. Now a days, price comparison website can be found in almost every domain such as technology, hospitality, automobiles, durables, apparels etc.

6. **People Analytics:** This application of analytics helps companies manage human resources. The aim is to discern which employees to hire, which to reward or promote, what responsibilities to assign, and similar human resource problems. For example, an analysis may find that individuals that fit a certain type of profile are those most likely to succeed at a particular role, making them the best employees to hire. HR analytics is

becoming increasingly important to understand what kind of behavioral profiles would succeed and fail. While HR analytics is done for employees within the organisation , Customer Segmentation techniques are used on the market to study customer profiles and identify which customers most likely form the target market.

7. **Portfolio analytics:** A common application of business analytics is portfolio analysis. In this, a bank or lending agency has a collection of accounts of varying value and risk. The accounts may differ by the social status (wealthy, middle-class, poor, etc.) of the holder, the geographical location, its net value, and many other factors. The lender must balance the return on the loan with the risk of default for each loan. The question is then how to evaluate the portfolio as a whole.

   The least risk loan may be to the very wealthy, but there are a very limited number of wealthy people. On the other hand, there are many poor that can be lent to, but at greater risk. Some balance must be struck that maximizes return and minimizes risk. The analytics solution may combine time series analysis with many other issues in order to make decisions on when to lend money to these different borrower segments, or decisions on the interest rate charged to members of a portfolio segment to cover any losses among members in that segment.

8. **Risk analytics:** Predictive models in the banking industry are developed to bring certainty across the risk scores for individual customers. Credit scores are built to predict individual's delinquency behavior and widely used to evaluate the credit worthiness of each applicant. Furthermore, risk analyses are carried out in the scientific world and the insurance industry. It is also extensively used in financial institutions like Online Payment Gateway companies to analyse if a transaction was genuine or fraud. For this purpose they use the transaction history of the customer. This is more commonly used in Credit Card purchase, when there is a sudden spike in the customer transaction volume the customer gets a call of confirmation if the transaction was initiated by him/her. This helps in reducing loss due to such circumstances.

9. **Digital analytics:** Digital analytics is a set of business and technical activities that define, create, collect, verify or transform digital data into reporting, research, analyses, recommendations, optimizations, predictions, and automations. This also includes the SEO (Search Engine Optimization) where the keyword search is tracked and that data is used for marketing purposes. Even banner ads and clicks come under digital analytics. A growing number of brands and marketing firms rely on digital analytics for their digital marketing assignments, where MROI (Marketing Return on Investment) is an important key performance indicator (KPI).

10. **Security analytics:** Security analytics refers to information technology (IT) to gather and analyze security events to understand and analyze events that pose the greatest risk. Products in this area include security information and event management and user behavior analytics.

11. **Miscellaneous:** Apart from the applications mentioned above, data science is also used in Marketing, Finance, Human Resources, Health Care, Government Policies and every possible industry where data gets generated. Using data science, the marketing

departments of companies decide which products are best for Up selling and cross selling, based on the behavioural data from customers. In addition, predicting the wallet share of a customer, which customer is likely to churn, which customer should be pitched for high value product and many other questions can be easily answered by data science. Finance (Credit Risk, Fraud), Human Resources (which employees are most likely to leave, employees performance, decide employees bonus) and many other tasks are easily accomplished using data science in these disciplines.

REFERENCES

1. Dhar, V. (2013). "Data science and prediction". Communications of the ACM. 56 (12): 64. doi:10.1145/2500499.
2. Jeff Leek (2013-12-12). "The key word in "Data Science" is not Data, it is Science". Simply Statistics.
3. Hayashi, Chikio (1998-01-01). "What is Data Science? Fundamental Concepts and a Heuristic Example". In Hayashi, Chikio; Yajima, Keiji; Bock, Hans-Hermann; Ohsumi, Noboru; Tanaka, Yutaka; Baba,.
4. Stewart Tansley; Kristin Michele Tolle (2009). The Fourth Paradigm: Data-intensive Scientific Discovery. Microsoft Research. ISBN 978-0-9825442-0-4.
5. Bell, G.; Hey, T.; Szalay, A. (2009). "COMPUTER SCIENCE: Beyond the Data Deluge". Science. 323 (5919): 1297–1298. doi:10.1126/science.1170411. ISSN 0036-8075.
6. Naina sethi, Spring Board article at https://www.springboard.com/blog/data-science-toolkit
7. Raj Bandyopadhyay, Springboard's Director of Data Science Education,"the Data Science Process", which he outlines in detail in his a short 5-day email course.

Chapter 2

DATA MANAGEMENT USING 1BM SPSS

☞ Learning Objectives and Outcomes

After reading the matter of this chapter, the student shall be able to grasp

- ☞ Data collection methods and Management
- ☞ Availability of Data Sources
- ☞ Recognising the functions of APIs,
- ☞ Exploring and fixing data,
- ☞ Learning Data storage and Management Techniques,
- ☞ Knowing how to work with multiple data Sources

2.1 DATA MANAGEMENT PLANNING

A data management plan is an integral part of the research plan. The data plan can be reviewed and expanded during research but main principles and procedures should be determined before the research starts, at the latest before data collection begins.

The aim with data management planning is to ensure that good scientific practice is followed in the research, data are kept safe and secure at all stages of research, and data sharing is possible after the original research has been completed.

Data collection and management aims to maximise efficiency of staff and resources, ensure the collection of accurate and reliable data, and focus on careful management of data once they have been collected. The collection, management and analysis of data, is often a neglected aspect of programme planning and implementation, but has significant effects on programme effectiveness. At the planning stage of the research, researchers should find out whether the research requires ethical review.

2.1.1 Data analysis

Data analysis is at the heart of any scientific investigation. Using weather as an example, this module takes readers through the steps of data collection, analysis, interpretation, and evaluation. The module explores how scientists collect and record data, find patterns in data, explain those patterns, and share their research with the larger scientific community.

Key Concepts

1. Data collection is the systematic recording of information; data analysis involves working to uncover patterns and trends in datasets; data interpretation involves explaining those patterns and trends.
2. Scientists interpret data based on their background knowledge and experience; thus, different scientists can interpret the same data in different ways.
3. By publishing their data and the techniques they used to analyze and interpret those data, scientists give the community the opportunity to both review the data and use them in future research.

2.2 Data Quality

Describe procedures for ensuring data quality during the project. Technical and content decisions made at data entry stage influence the quality of data. Solutions chosen for post-collection processing also have an impact on data quality. Following are the measure to be adopted:

1. Systematic and consistent naming of data files facilitates data management during research as well as data archiving and reuse.
2. Always test the technical instruments and equipment before collecting data.
3. Be systematic and consistent when transcribing data even if you feel that you will only need parts of the data.
4. When recoding variables, use statistical software and, if possible, consider recoding the variables by using syntax.
5. Be consistent in determining values for missing data and 'can't say' type of responses.

The quality and value of any data collection exercise is enhanced by clearly establishing the following elements in advance[14]:

1. the purpose, scope and methodology for the data collection exercise;
2. relevant statistical variables and indicators 1 (e.g. age, gender, country of origin);
3. data collection tools (e.g. questionnaires, surveys, participatory assessments); and
4. parameters for data collection and sharing, such as the inclusion of safeguards to preserve privacy, confidentiality and security of personal information in accordance with data collection standards.

How will ethical issues concerning data management be taken into account?

A good data management plan contains a solution to all the questions specified below.

2.2.1 The Data

- What kind of data are collected/generated?
- In what way are data collected/generated?

What kind of data are collected is mainly determined by the research questions. Research data are typically questionnaire surveys, interviews, focus group discussions, written material, visit or meeting recordings, official documents, archival material, websites, or register or media data.

2.2.2 Ethical Issues : Copy Rights

- Who owns the copyright, Intellectual Property Rights and management rights to data?
- Who has the right to grant access to data?
- What procedures are used to inform research participants?

Copyright issues may be relevant for research data even though most empirical research data are outside the scope of the Finnish Copyright Act. If there are copyright issues involved, the owner of the copyright determines how the data can be used. Data use requires permission from the copyright owner. Regardless of whether data are protected by copyright or not, it is important to clarify the roles of persons involved in the research, since reusers of the data will cite the creators of the data when using it.

Research teams should always make an agreement on data ownership and usage rights. Usage rights should be determined both for the research project and for usage after the project has been completed. Before making any agreements, the requirements of the research funder(s) should be investigated in order to make the agreement follow their guidelines.

If an external contractor is used for data collection, the research team should determine, at the latest when the contract is being made, who is the owner of the data, who has data management responsibility and in what ways research participants are informed of future uses of the data.

Data archives specify access rights to archived data. Official documents are generally freely accessible to researchers. If data created from research have access restrictions, the depositor of the data will determine access conditions to it.

When information is collected directly from research participants, reuse possibilities of the data are determined by the information given to participants on the future uses of the data.

All human subject research must adhere to research ethical principles and data protection legislation. It is essential to carefully plan the information sheets, the procedures of obtaining informed consent from participants, and the anonymisation of data. It is also very important to inform research participants about the fact that the data will be archived.

2.2.3 Confidentiality and Data Security

Confidentiality in the research environment basically means planned and careful processing of personal data. Personal data should only be collected and processed to the degree necessary for the research, and unauthorised access to the data must be prevented. In cases where it is necessary to include personal identification numbers in the data, there must be clear rules about who can process such confidential material.

When data contain personal data, the various Personal Data Act requires that researchers completes a description of the file. There is a separate form for the description of scientific research data files. The data file description adds to the transparency of personal data processing. The description must be shown to research participants if they ask to see it. If data are collected through the Internet, it is also possible to use Privacy Notice form. Privacy Notice is an extended description of a personal data file and provides more detailed information. To avoid any ambiguity, the data file description should contain all information supplied to research participants on data collection, processing and use.

Data security means keeping personal information collected, as well as computer systems, data files and transfers of data safe. It is easy to copy and disseminate digital research data files, or unintentionally destroy or change them. Making back-ups of data files and preventing unauthorised access to them are thus integral parts of data security.

The process of data collection, analysis, and interpretation happens on multiple scales. It occurs over the course of a day, a year, or many years, and may involve one or many scientists whose priorities change over time. One of the fundamentally important components of the practice of science is therefore the publication of data in the scientific literature. Properly collected and archived data continues to be useful as new research questions emerge. In fact, some research involves re-analysis of data with new techniques, different ways of looking at the data, or combining the results of several studies.

One of the most exciting advances in science today is the development of public databases of scientific information that can be accessed and used by anyone. For example, climatic and oceanographic data, which are generally very expensive to obtain because they require large-scale operations like drilling ice cores or establishing a network of buoys across the Pacific Ocean, are shared online through several web sites run by agencies responsible for maintaining and distributing those data, such as the Carbon Dioxide Information Analysis Center run by the US Department of Energy. Anyone can download those data to conduct their own analyses and make interpretations. Likewise, the Human Genome Project has a searchable database of the human genome, where researchers can both upload and download their data.

The number of these widely available datasets has grown to the point where the National Institute of Standards and Technology actually maintains a database of databases. Some organizations require their participants to make their data publicly available, such as the Incorporated Research Institutions for Seismology (IRIS): The instrumentation branch of IRIS provides support for researchers by offering seismic instrumentation, equipment maintenance and training, and logistical field support for experiments. Anyone can apply to use the instruments as long as they provide IRIS with the data they collect during their seismic experiments. IRIS then makes these data available to the public.

2.3 DATA MANAGEMENT PLAN

A data management plan describes how research data are collected or created, how data are used and stored during research and how made accessible for others after the research has been completed.

1. Describe briefly what kind of data will be collected and how they will be collected.
2. Outline the type(s) of data (e.g. survey, interview, observation, face-to-face focus group, self-administered writings/diaries, photographs, news articles etc.) and estimate the foreseeable amount/volume of each datatype.
3. Describe also any existing data you will reuse.

Data file format

File format is a primary factor in accessing and reusing your data in the future. List the file formats you use to save the data, such as CSV, TXT or MP3.

What metadata standard will be used?

Detailed documentation of data contains information on the topic and authors/creators of the data, sampling and data collection methods, and target population, time period and geographic coverage of the data.

1. Create a detailed document that explain terms, variable names and labels, and abbreviations used.
2. Save one empty copy of the questionnaire. If you create a web-based/computer-assisted questionnaire, save the questions and response alternatives in a text file in the order they are presented to the respondents.
3. If the data are created by using source information (books, registers etc.), list the data sources and describe their selection method and define the variables that are used.

Preserving Qualitative Data

Separately preserve all the documents that refer to or have affected the data. These may include interview questions, writing instructions, transcription methods used and information sheets given to research participants.

Documentation of each data unit (e.g. an interview, a text written by a participant, a newspaper article) is necessary to enable archiving and reuse of the data.

2.4 DATA COLLECTION AND MANAGEMENT

Data collection is the process of gathering and measuring information on targeted variables in an established systematic fashion, which then enables one to answer relevant questions and evaluate outcomes. Data collection is a component of research in all fields of study including physical and social sciences, humanities, and business. While methods vary by discipline, the emphasis on ensuring accurate and honest collection remains the same. The goal for all data collection is to capture quality evidence that allows analysis to lead to the formulation of convincing and credible answers to the questions that have been posed.

But collecting data is only one step in a scientific investigation, and scientific knowledge is much more than a simple compilation of data points. The world is full of observations that can be made, but not every observation constitutes a useful piece of data. For example, your meteorologist could record the outside air temperature every second of the day, but would that make the forecast any more accurate than recording it once an hour? Probably not. All scientists make choices about which data are most relevant to their research and what to do with those data: how to turn a collection of measurements into a useful dataset through processing and analysis, and how to interpret those analyzed data in the context of what they already know. The thoughtful and systematic collection, analysis, and interpretation of data allow them to be developed into evidence that supports scientific ideas, arguments, and hypotheses.

Regardless of the field of study or preference for defining data (quantitative or qualitative), accurate data collection is essential to maintaining the integrity of research.

A formal data collection process is necessary as it ensures that the data gathered are both defined and accurate and that subsequent decisions based on arguments embodied in the findings are valid. [1]

A data collection system (DCS) is a computer application that facilitates the process of data collection, allowing specific, structured information to be gathered in a systematic fashion, subsequently enabling data analysis to be performed on the information.[2] Typically a DCS displays a form that accepts data input from a user and then validates that input prior to committing the data to persistent storage such as a database.

Many computer systems implement data entry forms, but data collection systems tend to be more complex, with possibly many related forms containing detailed user input fields, data validations, and navigation links among the forms.

Data collection methods are determined by the type of data sought for. Quantitative data can be collected through interviews, postal or online questionnaires, by using existing source material, or by measuring. Qualitative data are often collected by recording individual interviews, group interviews, sessions or meetings as audio or video files. Written material collection is usually initiated by publishing writing requests or invitations, and then collecting the writings via email, post or a specifically created website. Official documents can nowadays often be obtained from the Internet but some are available only by request or by obtaining permission to use them for research purposes. Access to register data generally requires applying for permission.

Researchers and research teams can collect the data themselves or can contract a data collection company to do it. If data collection is contracted out, it is best to send the call for tender to several companies. Data management plans are useful for drawing up tender calls.

The assumptions here are that an evaluation strategy has been developed that will include data collection in the form of the following quantitative and/or qualitative methods:

1. surveys of adults and/or children in workplaces, schools, health care settings and local communities
2. focus groups
3. key informant interviews
4. environmental scans
5. policy reviews.

The collection of both "qualitative" and "quantitative" data can be helpful to understand the complexities of mixed movements. Qualitative data is data that is non-measurable. It captures feelings, personal experience, attitudes and intentions. It can be obtained from sources such as focus groups, interviews, narrative texts and reports. It can be useful in understanding cultural context or establishing baseline information. By contrast, quantitative data, which is numerical and measurable, allows for an objective assessment of a situation in order to compare one situation with another and to track conditions within the same situation over time. It is produced by observing and measuring things that can be counted or calculated.

The collection of "primary data" (i.e. data collected directly from individuals for a specified purpose by using methods such as interviews or questionnaires), where possible, allows for a more in-depth and comprehensive analysis. Primary data can be collected at points of departure, entry points and reception centres.

For example, "profiling" exercises and the results of individual interviews undertaken during the processing of asylum claims are particularly useful. In addition, secondary data (i.e. data compiled from existing information sources and which may have been collected for other purposes) may also be available and ready for analysis. The collection of data using a range of different methodologies (i.e. primary, secondary, qualitative and quantitative) can assist to ensure that accurate and comprehensive information is obtained about a particular mixed movement situation. However, in order for data to properly inform policy development and responses to mixed movements, it requires processing and analysis In case of human settlement,

Defining the objective(s), scope and methodology of the data collection

Before a data collection exercise commences, its objectives, scope, methodology and data protection safeguards need to be clearly established. Factors such as the national and regional context, as well as existing research and data on migration and refugee related issues, will be relevant. International migration data, for example, can be used to extrapolate the number of persons in need of international protection in a given country.

It can also be used to assess migratory trends and patterns.

Safeguards are necessary in data collection and data sharing in order to preserve the privacy, confidentiality and security of personal information in accordance with data collection standards.

The evaluation plan may be simple or complex with a clear idea of how the data that are collected will be analysed and used to inform programme improvements and efficacy.

Generally the computer software used for data collection falls into one of the following categories of practical application.[3]

1. Surveys or questionnaires[4][5]
2. Data registries[6][7]
3. Case management systems[8]
4. Performance measurement systems[9][10]
5. Exams and quizzes[11][12]
6. Online forms and form filing and reporting systems

While collecting the data, the researcher must identify the type of data to be collected, source of data, and the method to be used to collect the data. Also, the answers to the questions that who, when and where the data is to be collected should be well addressed by the researcher.

2.4.1 Data Collection Methods

The choice of data collection methods depends on the research problem under study, the research design and the information gathered about the variable. Broadly, the data collection methods can be classified into two categories:

1. **Primary Data Collection Methods:** The primary data are the first-hand data, collected

by the researcher for the first time and is original in nature. The researcher collects the fresh data when the research problem is unique, and no related research work is done by any other person. The results of the research are more accurate when the data is collected directly by the researcher but however it is costly and time-consuming.

2. **Secondary Data Collection Methods:** When the data is collected by someone else for his research work and has already passed through the statistical analysis is called the secondary data. Thus, the secondary data is the second-hand data which is readily available from the other sources. One of the advantages of using the secondary data is that it is less expensive and at the same time easily available, but however the authenticity of the findings can be questioned.

Thus, the researcher can obtain data from either of the sources depending on the nature of his study and the pursued research objective.

2.4.2 Documentation on Data Processing and Contents

Technical and content decisions made at data entry stage influence the quality of data. Decisions to be made include, for example, whether to enter information into a matrix or the technical solution chosen for audio or video recording. Solutions chosen for post-collection processing also have an impact on data quality. For instance, in the case of quantitative data, the naming and organisation of data files, naming of variables, and documenting the codes and reasons for missing values. In the case of qualitative data, the transcription level chosen

1. How is the (technical) quality of data ensured?
2. How are data processing methods documented?
3. Where are metadata describing data collection methods and data content stored?

Sufficient data documentation in different stages of data collection and processing is a crucial factor for quality. Data documentation is also important for long-term preservation and usability. Good documentation, that is, carefully created metadata enable informed re-use of data and long data life cycle.

2.4.3 Processing Quantitative Data Files

A quantitative dataset is typically a data matrix consisting of rows and columns where one row corresponds to one observation and one column corresponds to one variable. To analyse quantitative data, software for statistical analysis is needed, as well as at least basic knowledge of statistics and quantitative methods.

In social sciences, empirical quantitative data are usually collected by surveys, for example, by a postal, telephone, face-to-face or Internet survey. When such collection methods are used, the unit of observation is most often the individual, and the variables in the data matrix represent the survey responses of these individuals. Data matrices are sometimes also called microdata (referring to individual response data) or numerical data.

1. **Recording a Data Matrix:** Data collection method and instrument affect how the data are stored in digital form. In online surveys, the responses are saved the moment they are

submitted. In computer-assisted face-to-face or phone interviews, the interviewer records the responses as the interview proceeds. Paper questionnaires can be optically read or the data can be entered manually. All recording methods have the potential to cause mistakes in the data. The quality of a dataset can be improved with the following measures:

1. check for and correct values out of range
2. check the entered data against a few randomly selected questionnaires
3. check the lengths of rows and the number of variables
4. do not recode variables (e.g. collapse categories) while entering the data
5. when the data have been entered, immediately create both a back-up file and a separate working copy
6. when recoding variables, use statistical software and, if possible, recode the variables by using syntax
7. be consistent in determining values for missing data and 'can't say' type of responses
8. check the accuracy of frequencies
9. create documentation of all changes made to the dataset

2 **Variable Names and Labels:** Be consistent when naming variables. Favour short names that correspond to the numbering of the instrument used in data collection. Examples:

1. Variables relating to actual survey questions. A good name for the variable that contains the responses to the first question in the questionnaire is q1. If a question has several subquestions (e.g. the so-called grid questions), the following form can be used: q2_1, q2_2, q2_3, ...
2. Variables relating to questions about background information. In addition to actual survey questions, the questionnaire often contains questions that chart the respondent's background. Generally, these questions do not have question numbers in the questionnaire. The background variables should be named in a consistent manner, for instance bv1, bv2, bv3, ...
3. Other variables. The dataset can contain information that is not directly related to the research instrument (e.g. observation id, date of response and time spent in responding). Data collected through online questionnaires often contain technical information, for instance, browser information, time of response and the respondent's IP address. The variables related to this sort of information should also be named in a logical manner, for example t1, t2, ... If there are only a few variables of this kind in the dataset, descriptive names, such as 'ID', 'date', 'time' and 'IP' can also be used.

If a dataset consists of several different sources or of datasets that are combined, it is sensible to name the variables in a manner that makes it possible to see which subset each variable originates from. Different subsets can be named, for instance, a, b, c etc. and the variables in these subsets could be named a1, a2_1, a2_2, b1_1 or, alternatively, a_q1, a_q2_1, b_q1_1 etc.

Even though some statistical packages allow long variable names, the recommendation is to avoid them because they may cause problems in file conversion. It is also best not to name variables according to their content, because this will basically lead to the use of abbreviated forms. The meanings of abbreviations can be ambiguous, which may make connecting a variable to the corresponding question in the questionnaire impossible. It is also recommended that using symbols and accented letters in variable names be avoided.

3. **A Variable Label:** A variable label refers to the description of the contents of a variable. Different statistical packages and file formats limit the length of variable labels (for example, SPSS Portable has a limit of 255 characters). Even if a label has to be shortened, it should provide relevant information on the contents of the variable. The label should follow the original question as accurately as possible.

   Values and value labels

   It is advisable to code the values of a variable to correspond to the numbering used in the research instrument, for instance:

Strongly disagree	1
Disagree to some extent	2
Neutral : Neither agree nor disagree	3
Agree to some extent	4
Strongly agree	5

   For missing data and 'can't say' types of classes, negative values and zero can be used. However, it should be made sure that the values are clearly distinguishable from each other. The pre-defined values for missing data provided in statistical packages can also be used.

   When creating value labels, it is advisable to follow the wording of the response alternatives used in the instrument. The maximum length of a value label depends on the software and file format. Often the maximum length of the label is very short (for example, 120 characters in SPSS 20.0.0 Portable). If a value label must be shortened, this should be done by using the wording and terminology in the research instrument as closely as possible to retain the original content.

4. **Recoding Variables:** When analysing the data, variables sometimes need to be recoded, or new variables based on them need to be formed. For example, the respondents' years of birth are often inquired in the questionnaires, but the results are reported as age groups. All such changes made to variables must be well-documented.

2.4.4 Missing Data

In almost all datasets, there are variables with missing data for some cases. For instance, a respondent may have decided not to answer a question in the questionnaire, or there may have been a failure in collecting the response. If the cases that have missing data are removed from the analysis, the total number of cases decreases and the accuracy of results may suffer. Results of analysis may become quite significantly skewed, if missing data are not evenly distributed among the cases. To ensure the accuracy of the results, it is important to process the missing data before analysing the dataset.

The missing data should be coded so that they can be clearly distinguished from the "actual" values of a variable. Often, values such as 9, 99 or 999 are used to signify missing data. Zero is also frequently used, but in those cases 0 should not be an acceptable value within the range.

Weight variables

If there are systematic errors in the dataset, it may be prudent to weight the observations. With weight variables, potential bias in age, gender and region distributions resulting from the sampling can be corrected. Clear documentation on the weighting methods and calculations used should be provided to ensure that people reusing the data also have an understanding of the variables created during the research process.

Using syntax

Most statistical packages allow users to process and analyse data with the help of a programming language, or syntax. Often the most effective features of statistical packages are available only through syntax commands, even though basic analyses can be performed through menus. The commands given in syntax can be saved to a separate file (syntax file).

It is advisable to always use syntax rather than menus when editing data. Syntax allows users to see what changes have been made to the data and how. This makes it easy to perform quality control, search for potential mistakes, and make corrections and adjustments. Moreover, executing often-used commands is faster with syntax. Many statistical packages are compatible with several programming languages, which enables the user to create custom features or analyses.

It is recommended to write comments in the syntax file beside the commands to explain why a certain command is executed (for instance, why a variable is recoded). The name of the dataset, version number, date created and the name of author are usually added as comments at the beginning of a syntax file.

2.4.5 Processing Qualitative Data Files

Qualitative research data may consist of many different types of research material. These may include transcribed interviews, audio recordings, still images, ethnographic diaries and various types of written texts.

1. Transcription

The most common formats of qualitative data are written texts, interview data and focus group discussion data. In most cases, interview and discussion data are first digitally recorded and then transcribed. Representing audiovisual data into written form is the most typical way of processing interview and discussion data into an analysable format. Occasionally, the recordings themselves are analysed, for instance, in studies focusing on language or interaction.

The level of transcription is always decided by the original researcher or research team and is dependent on the objectives set for the data. Transcription level decisions are often influenced by the resources available. In an ideal case, researchers understand how valuable the data may become for other researchers outside the original research team and thus allocate resources to the transcription. It is recommended that transcription of the recorded material is done as extensively as possible. As it is hard to say in advance for what kind of study the data will be used in future, it is often best to transcribe also those parts that do not seem relevant at the time. This also enables the researchers themselves to reuse the data later for other new research questions. Researchers can do the transcription themselves or buy it from a service provider.

There are no established names or definitions for different levels of transcription, although there is some agreement on the general guidelines. In practice, transcription does not follow any particular level but combines features from different levels, tailoring the transcription to the requirements of the material at hand. Whatever the level chosen, it is essential to be uniform and consistent throughout in the level of detail and logics of transcription.

(2) Levels of Transcription

Different levels of transcription can be classified in a following manner, for instance:

1. **Gisted/summary transcription:** Interview recordings are represented into written form only roughly, by listing or summarising main points/topics. Direct quotations or parts of speech are only rarely written down. Interpretation plays a big role in this kind of transcription because it is the transcriber who decides which parts are worth transcription.

   This type of summary can be used, for instance, for producing articles based on interview data. Does not enable in-depth analysis nor does it support rich and varied use and reuse of the data.

2. **Basic level transcription:** Will produce a verbatim (exact) transcription of utterances but leaves out repeats, cut-offs of words and sentences, fillers ('you know'), and non-lexical sounds ('uh', 'ah'). Utterances clearly not in context can also be left out. In addition to speech, significant expressions of emotion (laughter, getting upset etc.) are incorporated.

   Basic level transcription can be used when the main focus is analysing the content of speech. This is the minimum transcription level for data sharing and archiving.

3. **Exact transcription:** All speech is transcribed, nothing is left out. Transcription is a verbatim, word-for-word replication of the verbal data, using the most common standardized notation symbols. Fillers ('you know'), repeats, cut-offs of words and non-lexical sounds are incorporated in the transcription, as well as expressions of emotion (laughter, sighs, getting upset etc.) and emphasis or stress. Timed pauses (in seconds) and possible background noises and other disturbances are noted .

   Exact transcription is often used when there is intention to analyse expressions and interaction, at least to some extent. This level of transcription allows for varied and rich reuse of the data.

4. **Conversation analysis transcription:** Full verbal transcription using standardized notation symbols, with careful reproduction of colloquial speech patterns. Transcription includes all words, timed pauses (in seconds), cut-offs of a word, intonation, volume, word stress, as well as non-lexical action (sneezes, breaths, sighs, facial expressions) etc.

This is most detailed level of transcription. The goal is to represent the conversation event in as much detail as possible in textual format. Often used together with the audio and video recordings themselves.

Both for the sake of one's own research and for the sake of data reuse, it is always better for transcription to be too detailed than vice versa. If interview records have been represented into text only in a summary format, this may become a problem even for the original researchers at the analysis stage. The minimum transcription level for data reuse and sharing is basic level transcription. Data reuse is further enhanced if exact transcription has been used. Whether a yet more detailed transcription level is chosen is dependent on the research objectives and resources available.

If transcription notation symbols are used, it is good to remember that the symbol signs of word processor programs may change when converted to other software programs. Formatting, footnotes and links to other documents may also disappear in conversion. It is therefore advisable never to enter content or structural information using formatting (i.e. using bold, italics, underline, colours, indent etc.). It is safest to use only the symbols available in keyboards.

The notation symbols used in transcription should be described in interview guidelines and consequent data documentation. This way the same notations will be used systematically and consistently throughout. Having information on the notations used in transcription is essential for data reuse, or when data are collected and transcribed in different locations, and even in cases when it is the original researchers who are reusing the data, because memory is short. Without notation information, it soon becomes impossible to understand what each symbol means. When a standardised notation is used, it may be enough to enter a detailed reference to the original source of the notation.

Speaker demarcation should be consistent throughout the transcription to facilitate readability and to allow for automatic processing at some stage. Each time the person speaking changes, his or her speech should be transcribed as a discrete unit, always starting from a new row. For instance, at the beginning of the row, a speaker ID is entered, followed by colon (:). The speaker ID may be the name of the speaker, initials of the name or a pseudonym, as long as they are used consistently.

For instance,

Interviewer 1: Did they agree?

Interviewee 6: I'm guessing they did, for most part.

Interviewee 7: Oh, yes, I thought so as well.

2.4.6 Organizing Data Files

When the data have been collected, saved and possibly transcribed, it is time to decide how to organise the storage. The data collected are entered into data files which are then stored in a data folder. If the research involves several independent data collections, it is advisable to create a separate data folder for each collection.

The decision on how to organise the data files should be made on a case-by-case basis. All material relevant to the data should be entered into the data folders. This should include detailed information on the data collection and data processing procedures. Examples of relevant material:

1. interview guidelines
2. possible stimulus material

3. writing invitation
4. observation instructions
5. transcription guidelines
6. writing instructions

Depending on the amount of data, one data file can include one or more data units. Sometimes it is more convenient to store several short pieces of texts (=data units) into one data file instead of having a separate file for each unit, for instance, in case of several short writing competition texts. If the textual data as a whole are not very large, it might be more useful to store all units in one data file.

If the data consist of several types of data (e.g., both focus group and individual interviews) or of different types of data files collected in the same connection (e.g. transcriptions, audio tapes and photographs), the best option might be to store the files of each type in their own subfolders.

1. **Naming Data Files:** Systematic and consistent naming of data files facilitates data management during research as well as data archiving and reuse. Even during an ongoing research project, it is easier to manage and locate data files if they have descriptive names which means including some of the background information of the data unit in the file name (e.g. date, gender and age). However, it is good to be aware of certain problems which may arise for data reuse and archiving when this type of naming is used.

Example 2.1: An example on how to document data file conventions used

Data file names are formed in the following manner:

<date><type><ID1><gender><age><municipality><datatype><ID2>,

where

<date> is the date on which the data were collected,

<type> specifies the type of event/data material,

<ID1> is the ID of the collection event,

<gender> is the gender of the interviewee,

<age> is the age of the interviewee,

<municipality> is the municipality of residence of the interviewee,

<datatype> specifies the type of data the file contains, for instance,

"trans" means transcription, "audio" means audio recording, and "image" means photograph.

<ID2> is the ID number used to separate the images connected to the collection event.

2. **Documenting Background Information:** As mentioned above, from the point of view of data reuse and sharing it is not a good practise to document background information in the file names alone. Interpreting the background information appearing in a file name may be difficult or downright impossible for outsiders or even for researchers themselves if some time has passed. It may also cause difficulties for archiving processes. Automatic parsing is not possible when background information is coded in file names as the naming conventions vary greatly between research projects.

What background information is entered for each unit varies from data to data and is a decision of the original researchers. Background information may include information on the research subject and the data collection event, and notes of the researcher. Information relating to the collection event are typically time and location, and the name of the interviewer. Information on research subjects may include gender, age, municipality of residence, education, occupation, job, educational institute, family composition, marital status, mother tongue, and nationality or ethnic background. Other relevant information include the file name(s) and the research subject ID.

Recording background information which does not seem very relevant for the ongoing research may be of great importance in future when the data are reused for other research purposes. It is therefore better to record too much background information than too little. Removing superfluous information is always easier than complementing insufficient information. Even though background information should be as informative as possible, it is good to keep in mind what kind and level of identifying information is allowed in the consent obtained from research participants .

2.4.7 Life Cycle

What happens to data after research has been finalised?

Subsequent use value of research data is largely dependent on data management measures carried out during the research. Effective data management before and during data collection and processing is an essential requirement for generating data that can be used afterwards for new research, learning, or teaching of methodology.

If data are to be stored by an individual researcher, university department, research unit or organisation, data owners must provide a solution to all aspects of subsequent data management: storage, archival and dissemination packages, terms of use, data delivery, and dissemination of metadata. If data are deposited with the Finnish Social Science Data Archive, the archive will take care of all these aspects and in addition ensure confidentiality and data security.

It is not worthwhile to preserve all research data permanently. When considering whether to archive a dataset or not, uniqueness of the data, its usability, access conditions, re-use value in research and education, and archiving costs all need to be taken into consideration. Insufficient or poor data management during the research stage considerably increases the costs of archiving, as it often is time-consuming to process the data for reuse afterwards and find out information needed for metadata. Still, destroying a dataset must always be a conscious decision and not the result of an inadequate or careless data management.

2.5 APPLICATION PROGRAMMING INTERFACE (API)

An API is a set of subroutine definitions, protocols, and tools for building application software. In general terms, it is a set of clearly defined methods of communication between various software components. A good API makes it easier to develop a computer program by providing all the building blocks, which are then put together by the programmer. An API may be for a web-based system, operating system, database system, computer hardware or software library.

An API specification can take many forms, but often includes specifications for routines, data structures, object classes, variables or remote calls. POSIX, Windows API and ASPI are examples of different forms of APIs. Documentation for the API is usually provided to facilitate usage.

Just as a Graphical User Interface (GUI) makes it easier for people to use programs, Application Programming Interfaces (API) make it easier for developers to use certain technologies in building applications. By abstracting the underlying implementation and only exposing objects or actions the developer needs, an API simplifies programming. While a graphical interface for an email client might provide a user with a button that performs all the steps for fetching and highlighting new emails, an API for file input/output might give the developer a function that copies a file from one location to another without requiring that the developer understand the file system operations occurring behind the scenes.

An Example of an API

When you use an application on your mobile phone, the application connects to the Internet and sends data to a server. The server then retrieves that data, interprets it, performs the necessary actions and sends it back to your phone. The application then interprets that data and presents you with the information you wanted in a readable way. This is what an API is - all of this happens via API.

2.5.1 The Modern API

Over the years, what an "API" is has often described any sort of generic connectivity interface to an application. More recently, however, the modern API has taken on some characteristics that make them extraordinarily valuable and useful:

1. Modern APIs adhere to standards (typically HTTP and REST), that are developer-friendly, easily accessible and understood broadly
2. They are treated more like products than code. They are designed for consumption for specific audiences (e.g., mobile developers), they are documented, and they are versioned in a way that users can have certain expectations of its maintenance and lifecycle.
3. Because they are much more standardized, they have a much stronger discipline for security and governance, as well as monitored and managed for performance and scale
4. As any other piece of productized software, the modern API has its own software development lifecycle (SDLC) of designing, testing,, building, managing, and versioning. Also, modern APIs are well documented for consumption and versioning.

The API consists of:

1. Bring in the API module
2. Obtain database connection
3. Issue SQL statements and then store procedures
4. Close the connection

Data Acquisition

There are many ways to get a dataset like configuring an API, internet, database, etc. To convert binary data into a useful data, we need to perform certain tasks which includes-Decompress files, Querying relational database, etc.

It is very much important to track the origin of database and check whether that data is up to date or not, as it is very much important to match with the real time results.

Since each data is very important, so it is important that the data should be uploaded on server so that there will be enough space to hold that data for accurate result.

Pre-processing

It is the most important part of data science, when data is incomplete or some values are missing. We need to fill some value into it and process that data to avoid any error. We need to enter values with respect to certain conditions like from where we are getting that datasets and what are the useful patterns to follow or can we use random values by implementing random function so that it will not affect the accuracy with the results obtained.

Scrubbing Data

As we know the obtained data has inconsistencies, errors, weird characters, missing values or different problems. In this situation, you have to scrub, or clean the data before to use this data. So for scrubbing the data some techniques are used which are as follows:-

1. Filter lines
2. Extract certain columns or words
3. Replace values
4. Handle missing values
5. Convert data from one format to another

Filtering Lines

The first scrubbing operation is to filter lines. It means that from the input data every line will be calculated to determine whether it may be passed on as output.

1. **Based on location:** Based on their location is the simplest way to filter lines. It is useful when you want to inspect, say, the top 5 lines of a file, or when you want extract a particular row from the output of another command-line tool.
2. **Based on pattern:** If you want to extract or remove lines based on their contents then use grep which is canonical command-line tool for filtering lines. We can print every line that matches a certain pattern or regular expression.
3. **Based on randomness:** When you're in the process of formulating your data pipeline and have a bulk of data, then debugging your pipeline can be cumbersome. In that case, sampling from the data might be useful. The core reason of the command-line tool sample is to get a subset of the data by outputting only a particular percentage of the input on a line-by-line basis.

2.6 EXPLORING DATA

Actually it is the third step in the data mining process, as highlighted in the Fig. 2.1 is to explore the prepared data.

Building a mining model is part of a larger process that includes everything from asking questions about the data and creating a model to answer those questions, to deploying the model into a working environment. This process can be defined by using the following six basic steps:

1. Defining the Problem
2. Preparing Data
3. Exploring Data
4. Building Models
5. Exploring and Validating Models
6. Deploying and Updating Models

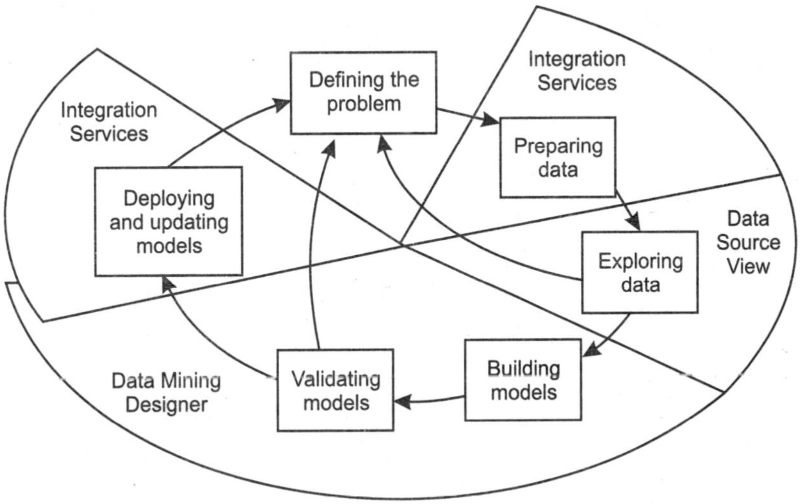

Fig. 2.1: Exploring data is third stage in Data Mining

The process illustrated in the Fig. 2.4 is cyclical, meaning that creating a data mining model is a dynamic and iterative process. After you explore the data, you may find that the data is insufficient to create the appropriate mining models, and that you therefore have to look for more data. Alternatively, you may build several models and then realize that the models do not adequately answer the problem you defined, and that you therefore must redefine the problem. You may have to update the models after they have been deployed because more data has become available. Each step in the process might need to be repeated many times in order to create a good model.

Exploration techniques include calculating the minimum and maximum values, calculating mean and standard deviations, and looking at the distribution of the data. For example, you might determine by reviewing the maximum, minimum, and mean values that the data is not representative of your customers or business processes, and that you therefore must obtain more balanced data or review the assumptions that are the basis for your expectations. Standard deviations and other distribution values can provide useful information about the stability and accuracy of the results. A large standard deviation can indicate that adding more data might help you improve the model. Data that strongly deviates from a standard distribution might be skewed, or might represent an accurate picture of a real-life problem, but make it difficult to fit a model to the data.

By exploring the data in light of your own understanding of the business problem, you can decide if the dataset contains flawed data, and then your can devise a strategy for fixing the problems or gain a deeper understanding of the behaviors that are typical of your business.

You can use tools such as Master Data Services to canvass available sources of data and determine their availability for data mining. You can use tools such as SQL Server Data Quality Services, or the Data Profiler in Integration Services, to analyze the distribution of your data and repair issues such as wrong or missing data.

2.7 BUILDING MODELS

Case Study. Data Collection for the CIH Programme

STEP 1: Prepare - know your population and develop survey sampling frames

Obtain demographic information and develop the sampling frame

- Obtain maps of the community, including any available GIS maps.
- Develop sampling frames.
- Collect demographic information from the intervention and control communities, including gender, age, socio-economic data.
- Collect demographic information from the individual settings involved (e.g. workplace, health care, schools), including gender, age, socio-economic data.

STEP 2: Finalise survey modules

- Translate and adapt modules provided in the Appendix (refer to a Translation Protocol, Appendix X).
- Conduct Field Test for all modules (refer to a Field Test Protocol, Appendix X).

STEP 3: Collect data

- Create and organise survey packages for each setting where surveys will be administered (neighbourhoods, schools, workplaces, health centres).
- Ensure survey modules are correctly labelled and create quality assurance measures to ensure all survey data will be correctly linked with data from biometric study.
- Verify that all surveys collected have signed consent forms (or passive consent for the Youth Module).

STEP 4: Prepare and create data entry strategy and environment

- Create SPSS data entry templates and Mapped Instruments.
- Set up quality assurance measures to facilitate accurate data entry.
- Train individuals for data entry.

STEP 5: Enter and clean data

- Perform ongoing quality assurance checks of data entered.
- Develop and run an error check programme. Double entry of at least 20% of all surveys is required (choose every 5th survey for double entry by a second data entry person).
- Re-keying will be necessary for improperly entered data. This is to make sure that the

values for each variable are consistent with the value codes of the mapped instruments and data entry templates.

- Provide error check programme and output to Evaluation Team.

STEP 6: Manage and analyse data

- Track data as it comes in.
- Analyze primary variables.
- Discuss preliminary data outcomes to direct and drive interventions.
- Create standard secondary variables for all sites to use for analysis.
- Review and analyse secondary variables.

2.7.1 Preparation for Data Collection

Organisation of the type of survery by setting is fundamental when there are multiple environments under study, as was the case in CIH. For baseline data collection, substantial effort was placed on organizing data packets and ensuring that a robust quality assurance system was developed for efficient and accurate collection and management of data.

2.7.2 Creating Survey Packages for Each Setting

The data preparation procedure for CIH was relatively complex given that there were numerous surveys and settings within which data had to be collected. The case study below provides an example of surveys that were organized by type of respondent in each setting.

Case Study. CIH surveys by setting				
Setting	**Person (s)**	**Policy Document Review**	**Key informant Survery**	**Scan**
School	Principal Food Manager	✓	✓	✓
Netghbourbhood	Community Leader			✓
Workplace	Seniro Manager Food Manager	✓	✓	✓
Health Setting	Senior Manager Food Manager	✓	✓	✓
Store	Manager		✓	✓
Broader Community	Mayor, Heath Department Transportation	✓		✓

2.7.3 Labelling Surveys

CIH surveys are labelled in the following format:

1. data collection time point – when follow up surveys are planned (TIME)
2. module type (MODULE)

3. participant identification number (ID)
4. region (Adult Module) or setting (Workplace, Clinical Practice, Youth Modules) code (REGION / SETTING)

CIH developed a coding strategy for multiple time points, settings, sites, and intervention and comparison areas. The case study below outlines a recommended coding scheme. This scheme assumes survey administration in all settings and utilizing intervention and control communities to measure the effect of interventions.

TIME	MODULE	ID	REGION/SETTING
• **T1** = baseline • **T2** = 1st 6-month interval (Cohort) • **T3** = 2nd 6-month interval (Cohort) • **T4** = 3rd 6-month interval (Cohort) • **T5** = follow up	• Adult Core **(A)** • Neighbourhood Family Cohort **(P)** • Work place **(WP)** • Clinical Practice **(C)** • Youth Core **(V)** • Youth Subset **(S)** • POPAR **(P)** • Biometric measures **(B)** • Optional 24-hour food and beverage recall **(D)**	**Adults in Neighbourhood** • **101000-102200** (intervention community), **201000-202200** (central community) **(Neighbourhood Cross-sectional)** • Number within the Cross-sectional sample (Neighbourhood Family Cohort)	**REGION** • Country-specific **SETTING** • **S1-SN** (Schools, N-number of schools) • **WP1-WPN** (Workplaces, N-number of workplaces in site) • **HC1-HCN** (Health centers, N-number of health centers in site)

Participant identification numbers are embedded on each survey instrument or interview, including forms to be completed with biometric measures and participant consent forms. Each person participating should have an independent identification number, or unique identifier where the coding is designed in advance. For example, in the CIH programme 6 digit codes were determined to be sufficient given the multiple settings and time points assessed. For CIH the coding numbers also took into consideration sampling for non-response and refusals.

Where multiple modules are administered to the same individual, each module should have the same ID number. For example, all modules administered to workers (Adult Module and Workplace Module) would have the same ID on the front covers, and all modules administered to the school subset (Youth Module and Youth Subset) have the same ID on the front covers. In this way, data for multiple surveys can be linked for a given individual.

2.7.4 Collecting Data: Surveys

An important initial step in collecting survey data is to establish a point-person for each setting. Once this person has been identified then a communication strategy should be developed between any evaluators and the point-person. The role of the evaluation team in distributing surveys is dictated by the setting with feasibility and confidentiality both important issues. Where possible, a bonus or incentive (tied to a certain % data return) is suggested for the point-person.

Depending on time, cost, and feasibility, interviews may be administered via paper and pencil, laptop or personal digital assistants (PDAs). In addition to considering the mechanical aspects of administration, it is also important to determine whether the survey will be administered by an interviewer or completed by the participant themselves. If administered via laptop or PDAs and completed by the individual participant, then it is important to ensure that the language used is simple and easy to understand in order to avoid confusion. The full protocol for distributing surveys including the KISH method (Kish 1949) for selecting persons within households is described in the Sampling Appendix. The case study below presents a summary of the types of data collection methods that could be used as well as their advantages and disadvantages.

Data Collection Method	Type of Administration	Advantage	Disadvantage
Paper and pencil	Self administered	• Can collect data in shorter period of time • Low cost in collecting data from a large sample • Requires less people for the implementation of data collection	• There might be issues when entering the data • There is lag time between data collection and data entry • Quality of data might be low depending on the length of survey and population survey is administered to
	Interview	• Have higher response rate and increased rate of survey completion • Can ensure better quality of data collected	• Will take longer time for data collection process • Might get biased response on sensitive questions
Electronic data collection method	Self-Administer	• Can review the data collected immediately after data is collected • Improved quality of data with skip patterns and set fields to ensure accuracy of responses	• Requires certain level infrastructure in order to use this method (e.g. electricity, internet, hardware devices PDAs) • May have more logistic challenges if setting for data collection does not have equipment for data collection (e.g. computers)
	Interview	• Can review the data collected immediately after data is collected • Improved quality of data with skip patterns and set fields to ensure accuracy of responses • Have higher response rate and increased rate of survey completion • Can ensure better quality of data collected	• Requires certain level infrastructure in order to use this method (e.g. electricity, internet, hardware devices PDAs) • Will take longer time for data collection process • Might get biased response on sensitive questions

Using computers/PDA's saves time, effort and data entry challenges. The decision to use technology should be based on feasibility issues including cost and up front time to programme the surveys into the device. In some settings it may not be safe to carry them.

The choice of survey administration methodology should remain consistent with any deviations from the determined protocol noted and controlled for. If the surveys are conducted by interviewers then their training must be standardized with each interviewer asking the questions in the same style and manner. For CIH an interviewer training protocol was developed by each site. In addition, if the interview is done face-to-face it should be administered verbally in the local language/dialect that is the stated preference of the household member.

2.8 STORAGE MANAGEMENT

The term storage management encompasses the technologies and processes organizations use to maximize or improve the performance of their data storage resources. It is a broad category that includes virtualization, replication, mirroring, security, compression, traffic analysis, process automation, storage provisioning and related techniques.

By some estimates, the amount of digital information stored in the world's computer systems is doubling every year. As a result, organizations feel constant pressure to expand their storage capacity. However, doubling a company's storage capacity every year is an expensive proposition. In order to reduce some of those costs and improve the capabilities and security of their storage solutions, organizations turn to a variety of storage management solutions.

2.8.1 Storage Management Benefits

Many storage management technologies, like storage virtualization, de-duplication and compression, allow companies to better utilize their existing storage. The benefits of these approaches include lower costs -- both the one-time capital expenses associated with storage devices and the ongoing operational costs for maintaining those devices.

Most storage management techniques also simplify the management of storage networks and devices. That can allow companies to save time and even reduce the number of IT workers needed to maintain their storage systems, which in turn, also reduces overall storage operating costs.

Storage management can also help improve a data center's performance. For example, compression and technology can enable faster I/Os, and automatic storage provisioning can speed the process of assigning storage resources to various applications.

In addition, virtualization and automation technologies can help an organization improve its agility. These storage management techniques make it possible to reassign storage capacity quickly as business needs change, reducing wasted space and improving a company's ability to respond to evolving market conditions.

Finally, many storage management technologies, such as replication, mirroring and security, can help a data center improve its reliability and availability. These techniques are often particularly important for backup and archive storage, although they also apply to primary storage. IT departments often turn to these technologies for help in meeting service-level agreement (SLA) or achieving compliance goals. SLA is a contract between a service provider and its internal or external customers that documents what services the provider will furnish and defines the performance standards the provider is obligated to meet

2.8.2 Storage Resource Management (SRM)

Storage management is very closely related to Storage Resource Management (SRM). SRM often refers particularly to software used to manage storage networks and devices. By contrast, the term "storage management" can refer to devices and processes, as well as actual software. In addition, SRM usually refers specifically to software for allocating storage capacity based on company policies and ongoing events. It may include asset management, charge back, capacity management, configuration management, data and media migration, event management, performance and availability management, policy management, quota management, and media management capabilities. In short, SRM is a subset of storage management; however, the two terms are sometimes used interchangeably.

2.8.3 Mass Storage Management

Mass storage refers to various techniques and devices for storing large amounts of data. The earliest storage devices were punched paper cards, which were used as early as 1804 to control silk-weaving looms. Modern mass storage devices include all types of disk drives and tape drives.

Mass storage is distinct from memory, which refers to temporary storage areas within the computer. Unlike main memory, mass storage devices retain data even when the computer is turned off.

2.8.4 Examples of Mass Storage Devices (MSD)

Common types of mass storage include the following:

1. Solid-state drives (SSD)
2. Hard drives
3. External hard drives
4. Optical drives
5. Tape drives
6. RAID storage
7. USB storage
8. Flash memory cards

Today, mass storage is measured in gigabytes (1,024 megabytes) and terabytes(1,024 gigabytes). Older mass storage technology, such as floppy drives, are measured in kilobytes (1,024 bytes), megabytes (1,024 kilobytes).

Storage management is also closely associated with networked storage solutions, such as storage area networks (SANs) and network-attached storage (NAS) devices. Because using SAN and NAS devices is more complicated than using direct-attached storage (DAS), many organizations deploy SRM software when they deploy their storage networking environments. However, storage management techniques like replication, mirroring, security, compression and others can be utilized with DAS devices as well as with SANs and NAS arrays.

Storage management is often used in virtualized or cloud computing environments.

Network-attached storage (NAS), storage-area networks (SANs) and unified storage (a combination of NAS and SAN approaches) provide storage capacity not directly attached to servers, but use different protocols for data.

They are not directly attached to servers. They pool storage on arrays of drives that are accessed by and independent of servers.NAS, SAN and unified storage differ depending on the network structure that servers and data storage use to connect to each other, as well as on the networking protocols each technology uses to deliver and receive data.

1. Network-attached Storage (NAS)

Before storage networking, computing environments used disks directly attached to servers to store data, while clients connected to servers over an Ethernet network using TCP/IP. Then Sun Microsystems developed the Network File System (NFS) that allowed data to be shared over an Ethernet network. NFS enabled local users to access files on a remote machine over a TCP/IP network and access it just as if it were on the local hard drive. Microsoft later created the Common Internet File System (CIFS) protocol to enable access in the same way for Windows computers.

Network-attached storage is a dedicated disk storage subsystem residing on a local-area network (LAN) that provides access to entire files using the CIFS (Windows) or NFS (Unix) protocols. NAS impacts LAN traffic and is generally seen as a solution for smaller businesses or remote offices who want to access whole files.

2. Storage-area Network (SAN)

A storage-area network addresses essentially the same challenge as a network-attached storage system – to allow server access to a shared pool of data storage.

The critical difference between SAN and NAS is that SAN storage delivers data in blocks rather than whole files, which makes storage-area networks – especially Fibre Channel (FC) SANs – well-suited to delivering large amounts of transactional data at very high levels of I/O performance, such as for databases.

Storage-area networks and network-attached storage were once also distinguishable by the way they delivered data. SAN used to be defined by residing on a network discrete from the LAN – known as a fabric – upon which SCSI commands were encapsulated within the specially developed low latency Fibre Channel protocol.

But in recent years, the iSCSI protocol has emerged, which contains SCSI block storage commands within TCP/IP and can be used over the LAN/WAN. For that reason, SAN has come to mean block storage as opposed to file storage.

A key advantage of Fibre Channel SANs is that the storage network is entirely separate from the local-area network. This can bring performance benefits to data storage and backup that iSCSI may not be able to because of its use of Ethernet networks, which may be shared with other traffic. The downside to Fibre Channel is that the staff training overhead is far greater than for iSCSI, which uses technology protocols familiar to networking professionals.

3. Unified Storage

Unified storage – also known as multiprotocol storage – is a single data storage system that supports both file and block access. The subsystem can support NAS (file-based access), as well as iSCSI and Fibre Channel (block-based access) storage protocols simultaneously.

Broadly speaking, there are two ways of achieving unified storage. You can buy arrays that are built as dedicated multiprotocol storage arrays with a NAS server and storage-area network controller combined under a single management interface. Or you can provide file-level access to a SAN disk array by adding a so-called network-attached storage head or gateway.

Dedicated unified storage systems are popular for small- to medium-sized enterprises (SMEs) and remote-office implementations where flexibility in how servers are attached to data storage is at a premium. The unified storage head/gateway approach is better suited to larger enterprises wanting more flexibility from their existing information technology investments. This approach may result in data storage managers having to manage two systems – the storage-area network array and the network-attached storage head.

2.8.5 Storage Management Implementation

Because storage management is such a broad category, it's difficult to provide detailed instructions on how to install or how to use storage management technologies. In general, storage management technology can be deployed as software or it can be included in a hardware device. Storage management techniques can be applied to primary, backup or archived storage. Deployment and implementation procedures will vary widely depending on the type of storage management selected and the vendor. In addition, the skills and training of storage administrators and other personnel add another level to an organization's storage management capabilities.

2.8.6 Storage Management Technology

The primary organization involved in establishing storage management standards is the Storage Networking Industry Association (SNIA). It has put forth several important storage specifications, including the Storage Management Initiative Specification (SMI-S) and the Cloud Data Management Interface (CDMI). SMI-S defines the attributes of storage hardware, such as Fibre Channel switches, Fibre Channel and iSCI arrays, NAS devices, tape libraries and host profiles. It also addresses storage management software issues, such as configuration discovery, provisioning and trending, security, asset management, compliance and cost management, event management and data protection. The CDMI specification provides standards for cloud storage services, enabling interoperability among various storage management solutions.

The work of the SNIA builds on previous work done by the Distributed Management Task Force (DMTF), which has also been involved in establishing storage management standards.

2.9 IMPORTING DATA

We shall be using IBM SPSS Statistics software for learning how to import data.

2.9.1 IBM SPSS Statistics

IBM SPSS Statistics 21 IBM® SPSS® Statistics 21 is a comprehensive system for analyzing data. SPSS Statistics can take data from almost any type of file and use them to generate tabulated reports, charts, and plots of distributions and trends, descriptive statistics, and complex statistical analyses. SPSS Statistics makes statistical analysis more accessible for the beginner and more convenient for the experienced user. Simple menus and dialog box selections make it possible to perform complex analyses without typing a single line of command syntax. The Data Editor offers a simple and efficient spreadsheet-like facility for entering data and browsing the working data file.

1. IBM SPSS Statistics 21 Student Version

The IBM® SPSS® Statistics 21 Student Version is a limited but still powerful version of SPSS Statistics.

(*a*) **Capability:** The Student Version contains many of the important data analysis tools contained in IBM® SPSS® Statistics, including: „

1. Spreadsheet-like Data Editor for entering, modifying, and viewing data files.
2. Statistical procedures, including t tests, analysis of variance, and crosstabulations.
3. Interactive graphics that allow you to change or add chart elements and variables dynamically; the changes appear as soon as they are specified.
4. Standard high-resolution graphics for an extensive array of analytical and presentation charts and tables.

(*b*) **Limitations:** Created for classroom instruction, the Student Version is limited to use by students and instructors for educational purposes only. The following limitations apply to the IBM® SPSS® Statistics 21 Student Version:

1. Data files cannot contain more than 50 variables.
2. Data files cannot contain more than 1,500 cases. SPSS Statistics add-on modules (such as Regression or Advanced Statistics) cannot be used with the Student Version.
3. SPSS Statistics command syntax is not available to the user. This means that it is not possible to repeat an analysis by saving a series of commands in a syntax or "job" file, as can be done in the full version of IBM® SPSS® Statistics.

Scripting and automation are not available to the user. This means that you cannot create scripts that automate tasks that you repeat often, as can be done in the full version of SPSS Statistics.

(*c*) Let us start working with IBM® SPSS® Statistics.

2.9.2 To open a data file:

1. From the menus choose:

File > Open > Data...

A dialog box for opening files is displayed.

By default, IBM® SPSS® Statistics data files (.sav extension) are displayed.

This example uses the file demo.sav.

About demo.sav. This is a hypothetical data file that concerns a purchased customer database, for the purpose of mailing monthly offers. Whether or not the customer responded to the offer is recorded, along with various demographic information.

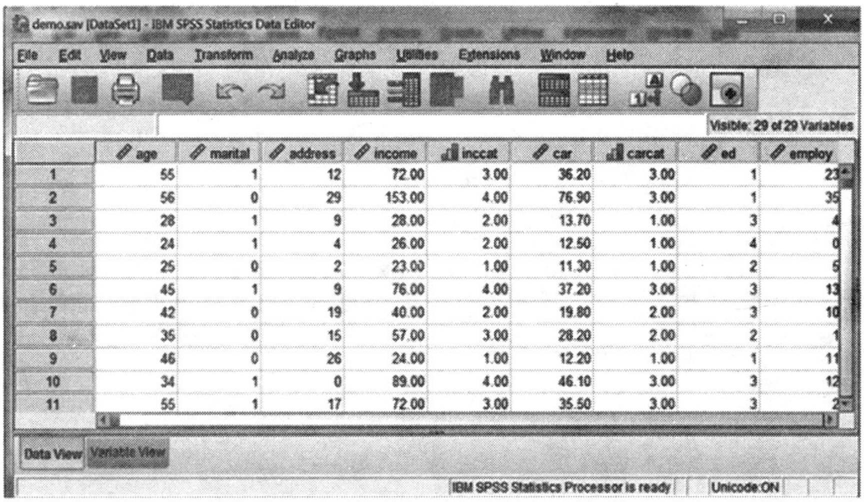

Fig. 2.2: Demo.sav file in Data Editor

The data file is displayed in the Data Editor. In Data View, if you put the mouse cursor on a variable name (the column headings), a more descriptive variable label is displayed (if a label has been defined for that variable).

By default, the actual data values are displayed. To display labels:

2. **From the menus choose:**
 View > Value Labels

Alternatively, you can use the Value Labels button on the toolbar.

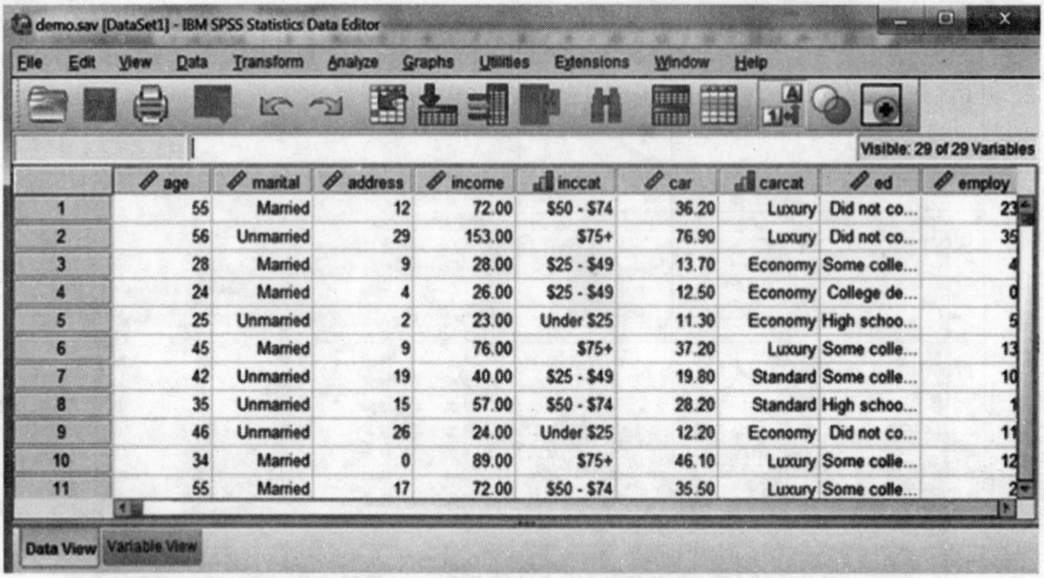

Fig. 2.3. Value labels displayed in the Data Editor

Descriptive value labels are now displayed to make it easier to interpret the responses.

If you have any add-on options, the Analyze menu contains a list of reporting and statistical analysis categories. We will start by creating a simple frequency table (table of counts). This example requires the Statistics Base option.

3. **From the menus choose:**

   Analyze > Descriptive Statistics > Frequencies...

   The Frequencies dialog box is displayed.

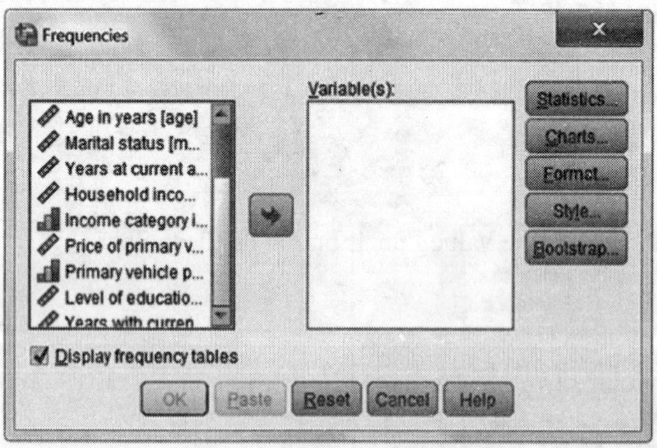

Fig. 2.4. Frequencies dialog box

An icon next to each variable provides information about data type and level of measurement.

	Numeric	String	Date	Time
Scale (Continuous)		n/a		
Ordinal				
Nominal				

If the variable label and/or name appears truncated in the list, the complete label/name is displayed when the cursor is positioned over it. The variable name inccat is displayed in square brackets after the descriptive variable label. Income category in thousands is the variable label. If there were no variable label, only the variable name would appear in the list box.

You can resize dialog boxes just like windows, by clicking and dragging the outside borders or corners. For example, if you make the dialog box wider, the variable lists will also be wider.

In the dialog box, you choose the variables that you want to analyze from the source list on the left and drag and drop them into the Variable(s) list on the right. Thc OK button, which runs the analysis, is disabled until at least one variable is placed in the Variable(s) list.

In many dialogs, you can obtain additional information by right-clicking any variable name in the list and selecting Variable Information from the pop-up menu.

- Click **Gender** [gender] in the source variable list and drag the variable into the target Variable(s) list.

Click Income category in thousands [inccat] in the source list and drag it to the target list.

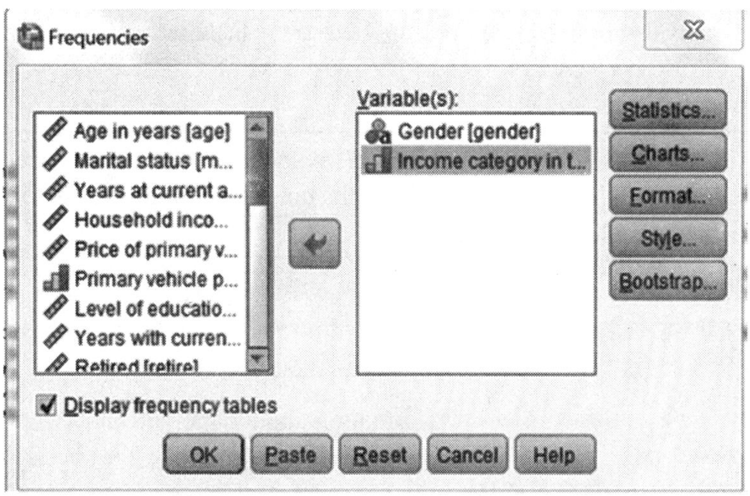

Fig. 2.5 Variables selected for analysis

Click **OK** to run the procedure.

Results are displayed in the Viewer window.

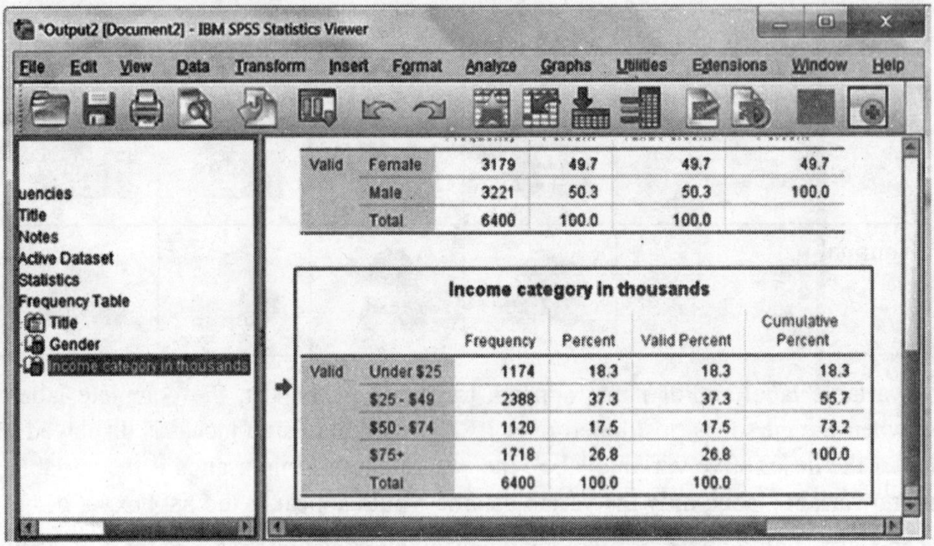

Fig. 2.6. Frequency table of income categories

Although some statistical procedures can create charts, you can also use the Graphs menu to create charts.

For example, you can create a chart that shows the relationship between wireless telephone service and PDA (personal digital assistant) ownership.

2.9.3 Importing Data

Data from database sources are easily imported using the Database Wizard. Any database that uses ODBC (Open Database Connectivity) drivers can be read directly after the drivers are installed. ODBC drivers for many database formats are supplied on the installation CD. Additional drivers can be obtained from third-party vendors. One of the most common database applications, Microsoft Access, is discussed in this example.

> **Note:** This example is specific to Microsoft Windows and requires an ODBC driver for Access. The steps are similar on other platforms but may require a third-party ODBC driver for Access

From the menus choose:

File > Import Data > Open Database > New Query...

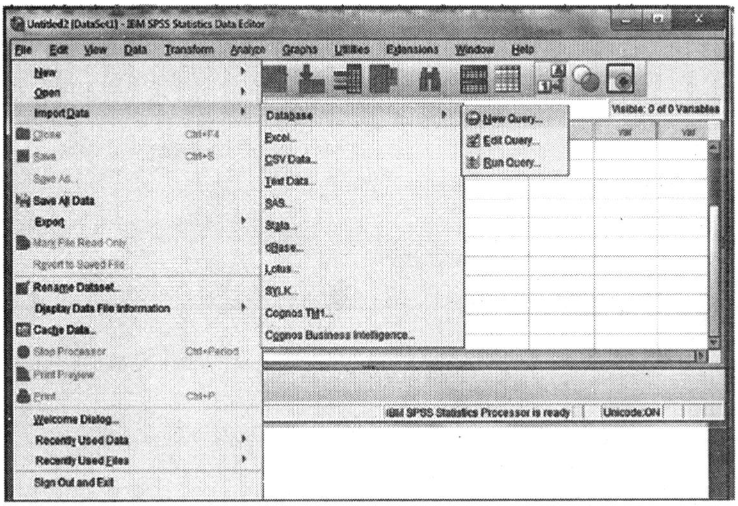

Fig. 2.6: Choosing New Query

After clicking over the **Run Query** option, following screen shall appear:

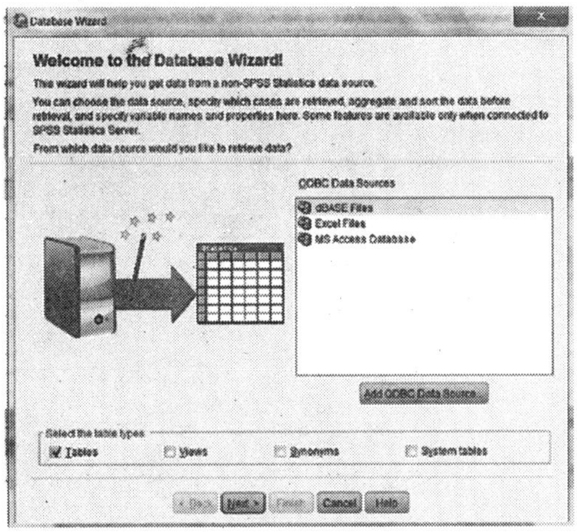

Fig. 2.7: Database Wizard Welcome dialog box

1. Select **MS Access Database** from the list of data sources and click **Next**.

	Note: Depending on your installation, you may also see a list of OLEDB data sources on the left side of the wizard (Windows operating systems only), but this example uses the list of ODBC data sources displayed on the right side.

2. Click **Browse** to navigate to the Access database file that you want to open.

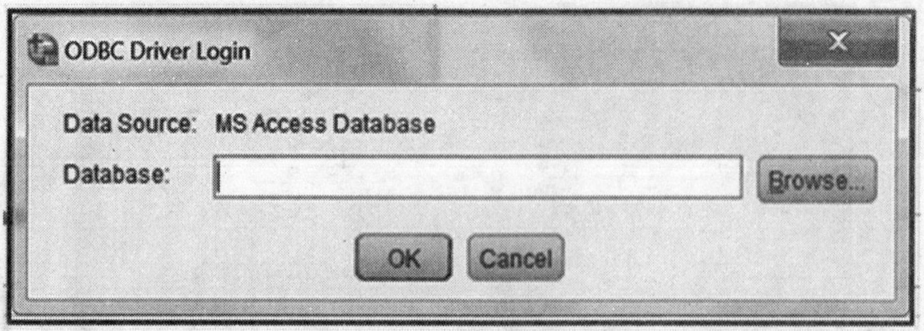

Fig. 2.8: Browsing the data file in MS Access Database

3. Open **demo.mdb.**
4. Click **OK** in the login dialog box.

   In the next step, you can specify the tables and variables that you want to import.

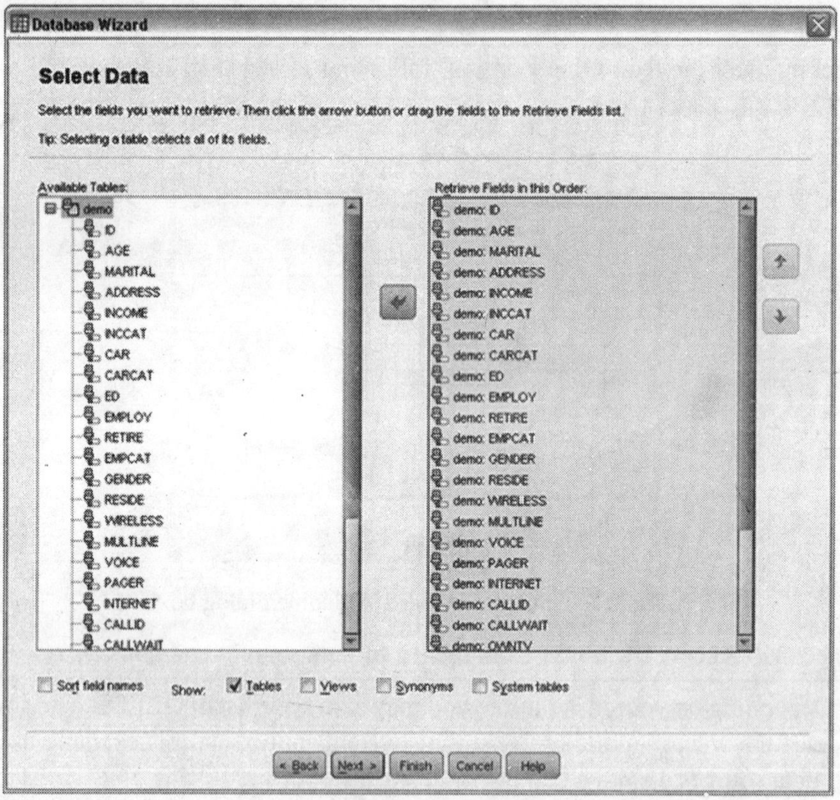

Fig. 2.9: Select Data step

5. Drag the entire demo table to the Retrieve Fields In This Order list.
6. Click **Next**.

   In the next step, you can select which records (cases) to import.

   If you do not want to import all cases, you can import a subset of cases (for example, males older than 30), or you can import a random sample of cases from the data source. For large data sources, you may want to limit the number of cases to a small, representative sample to reduce the processing time.

7. Click **Next** to continue.

   Field names are used to create variable names. If necessary, the names are converted to valid variable names. The original field names are preserved as variable labels. You can also change the variable names before importing the database.

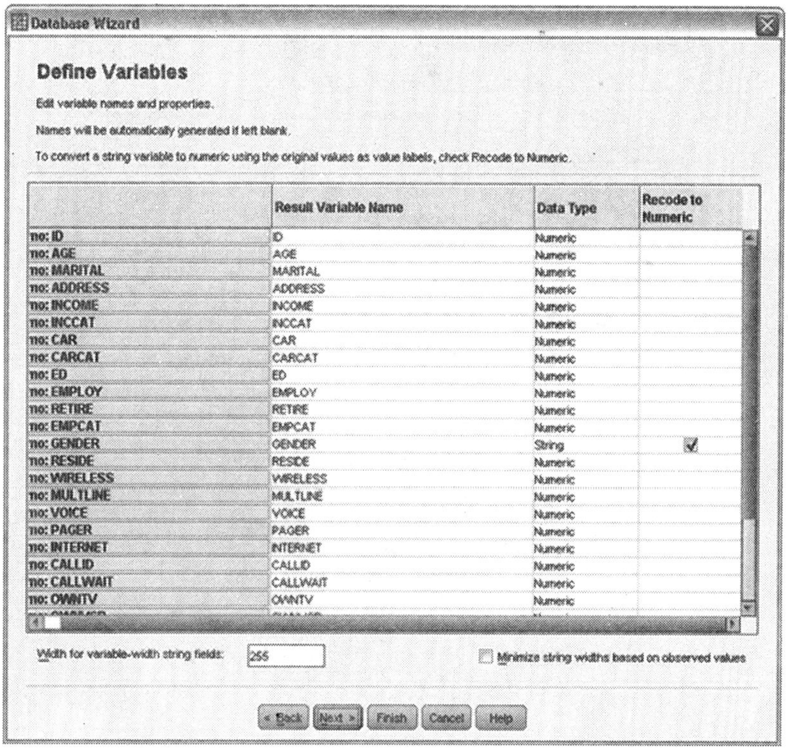

Fig. 2.10: Define Variables step

8. Click the **Recode to Numeric** cell in the Gender field. This option converts string variables to integer variables and retains the original value as the value label for the new variable.
9. Click **Next** to continue.

   The SQL statement created from your selections in the Database Wizard appears in the Results step. This statement can be executed now or saved to a file for later use.
10. Click **Finish** to import the data.

    All of the data in the Access database that you selected to import are now available in the Data Editor.

2.9.4 Dealing with Text Files

Text files are another common source of data. Many spreadsheet programs and databases can save their contents in one of many text file formats. Comma- or tab-delimited files refer to rows of data that use commas or tabs to indicate each variable. In this example, the data are tab delimited.

1. From the **menus** choose:

   File > Read Text Data...

2. Select **Text** (*.txt) as the file type you want to view.
3. Open **demo.txt.**

   The Text Import Wizard guides you through the process of defining how the specified text file should be interpreted.

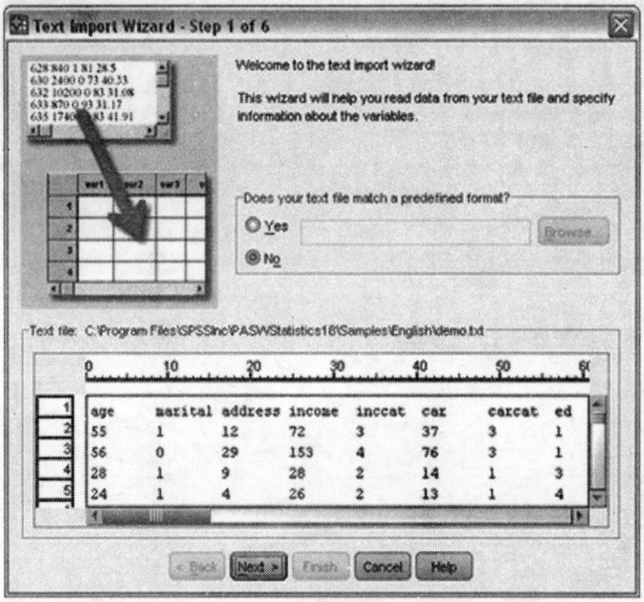

Fig. 2.11: Text Import Wizard: Step 1 of 6

4. In Step 1, you can choose a predefined format or create a new format in the wizard. Select **No** to indicate that a new format should be created.
5. Click **Next** to continue.

   As stated earlier, this file uses tab-delimited formatting. Also, the variable names are defined on the top line of this file.

6. In step 2 of the wizard, select Delimited to indicate that the data use a delimited formatting structure.
7. Select **Yes** to indicate that variable names should be read from the top of the file.
8. Click **Next** to continue.
9. In step 3, enter 2 for the line number where the first case of data begins (because variable names are on the first line).

   Keep the default values for the remainder of this step, and click **Next** to continue.

10. The Data preview in Step 4 provides you with a quick way to ensure that your data are being properly read.
11. Select Tab and deselect the other options for delimiters.

12. Click **Next** to continue.

    Because the variable names may have been modified to conform to naming rules, step 5gives you the opportunity to edit any undesirable names.

    Data types can be defined here as well. For example, it's safe to assume that the income variable is meant to contain a certain dollar amount.

13. To change a data type:

    Under **Data preview**, select the variable you want to change, which is Income in this case.

14. Select **Dollar** from the Data format drop-down list.

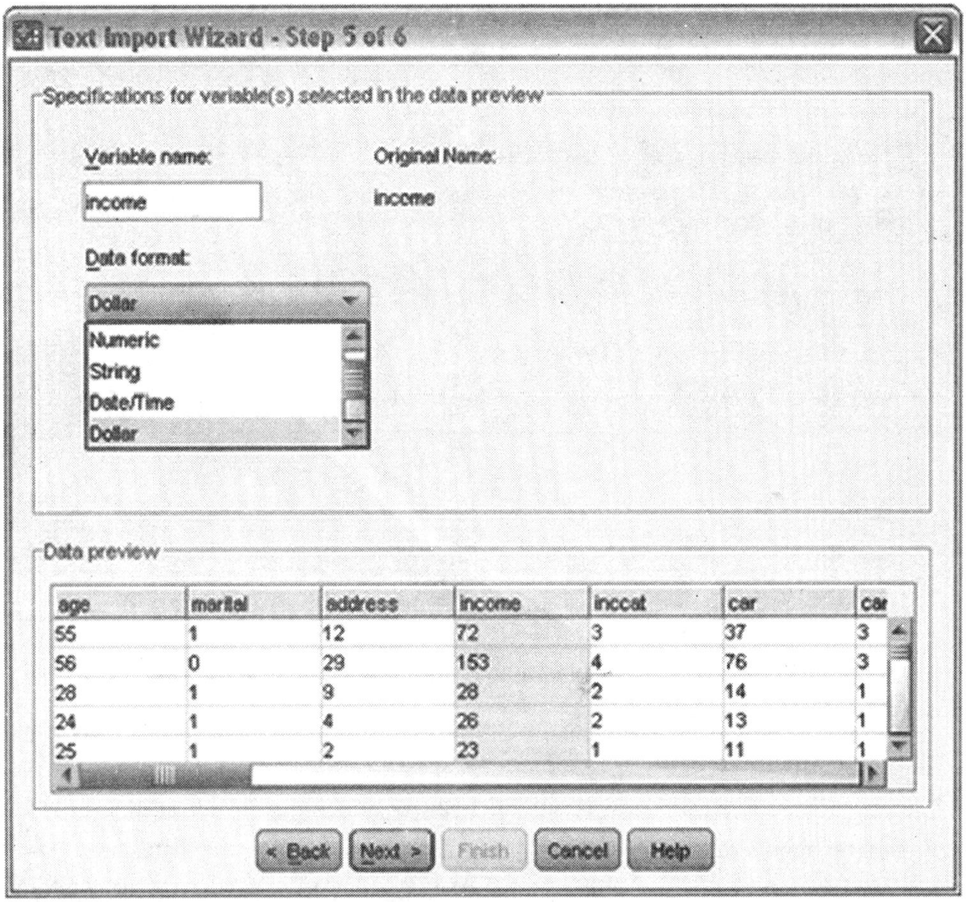

Fig. 2.12. Change the data type

15. Click **Next** to continue.

    Leave the default selections in the last step, and click Finish to import the data.

2.9.5 Working with Multiple Data Sources

Starting with version 14.0, multiple data sources can be open at the same time, making it easier to:

- Switch back and forth between data sources.
- Compare the contents of different data sources.
- Copy and paste data between data sources.
- Create multiple subsets of cases and/or variables for analysis.
- Merge multiple data sources from various data formats (for example, spreadsheet, database, text data) without saving each data source first.

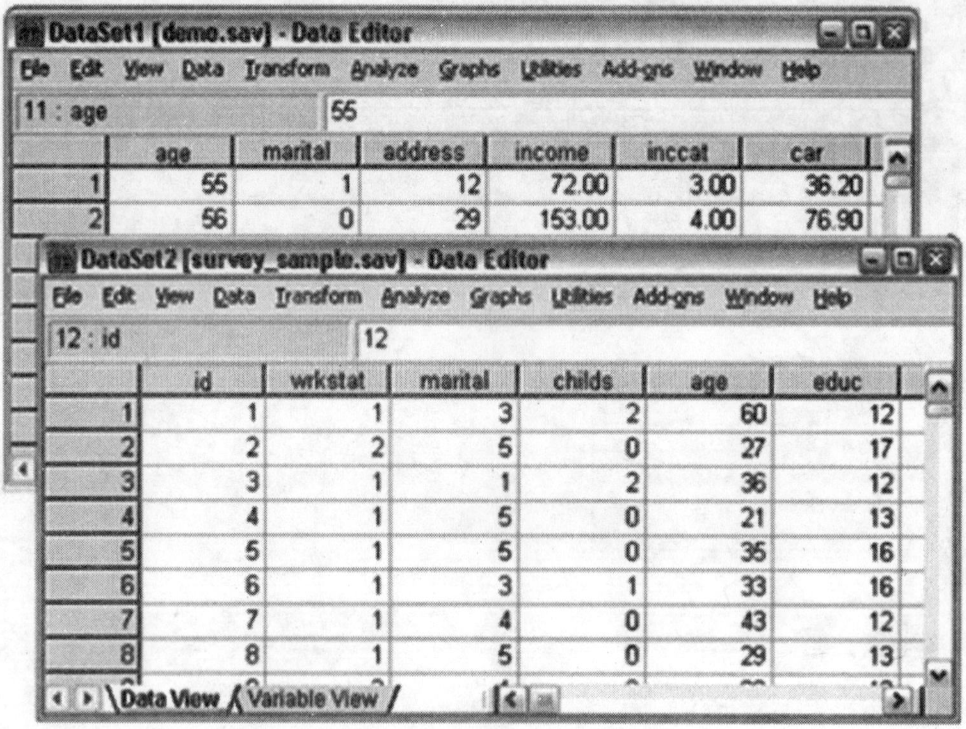

Fig. 2.13: Basic Handling of Multiple Data Sources

Two data sources open at same time By default, each data source that you open is displayed in a new Data Editor window. „

Any previously open data sources remain open and available for further use. „

When you first open a data source, it automatically becomes the active dataset. „

You can change the active dataset simply by clicking anywhere in the Data Editor window of the data source that you want to use or by selecting the Data Editor window for that data source from the Window menu.

Only the variables in the active dataset are available for analysis.

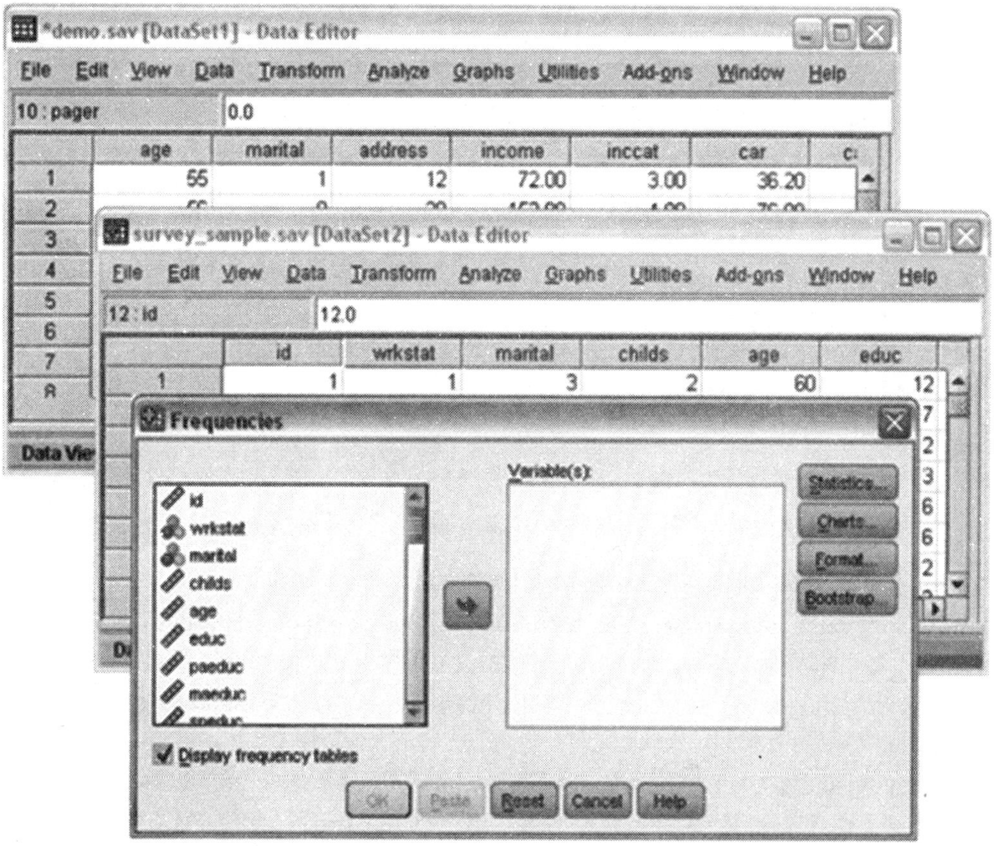

Fig. 2.14: Variable list containing variables in the active dataset „

You cannot change the active dataset when any dialog box that accesses the data is open (including all dialog boxes that display variable lists). „

At least one Data Editor window must be open during a session. When you close the last open Data Editor window, IBM® SPSS® Statistics automatically shuts down, prompting you to save changes first.

2.9.6 Working with Multiple Datasets in Command Syntax

If you use command syntax to open data sources (for example, GET FILE, GET DATA), you need to use the DATASET NAME command to name each dataset explicitly in order to have more than one data source open at the same time. When working with command syntax, the active dataset name is displayed on the toolbar of the syntax window.

All of the following actions can change the active dataset:

1. Use the DATASET ACTIVATE command.
2. Click anywhere in the Data Editor window of a dataset.
3. Select a dataset name from the toolbar in the syntax window.

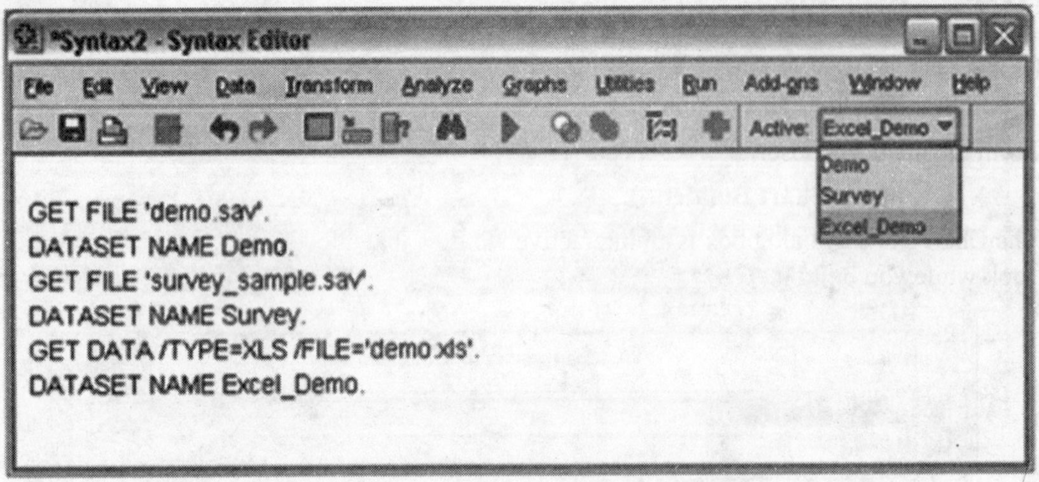

Fig. 2.15 Open datasets displayed on syntax window toolbar

Copying and Pasting Information between Datasets

You can copy both data and variable definition attributes from one dataset to another dataset in basically the same way that you copy and paste information within a single data file.

1. Copying and pasting selected data cells in Data View pastes only the data values, with no variable definition attributes.
2. Copying and pasting an entire variable in Data View by selecting the variable name at the top of the column pastes all of the data and all of the variable definition attributes for that variable.
3. Copying and pasting variable definition attributes or entire variables in Variable View pastes the selected attributes.

2.9.7 Renaming Datasets

When you open a data source through the menus and dialog boxes, each data source is automatically assigned a dataset name of DataSetn, where n is a sequential integer value, and when you open a data source using command syntax, no dataset name is assigned unless you explicitly specify one with DATASET NAME.

To provide more descriptive dataset names: E From the menus in the Data Editor window for the dataset whose name you want to change choose:

File > Rename Dataset... E

Enter a new dataset name that conforms to variable naming rules. Suppressing Multiple Datasets If you prefer to have only one dataset available at a time and want to suppress the multiple dataset feature: E From the menus choose:

Edit > Options...

Click the **General tab**. Select (check) **Open only one dataset at a time**.

2.9.8 Creating Charts

To demonstrate the basics of chart creation, we will create a bar chart of mean income for different levels of job satisfaction. This example uses the data file demo.sav.

From the menus choose:

Graphs > Chart Builder...

The Chart Builder dialog box is an interactive window that allows you to preview how a chart will look while you build it.

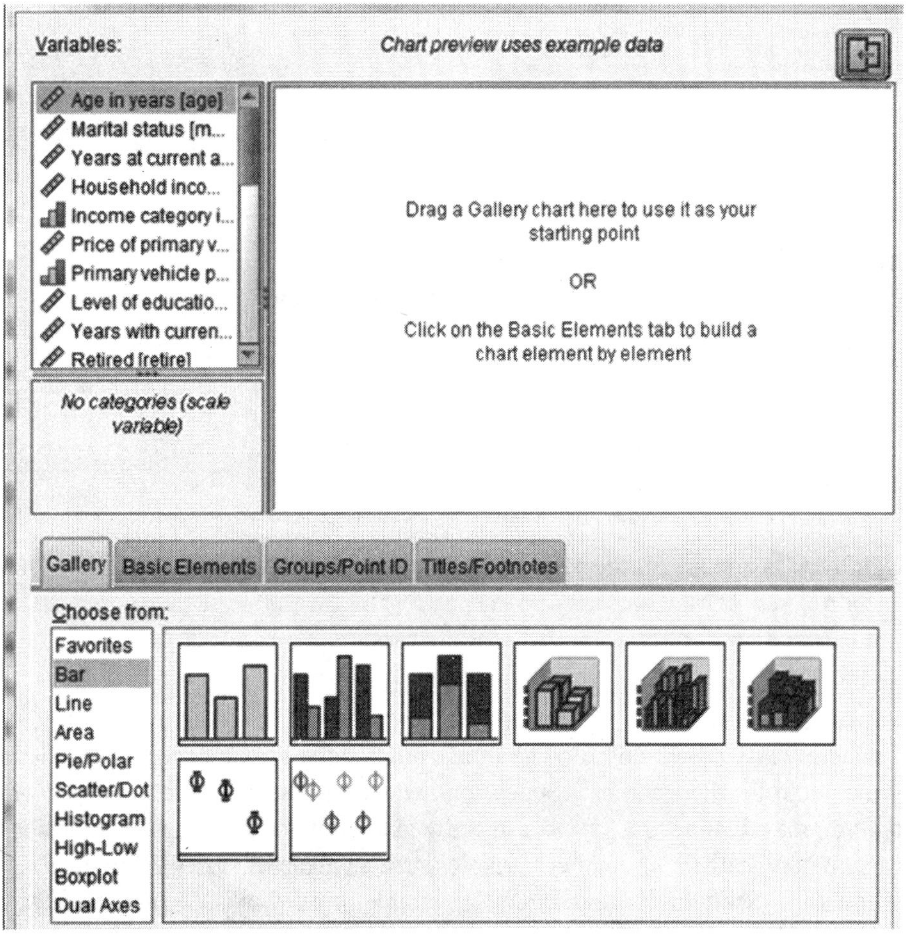

Fig. 2.16 Chart Builder dialog box

1. **Click the Gallery tab if it is not selected:** The Gallery includes many different predefined charts, which are organized by chart type. The Basic Elements tab also provides basic elements (such as axes and graphic elements) for creating charts from scratch, but it's easier to use the Gallery.
2. **Click Bar if it is not selected:** Icons representing the available bar charts in the Gallery appear in the dialog box. The pictures should provide enough information to identify

the specific chart type. If you need more information, you can also display a ToolTip description of the chart by pausing your cursor over an icon.

3. Drag the icon for the simple bar chart onto the "canvas," which is the large area above the Gallery. The Chart Builder displays a preview of the chart on the canvas. Note that the data used to draw the chart are not your actual data. They are example data.

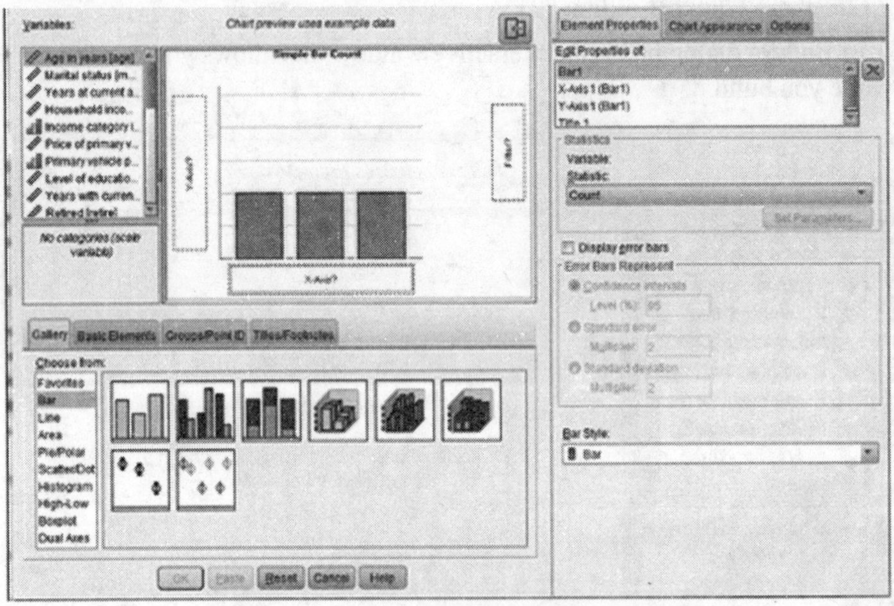

Fig. 2.17: Bar chart on Chart Builder canvas

Although there is a chart on the canvas, it is not complete because there are no variables or statistics to control how tall the bars are and to specify which variable category corresponds to each bar. You can't have a chart without variables and statistics. You add variables by dragging them from the Variables list, which is located to the left of the canvas.

When you drag the variables, the targets are "drop zones" on the canvas. Some drop zones require a variable while others do not. The drop zone for the x axis is required. The variable in this drop zone controls where the bars appear on the x axis. Depending on the type of chart you are creating, you may also need a variable in the y axis drop zone. For example, when you want to display a summary statistic of another variable (such as mean of salary), you need a variable in the y axis drop zone. Scatterplots also require a variable in the y axis. In that case, the drop zone identifies the dependent variable.

You are going to create a chart that shows bars for the mean income of each job satisfaction category, so both drop zones are needed. There will be a categorical variable on the x axis and a scale variable on the y axis for calculating the mean.

A variable's measurement level is important in the Chart Builder. You are going to use the Job satisfaction variable on the xaxis. However, the icon (which looks like a ruler) next to the variable indicates that its measurement level is defined as scale. To create the correct chart, you must use a categorical measurement level. Instead of going back and changing the measurement level in the Variable View, you can change the measurement level temporarily in the Chart Builder.

1. Right-click **Job satisfaction** in the Variables list and choose Ordinal. Ordinal is an appropriate measurement level because the categories in Job satisfaction can be ranked by level of satisfaction. Note that the icon changes after you change the measurement level.
2. Now drag **Job satisfaction** from the Variables list to the x axis drop zone.

   The y axis drop zone defaults to the Count statistic. If you want to use another statistic (such as percentage or mean), you can easily change it. You will not use either of these statistics in this example, but we will review the process in case you need to change this statistic at another time.

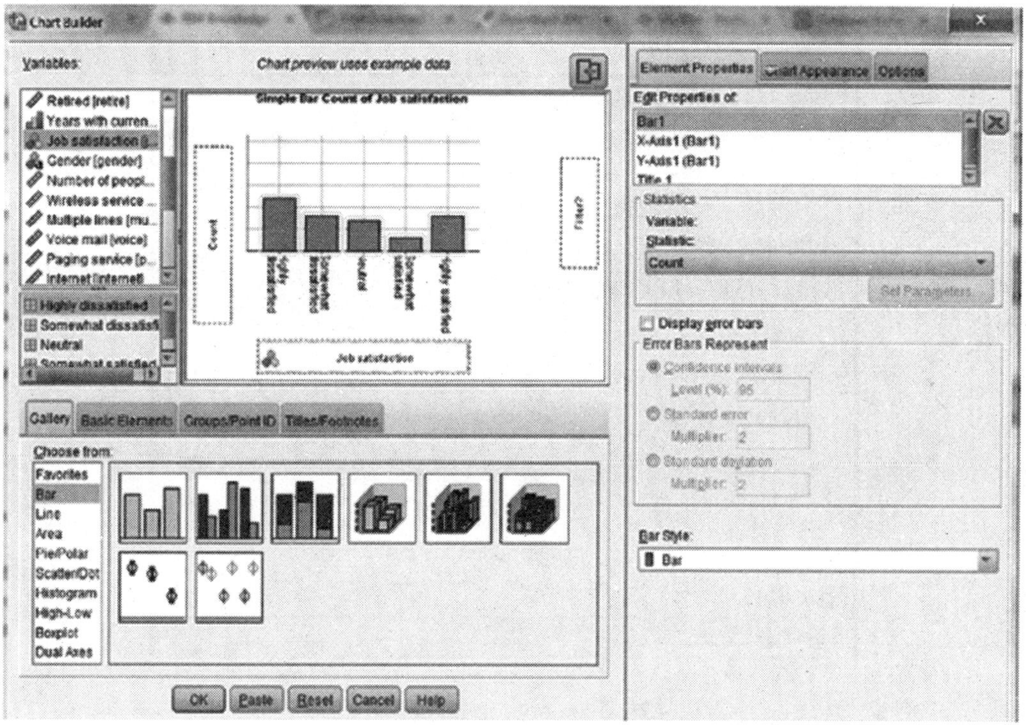

Fig. 2.18: Defining X- Axis.

3. Click **Element Properties** to display the Element Properties window.

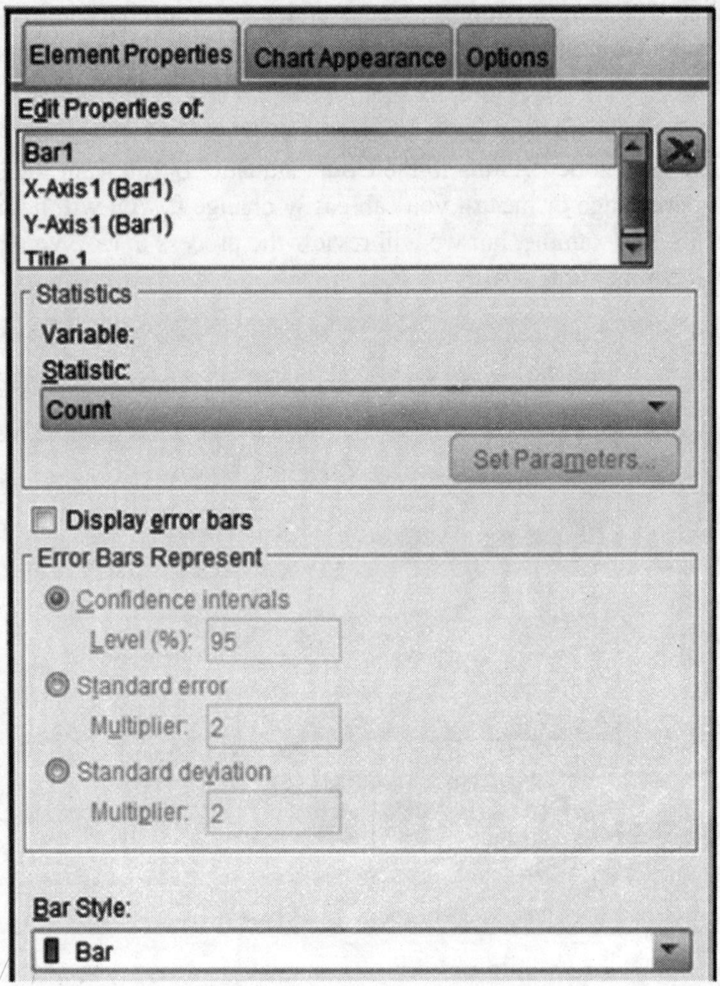

Fig. 2.19: Element Properties window

1. The **Element Properties** window allows you to change the properties of the various chart elements. These elements include the graphic elements (such as the bars in the bar chart) and the axes on the chart. Select one of the elements in the Edit Properties of list to change the properties associated with that element. Also note the red X located to the right of the list. This button deletes a graphic element from the canvas. Because **Bar1** is selected, the properties shown apply to graphic elements, specifically the bar graphic element.

   The Statistic drop-down list shows the specific statistics that are available. The same statistics are usually available for every chart type. Be aware that some statistics require that the y axis drop zone contains a variable.

2. Return to the **Chart Builder** dialog box and drag Household income in thousands from the Variables list to the y axis drop zone. Because the variable on the y axis is scalar and the x axis variable is categorical (ordinal is a type of categorical measurement level), the y axis drop zone defaults to the Mean statistic. These are the variables and statistics you want, so there is no need to change the element properties.

You can also add titles and footnotes to the chart.

1. Click the **Titles/Footnotes** tab.
2. Select Title 1.

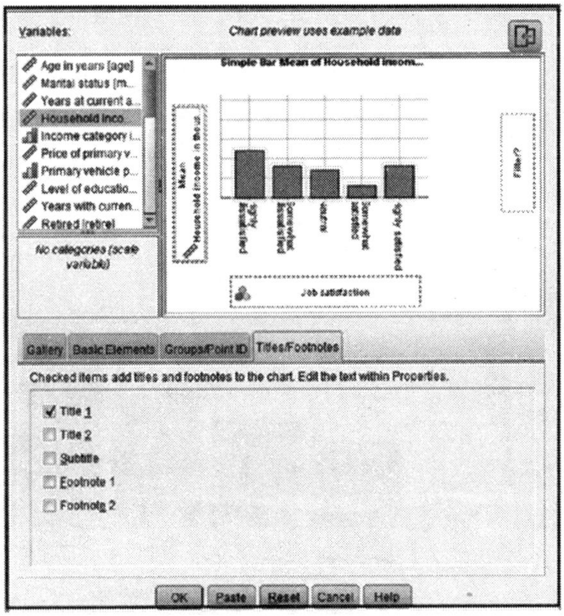

Fig. 2.20. Title 1 displayed on canvas

3. The title appears on the canvas with the label T1.
4. In the Element **Properties window**, select **Title 1** in the **Edit Properties of list**.

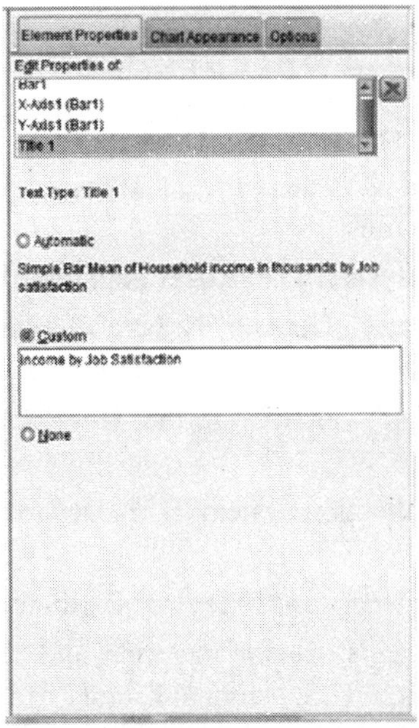

Fig. 2.21: Text for Title 1

5. In the Custom box, type Income by Job Satisfaction. This is the text that the title will display
6. Click **OK** and select **File -> Output to generate** and see the Graph as shown below:

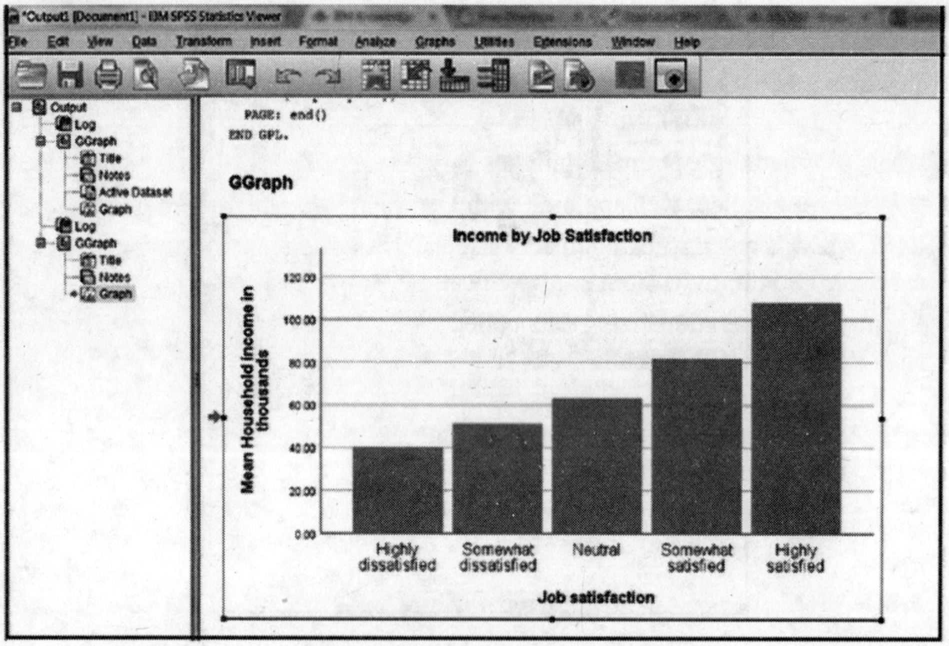

Fig. 2.22: The completed Bar Chart

The bar chart reveals that respondents who are more satisfied with their jobs tend to have higher household incomes.

REFERENCES

1. Lescroël, A. L.; Ballard, G.; Grémillet, D.; Authier, M.; Ainley, D. G. (2014). Descamps, Sébastien, ed. "Antarctic Climate Change: Extreme Events Disrupt Plastic Phenotypic Response in Adélie Penguins".
2. Data Collection and Analysis By Dr. Roger Sapsford, Victor Jupp ISBN 0-7619-5046-X
3. "Data Collection Software". GetApp. Nubera eBusiness S.L. Retrieved 20 December 2016.
4. "Survey Data Collection". NORC at the University of Chicago. 2016. Retrieved 2016-10- 14.
5. Jump "Using the Data Collection System". U.S. Department of Education. 2016. Retrieved 2016-10-14.
6. "How to Collect Data". American College of Cardiology. 2016. Retrieved 2016-10-14.
7. "Registries: Electronic registries for maternal and child health". National Center for Biotechnology Information. U.S. National Library of Medicine. PMC 4721069.
8. "Electronic Data Collection Options for Practice-Based Research Networks". National Center for Biotechnology Information. U.S. National Library of Medicine. PMC 1466955.

9. "Managing Data for Performance Improvement". HHS Bird Health Resources & Services Administration. U.S. Department of Health and Human Services. Retrieved 4 February 2017.
10. "Collecting and Reporting Data for Performance Measurement: Moving Toward Alignment". Proceedings of the AHRQ Conference on Health Care Data Collection and Reporting. U.S. Department of Health and Human Services. AHRQ Publication No. 07-0033-EF (March 2007). November 8–9, 2006. Retrieved 4 February 2017.
11. "Quiz - Drupal.org". Drupal.org. Dries Buytaert. Retrieved 20 December 2016.
12. "Online QuizBuilder web app built with Laravel". Webxity. Webxity Technologies.
13. IOM, ASEAN and trafficking in persons: Using data as a tool to combat trafficking, 2007, available at: http://www.iom.or.id/publications/pdf/16_MIL6010112_ASEAN_lo.pdf
14. Chapter 2 of Operationalizing data collection and analysis: Suggestions for stakeholders andsupport UNHCR Somalia

Chapter 3

DATA ANALYSIS USING R PROGRAMMING LANGUAGE

☞ Learning Objectives and Outcomes

In this unit student will be able to learn essentials of :

- ☞ Data analysis
- ☞ Terminology and concepts of data Analysis
- ☞ Introduction to statistics,
- ☞ Central tendencies and distributions,
- ☞ Defining Variance, Distribution properties and arithmetic,
- ☞ Samples and Central Limit Theorem (CLT),
- ☞ Basic machine learning algorithms,
- ☞ Linear regression,
- ☞ Support Vector Machine (SVM),
- ☞ Naive Bayes.

3.1 INTRODUCTION TO APPLIED STATISTICAL TECHNIQUES

Statistics is a branch of mathematics dealing with the collection, analysis, interpretation, presentation, and organization of data. In applying statistics to, e.g., **a scientific, industrial,** or **social problem**, it is conventional to begin with a statistical population or a **statistical model** process to be studied. Populations can be diverse topics such as "all people living in a country" or "every atom composing a crystal." Statistics deals with all aspects of **data including the planning of data collection in terms of the design of surveys and experiments.**

Applied statistics is a branch which covers natural processes and phenomena and provides us the knowledge for decision making as detailed in sketch shown in Figure 3.1.

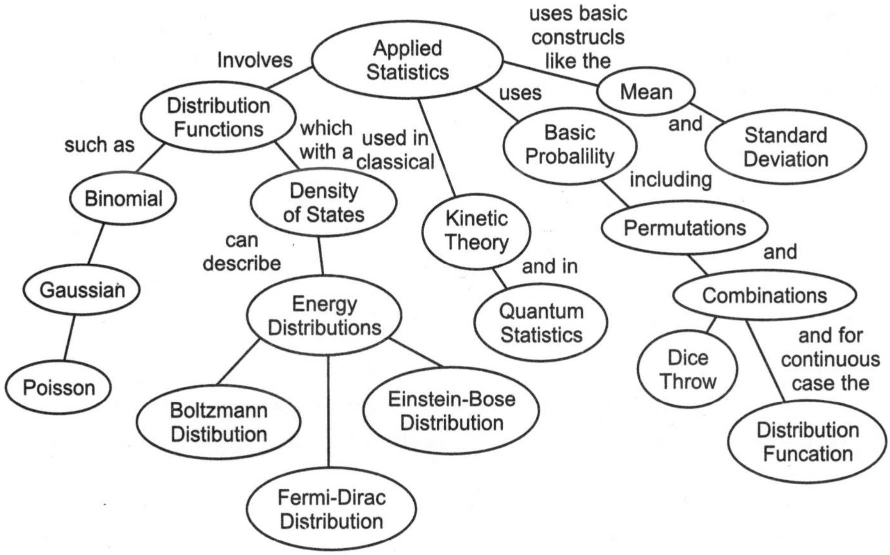

Fig. 3.1: Coverage of Applied Statistics.

3.1.1 Data Analysis

Analysis is the process of breaking a complex topic or substance into smaller parts in order to gain a better understanding of it. As such it refers to breaking a whole into its separate components for individual examination. Data analysis is a process for obtaining raw data and converting it into information useful for decision-making by users. Data is collected and analyzed to answer questions, test hypotheses or disprove theories. The term data analysis is sometimes used as a synonym for data modelling.

3.1.2 Data Analytics

Analytics is the discovery, interpretation, and communication of meaningful patterns in data. Especially valuable in areas rich with recorded information, analytics relies on the simultaneous application of statistics, computer programming and operations research to quantify performance. Data analytics uses analysed data to draw conclusions from it. It is the technique of getting automated insights into a given dataset. Data analytics can be described as a part of data science and it does find its applications in analyzing big data. The main focus of data analytics is inferencing some conclusion from the given data.

According to Merriam-Webster dictionary, *analysis* is the separation of a whole into its component parts, and *analytics* is the method of logical analysis. Marketers leverage both to drive all types of decisions, and each specific application supports the unique insight challenges inherent in dissecting customer behaviors.

Sole Difference

Analysis looks backwards over time, providing marketers with a historical view of what has happened. Typically, analytics look forward to model the future or predict a result.

Data analytics is a broader term and includes data analysis as necessary subcomponent. Analytics defines the science behind the analysis. The science means understanding the cognitive processes an analyst uses to understand problems and explore data in meaningful ways. Analytics also include data extract, transform, and load; specific tools, techniques, and methods; and how to successfully communicate results.

The growing maturity of the concept more starkly delineates the difference between big data and Business Intelligence:

1. Business Intelligence uses descriptive statistics with data with high information density to measure things, detect trends, etc..
2. Big data uses inductive statistics and concepts from nonlinear system identification to infer laws (regressions, nonlinear relationships, and causal effects) from large sets of data with low information density to reveal relationships and dependencies, or to perform predictions of outcomes and behaviors.

3.1.3 Statistical Data Analysis

The goal of statistical data analysis is to understand a complex, real-world phenomenon from partial and uncertain observations. The uncertainty in the data results in uncertainty in the knowledge we get about the phenomenon. A major goal of the theory is to quantify this uncertainty.

It is important to make the distinction between the mathematical theory underlying statistical data analysis, and the decisions made after conducting an analysis. The former is perfectly rigorous; perhaps surprisingly, mathematicians were able to build an exact mathematical framework to deal with uncertainty. Nevertheless, there is a subjective part in the way statistical analysis yields actual human decisions. Understanding the risk and the uncertainty behind statistical results is critical in the decision-making process.

In this unit, we will see the basic notions, principles, and theories behind statistical data analysis, covering in particular how to make decisions with a quantified risk. Of course, we will always show how to implement these methods with Python.

Exploratory methods allow us to get a preliminary look at a dataset through basic statistical aggregates and interactive visualization.

Statistical inference consists of getting information about an unknown process through partial and uncertain observations. In particular, estimation entails obtaining approximate quantities for the mathematical variables describing this process.

Decision theory allows us to make decisions about an unknown process from random observations, with a controlled risk.

Prediction consists of learning from data, that is, predicting the outcomes of a random process based on a limited number of observations.

Univariate and multivariate methods

In most cases, you can consider two dimensions in your data:

1. Observations (or samples, for machine learning people)
2. Variables (or features)

Typically, observations are independent realizations of the same random process. Each observation is made of one or several variables. Most of the time, variables are either numbers, or elements belonging to a finite set (that is, taking a finite number of values). The first step in an analysis is to understand what your observations and variables are.

Your problem is univariate if you have one variable. It is bivariate if you have two variables and multivariate if you have at least two variables. Univariate methods are typically simpler. That being said, univariate methods may be used on multivariate data, using one dimension at a time. Although interactions between variables cannot be explored in that case, it is often an interesting first approach.

When working with statistics, it's important to recognize the different types of data:

3.2 TYPES OF STATISTICAL DATA

Data are the actual pieces of information that you collect through your study.

When working with statistics, it's important to recognize the different types of data:

1. Numerical *(discrete and continuous)*,
2. Categorical, and
3. Ordinal.

Discrete data are called *digital or Binary* data and Continuous data types are called *Analog data* in information technology

3.2.1 Numerical Data

These data have meaning as a measurement, such as a person's height, weight, IQ, or blood pressure; or they're a count, such as the number of stock shares a person owns, how many teeth a dog has, or how many pages you can read of your favourite book before you fall asleep. (Statisticians also call numerical data ***quantitative*** *data.*)

Numerical data can be further broken into two types: **discrete and continuous.**

Discrete data represent items that can be counted; they take on possible values that can be listed out. The list of possible values may be fixed (also called *finite*); or it may go from 0, 1, 2, on to infinity (making it *countably infinite*). For example, the number of heads in 100 coin flips takes on values from 0 through 100 (finite case), but the number of flips needed to get 100 heads takes on values from 100 (the fastest scenario) on up to infinity (if you never get to that 100th heads). Its possible values are listed as 100, 101, 102, 103, . . . (representing the countably infinite case).

Continuous data represent measurements; their possible values cannot be counted and can only be described using intervals on the real number line. For example, the exact amount of gas purchased at the pump for cars with 20-gallon tanks would be continuous data from 0 gallons to 20 gallons, represented by the interval [0, 20], inclusive. You might pump 8.40 litres, or 8.41, or 8.414863 litress, or any possible number from 0 to 20. In this way, continuous data can be thought of as being uncountably infinite. For ease of recordkeeping, statisticians usually pick some point in the number to round off. Another example would be that the lifetime of a C battery can be anywhere from 0 hours to an infinite number of hours (if it lasts forever), technically, with all possible values in between. Granted, you don't expect a battery to last more than a few hundred hours, but no one can put a cap on how long it can put on service.

3.2.2 Categorical Data or Qualitative Data

Categorical data represent characteristics such as a person's gender, marital status, hometown, or the types of movies they like. Categorical data can take on numerical values (such as "1" indicating male and "2" indicating female), but those numbers don't have mathematical meaning. You couldn't add them together, for example. (Other names for categorical data are *qualitative data*, or *Yes/No data.*)

3.2.3 Ordinal Data

Ordinal data mixes numerical and categorical data. The data fall into categories, but the numbers placed on the categories have meaning. For example, rating a restaurant on a scale from 0 (lowest) to 4 (highest) stars gives ordinal data. Ordinal data are often treated as categorical, where the groups are ordered when graphs and charts are made. However, unlike categorical data, the numbers do have mathematical meaning. For example, if you survey 100 people and ask them to rate a restaurant on a scale from 0 to 4, taking the average of the 100 responses will have meaning. This would not be the case with categorical data.

3.2.4 Constant and Variable Data

Variables conforming only to nominal or ordinal measurements cannot be reasonably measured numerically, sometimes they are grouped together as categorical variables, whereas ratio and interval measurements are grouped together as quantitative variables, which can be either discrete or continuous, due to their numerical nature. Such distinctions can often be loosely correlated with data type in computer science, in that dichotomous categorical variables may be represented with the Boolean data type, polytomous categorical variables with arbitrarily assigned integers in the integral data type, and continuous variables with the real data type involving floating point computation. But the mapping of computer science data types to statistical data types depends on which categorization of the latter is being implemented.

3.3 TYPES OF BIG DATA ANALYTICS

It is useful to distinguish between different kinds of analytics because the differences have implications for the technologies and architectures used for big data analytics.

Some types of analytics are better performed on some platforms than on others. Fig. 3.2 provides with the historical evolution of big data Analytics.

1.

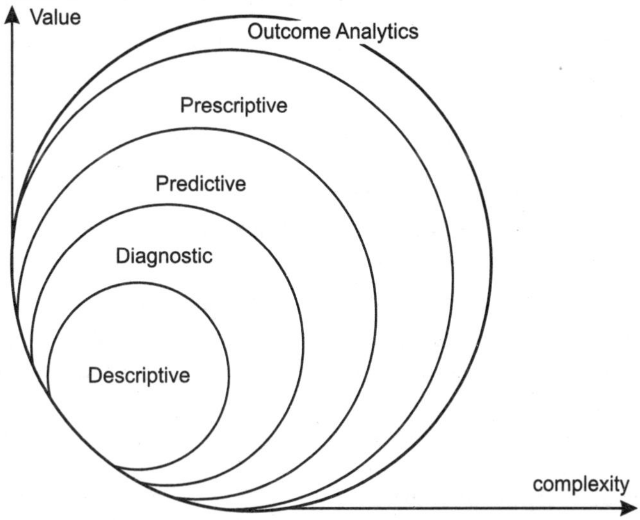

Descriptive: *What's happening in my business?*

- Comprehensive, accurate and live data.
- Effective visualisation

Diagnostic: *Why is it happening?*

- Ability to drill down to the root-cause
- Ability to isolate all confounding information

Predictive: *What's likely to happen?*

- Business strategies have remained fairly consistent over time
- Historical patterns being used to predict specific outcomes using algorithms
- Decisions are automated using algorithms and technology

Prescriptive: *What do I need to do?*

- Recommended actions and strategies based on champion/challenger testing strategy outcomes.
- Applying advanced analytical techniques to make specific recommendations.

Fig. 3.2: Evolution Of Analytics Within the Data Science

In general we find *five types* of big data analytics in most current (Year 2018) literature[1] :

3.3.1 Descriptive: What is happening?

The first stage of business analytics is descriptive analytics, which still accounts for the majority of all business analytics today. This is the most common of all forms. In business it provides the analyst a view of key metrics and measures within the business.

Descriptive analytics looks at past performance and understands that performance by mining historical data to look for the reasons behind past success or failure. Most management reporting – such as sales, marketing, operations, and finance – uses this type of post-mortem analysis.

Descriptive analytics, such as reporting/OLAP, dashboards/scorecards, and data visualization, have been widely used for some time, and are the core applications of traditional BI. This technique is the most time-intensive and often produces the least value; however, it is useful for uncovering patterns within a certain segment of customers. Descriptive analytics provide insight into what has happened historically and will provide you with trends to dig into in more detail. It gains insight from historical data with reporting, scorecards, clustering etc.

An examples of this could be a monthly profit and loss statement. Similarly, an analyst could have data on a large population of customers. Understanding demographic information on their customers (e.g. 30% of our customers are self-employed) would be categorised as "descriptive analytics". Utilising effective visualisation tools enhances the message of descriptive analytics.One trend, however, is to include the findings from predictive analytics, such as forecasts of future sales, on dashboards/scorecards.

Descriptive Statistics Application

In applying statistics to a problem, it is common practice to start with a population or process to be studied. Populations can be diverse topics such as "all persons living in a country" or "every atom composing a crystal".

Ideally, statisticians compile data about the entire population (an operation called census). This may be organized by governmental statistical institutes. Descriptive statistics can be used to summarize the population data. Numerical descriptors include mean and standard deviation for continuous data types (like income), while frequency and percentage are more useful in terms of describing categorical data (like race).

When a census is not feasible, a chosen subset of the population called a **sample** is studied. Once a sample that is representative of the population is determined, data is collected for the sample members in an observational or experimental setting

Again, descriptive statistics can be used to summarize the sample data. However, the drawing of the sample has been subject to an element of **randomness**, hence the established numerical descriptors from the sample are also due to uncertainty.

Examples of descriptive analytics also include summary statistics, clustering and association rules used in market basket analysis.

Key points:

- Backward looking
- Focused on descriptions and comparisons
- Pattern detection and descriptions
- MECE (mutually exclusive and collectively exhaustive) categorization
- Category development based on similarities and differences (segmentation)

3.3.2 Diagnostic Inferential Analytics : Why is it happening?

This is the next step of complexity in data analytics is descriptive analytics. On assessment of the descriptive data, diagnostic analytical tools will empower an analyst to drill down and in so doing isolate the root-cause of a problem.

Well-designed business information (BI) dashboards incorporating reading of time-series data (i.e. data over multiple successive points in time) and featuring filters and drill down capability allow for such analysis.

Data scientists turn to this technique when trying to determine why something happened. It is useful when researching leading churn indicators and usage trends amongst your most loyal customers. Examples of diagnostic analytics include churn reason analysis and customer health score analysis.

Key points:

- Backward looking
- Focused on causal relationships and sequences
- Relative ranking of dimensions/variable based on inferred explanatory power)
- Target/dependent variable with independent variables/dimensions
- Includes both frequentist and Bayesian causal inferential analyses

3.3.3 Predictive Analytics : What is likely to happen?

Predictive analytics is all about forecasting. Whether it's the likelihood of an event happening in future, forecasting a quantifiable amount or estimating a point in time at which something might happen – these are all done through predictive models.

Predictive models typically utilise a variety of variable data to make the prediction. The variability of the component data will have a relationship with what it is likely to predict (e.g. the older a person, the more susceptible they are to a heart-attack – we would say that age has a linear correlation with heart-attack risk). These data are then compiled together into a score or prediction.

In a world of great uncertainty, being able to predict allows one to make better decisions. Predictive models are some of the most important utilised across a number of fields.

In this forecasting method , historical data is combined with rules, algorithms, and occasionally external data to determine the probable future outcome of an event or the likelihood of a situation occurring.

The most commonly used technique; predictive analytics use models to forecast what might happen in specific scenarios. Examples of predictive analytics include next best offers, churn risk and renewal risk analysis.

Key points:

- Forward looking
- Focused on non-discrete predictions of future states, relationship, and patterns
- Description of prediction result set probability distributions and likelihoods
- Model application
- Non-discrete forecasting (forecasts communicated in probability distributions)

3.3.4 Prescriptive Analytics : What do I need to do?

The next step up in terms of value and complexity is the prescriptive model. The prescriptive model utilises an understanding of what has happened, why it has happened and a variety of "what-might-happen" analysis to help the user determine the best course of action to take. Prescriptive analysis is typically not just with one individual action, but is in fact a host of other actions.

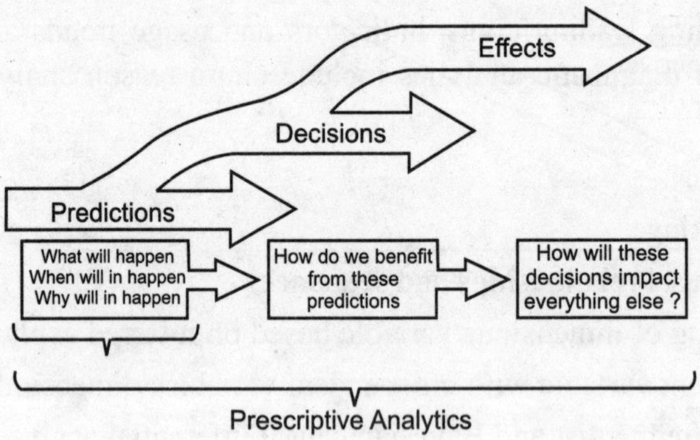

Fig. 3.3: Development of Prescriptive Analytics

Prescriptive Analytics extends beyond predictive analytics by specifying both the actions necessary to achieve predicted outcomes, and the interrelated effects of each decision

It is most valuable and most underused big data analytics technique, prescriptive analytics gives you a laser-like focus to answer a specific question. It helps to determine the best solution among a variety of choices, given the known parameters and suggests options for how to take advantage of a future opportunity or mitigate a future risk. It can also illustrate the implications of each decision to improve decision-making. Examples of prescriptive analytics for customer retention include next best action and next best offer analysis.

Key points:

- Forward looking
- Focused on optimal decisions for future situations
- Simple rules to complex models that are applied on an automated or programmatic basis
- Discrete prediction of individual data set members based on similarities and differences
- Optimization and decision rules for future events

A good example of this is a traffic application helping you choose the best route home and taking into account the distance of each route, the speed at which one can travel on each road and, crucially, the current traffic constraints.

Another example might be producing an exam time-table such that no students have clashing schedules.

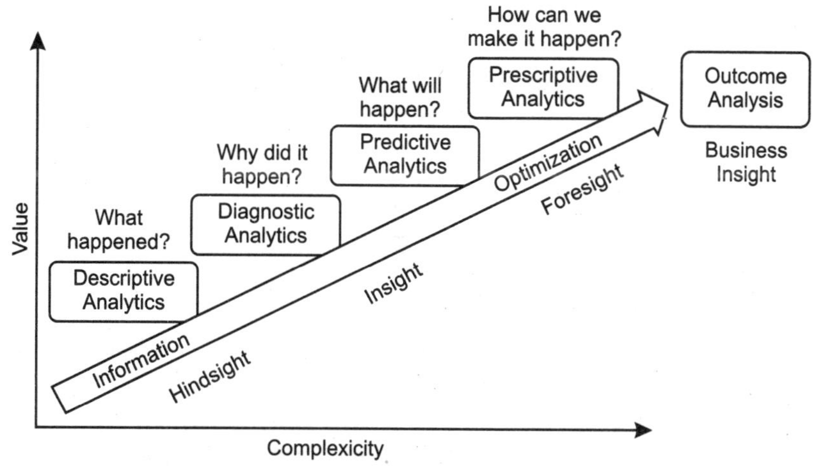

Fig. 3.4: Optmization of business data to Create Business Insights

3.3.5 Outcome Analytics

Also referred to as consumption analytics, this technique provides insight into customer behavior that drives specific outcomes. This analysis is meant to help you know your customers better and learn how they are interacting with your products and services. Creating increased value for customers is, today, a business imperative, as is the need to contain costs, and adopt new technologies to meet consumer expectations. Here's where Business Process Management (BPM) players can step in to develop customized analytics solutions that deliver targeted business outcomes. These outcomes can be varied – optimized marketing efforts, increased cash flow, accurate prediction of customer behavior and improved customer engagement, among others.

Key points:

1. Backward looking, Real-time and Forward looking
2. Focused on consumption patterns and associated business outcomes
3. Description of usage thresholds
4. Model application

3.4 COLLECTING DATA FOR SAMPLING AND DISTRIBUTION

Accurate data collection is essential to many business processes,[2][3][4] to the enforcement of many government regulations,[5] and to maintaining the integrity of scientific research.[6]

The problem with collecting data is that you do not generally know what distribution the data follows. So you have a sample, but no distribution to help figure it out. The true distribution is generally not knowable, but you could often find something workable distribution as per central limit theorem. It implies under fairly easy to satisfy conditions that some of the summary statistics you'd calculate from your sample do have a known distribution even if you do not know the distribution of your sample.

3.5 PROBABILITY

Probability is the *measure* of the likelihood that an *event* will occur. Probability is quantified as a number between 0 and 1, where, loosely speaking, 0 indicates **impossibility** and 1 indicates **certainty**. The higher the probability of an event, the more likely it is that the event will occur. A simple example is the tossing of a fair (unbiased) coin. Since the coin is fair, the two outcomes ("heads" and "tails") are both equally probable; the probability of "heads" equals the probability of "tails"; and since no other outcomes are possible, the probability of either "heads" or "tails" is 1/2 (which could also be written as 0.5 or 50%).

When dealing with experiments that are *random* and *well-defined* in a purely theoretical setting (like tossing a fair coin), probabilities can be numerically described by the number of desired outcomes divided by the total number of all outcomes. For example, tossing a fair coin twice will yield "head-head", "head-tail", "tail-head", and "tail-tail" outcomes. The probability of getting an outcome of "head-head" is 1 out of 4 outcomes or 1/4 or 0.25 (or 25%).

In probability theory, a probability distribution is a mathematical function that, stated in simple terms, can be thought of as providing the probabilities of occurrence of different possible outcomes in an experiment. For instance, if the random variable X is used to denote the outcome of a coin toss ("the experiment"), then the probability distribution of X would take the value 0.5 for X = heads, and 0.5 for X = tails (assuming the coin is fair).Normally in casinos, the coins are not fair and aredesired to bring the outcome result according to whim of the skilled but wicket person tossing the coin.

Throwing Dice

When a single die is thrown, there are six possible outcomes: **1, 2, 3, 4, 5, 3.** The probability of any one of them is 1/6

$$\text{Probability of an event happening} = \frac{\text{Number of ways it can happen}}{\text{Total number of outcomes}}$$

Example 3.1 (*a*): The chances of rolling a "4" with a die

Number of ways it can happen: 1 (there is only 1 face with a "4" on it)

Total number of outcomes: 6 (there are 6 faces altogether)

$$\text{So the probability} = \frac{1}{6}$$

Probability is Just a Guide

Probability does not tell us exactly what will happen, it is just a guide

Example 3.1 (*b*): Toss a coin 100 times, how many Heads will come up?

Probability says that heads have a ½ chance, so we can expect 50 Heads.

But when we actually try it we might get 48 heads, or 55 heads ... or anything really, but in most cases it will be a number near 50.

3.5 FREQUENCY DISTRIBUTION

A frequency distribution is a table that displays the frequency of various outcomes in a sample.. A frequency distribution is a table or graph that displays the frequency of various outcomes in a sample. Each entry in the table contains the frequency or count of the occurrences of values within a particular group or interval, and in this way, the table summarizes the distribution of values in the sample.

Frequency shows how often an event happens in any phenomena.

Example 3.2: Amit played football on

- Saturday Morning,
- Saturday Afternoon
- Thursday Afternoon

The frequency was 2 on Saturday, 1 on Thursday and for the whole week.

Frequency Distribution Table

By counting frequencies we can make a Frequency Distribution Table.

Example 3.3: Goals

Shyam's team has scored the following numbers of goals in recent games:

2, 3, 1, 2, 1, 3, 2, 3, 4, 5, 4, 2, 2, 3

Shyam put the numbers in order, then added up:

- how often 1 occurs (2 times),
- how often 2 occurs (5 times), ano so on.

Scores: 1, 1, 2, 2, 2, 2, 2, 3, 3, 3, 3, 4, 4, 5	
Score	**Frequency**
1	2
2	5
3	4
4	2
5	1

From the table (which is also called as *contingency table*), we can see interesting things such as getting 2 goals happens most often only once did they get 5 goals.

Bivariate (two way)

Bivariate (two way) frequency distributions are often presented as (two-way) contingency tables:

♦	Dance ♦	Sports ♦	TV ♦	Total ♦
Men	2	10	8	20
Women	16	6	8	30
Total	18	16	16	50

Fig. 3.4: A Two Way (Bivariate) Contingency Table

Managing and operating on frequency tabulated data is much simpler than operation on raw data. There are simple algorithms to calculate median, mean, standard deviation etc. from these tables.

Statistical hypothesis testing is founded on the assessment of differences and similarities between frequency distributions.

3.6 POPULATION AND PARAMETERS

In statistics, a population is a set of similar items or events which is of interest for some question or experiment.[7] A statistical population can be a group of actually existing objects (e.g. the set of all stars within the Milky Way galaxy) or a hypothetical and potentially infinite group of objects conceived as a generalization from experience (e.g. the set of all possible hands in a game of poker).[8]

We have seen that descriptive statistics provide information about our immediate group of data. For example, we could calculate the mean and standard deviation of the exam marks for the 100 students and this could provide valuable information about this group of 100 students. Any group of data like this, which includes all the data you are interested in, is called a **population**. A population can be small or large, as long as it includes all the data you are interested in. For example, if you were only interested in the exam marks of 100 students, the 100 students would represent your population. Descriptive statistics are applied to populations, and the properties of populations, like the mean or standard deviation, are called **parameters** as they represent the whole population (i.e., everybody you are interested in).

Statistical sampling is used quite often in statistics. sampling is the selection of a subset (a statistical sample) of individuals from within a statistical population to estimate characteristics of the whole population. Two advantages of sampling are that the cost is lower and data collection is faster than measuring the entire population. In this process we aim to determine something about a population. Since populations are typically large in size, we form a statistical sample by selecting a subset of the population that is of a predetermined size. By studying the sample we can use inferential statistics to determine something about the population.

A statistical sample of size n involves a single group of n individuals or subjects that have been randomly chosen from the population.

3.7 CENTRAL TENDENCY OR CENTRAL VALUE

In statistics, a central tendency (or measure of central tendency) is a central or typical value for a probability distribution.[9] It may also be called a center or location of the distribution. Colloquially, measures of central tendency are often called averages.

The most common measures of central tendency are the arithmetic mean, the median and the mode. A central tendency can be calculated for either a finite set of values or for a theoretical distribution, such as the normal distribution.

The central tendency of a distribution is typically contrasted with its dispersion or variability; dispersion and central tendency are the often characterized properties of distributions. Analysts may judge whether data has a strong or a weak central tendency based on its dispersion.

3.7.1 Central Value

Example 3.4: *What is the central value for 3 and 7?*

Answer: Half-way between, which is 5.

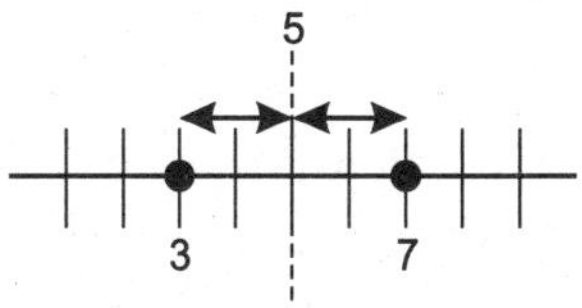

You can calculate it by adding 3 and 7 and then dividing the result by 2:

→ $(3 + 7)/2 = 10/2 = 5$

Example 3.5: *What is the central value of 3, 7 and 8?*

Answer: You calculate it by adding 3, 7 and 8 and then dividing the results by 3 (because there are 3 numbers):

→ $(3 + 7 + 8)/3 = 18/3 = 6$

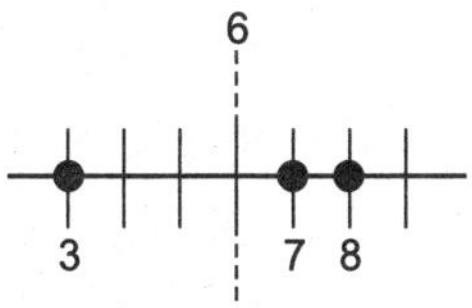

3.8 MEASURES OF CENTRAL TENDENCY

They are a combination of two words i.e. 'measure' and 'Central tendency'. Measure means methods and central tendency means average value of any statistical series. Thus we can say that central tendency means the methods of finding out the central value or average value of a statistical series of quantitative information. A measure of central tendency is a single value that attempts to describe a set of data by identifying the central position within that set of data. As such, measures of central tendency are sometimes called measures of central location. They are also classed as summary statistics.

In statistics we always find measures of central tendency because it always makes sense to compare individual scores to the overall group of scores in order to be able to correctly interpret the result.

Individual scores by themselves may mean little but when looked at from a group point of view, they may reveal the whole picture.

For example, if you say you saw an insect of length of 10mm it doesn›t mean anything by itself. However, if you say that the normal length of the insect is about 6cm and the maximum recorded length ever is 10.4cm, then it may mean you saw a particularly large insect. Therefore it is important to be able to quantify the «normal length» as used above, and this is what central tendency is all about.

There are **three main measures of central tendency**: the

1. Mean
2. Median
3. Mode

Each of these measures describes a different indication of the typical or central **value** in the distribution. The mean (often called the average) is most likely the measure of central tendency that you are most familiar with.

The mean, median and mode are all valid measures of central tendency, but under different conditions, some measures of central tendency become more appropriate to use than others.

3.8.1 The Mean

So far we have been calculating the Mean (or the Average):

Mean: Add up the numbers and divide by how many numbers. But sometimes the Mean can let you down: This may be some time embarassive.

Example 3.6: *Birthday Activities*

Uncle Bob wants to know the average age at the party, to choose an activity.

There will be 6 kids aged 13, and also 5 babies aged 1.

Add up all the ages, and divide by 11 (because there are 11 numbers):

(13 + 13 + 13 + 13 + 13 + 13 + 1 + 1 + 1 + 1 + 1)/11 = 7.5..

The mean age is about 7½, so he gets a Jumping Castle! The 13 year olds are embarrassed, and the 1 year olds can't jump!

The Mean was **accurate**, but in this case it was not **useful**.

The mean (or average) is the most popular and well known **measure of central tendency**. It can be used with both discrete and continuous data, although its use is most often with continuous data. The mean is equal to the sum of all the values in the data set divided by the number of values in the data set. So, if we have n values in a data set and they have values $x_1, x_2, ..., x_n$, the sample mean, usually denoted by (pronounced **x bar**), is:

$$\bar{x} = \frac{(x_1 + x_2 + ... + x_n)}{n}$$

This formula is usually written in a slightly different manner using the Greek capitol letter, , pronounced "**sigma**", which means "sum of...":

$$\bar{x} = \frac{\Sigma x}{n}$$

You may have noticed that the above formula refers to the sample mean. So, why have we called it a sample mean? This is because, in statistics, samples and populations have very different meanings and these differences are very important, even if, in the case of the mean, they are calculated in the same way. To acknowledge that we are calculating the population mean and not the sample mean, we use the Greek lower case letter "mu", denoted as μ:

$$\mu = \frac{\Sigma x}{n}$$

The mean is essentially a model of your data set. It is the value that is most common. You will notice, however, that the mean is not often one of the actual values that you have observed in your data set. However, one of its important properties is that it minimises error in the prediction of any one value in your data set. That is, it is the value that produces the lowest amount of error from all other values in the data set.

When not to use the mean

The mean has one main disadvantage: it is particularly susceptible to the influence of outliers. These are values that are unusual compared to the rest of the data set by being especially small or large in numerical value. For example, consider the wages of staff at a factory below:

Staff	1	2	3	4	5	6	7	8	9	10
Salary	15k	18k	16k	14k	15k	15k	12k	17k	90k	95k

The mean salary for these ten staff is $30.7k. However, inspecting the raw data suggests that this mean value might not be the best way to accurately reflect the typical salary of a worker, as most workers have salaries in the $12k to 18k range. **The mean is being skewed by the two large salaries.** Therefore, in this situation, we would like to have a better measure of central tendency. As we will find out later, taking the median would be a better measure of central tendency in this situation. **Skewness** is a measure of symmetry, or more precisely, the **lack of symmetry**. A distribution, or data set, is symmetric if it looks the same to the left and right of the center point.

Another time when we usually prefer the median over the mean (or mode) is when our data is **skewed** (i.e., the frequency distribution for our data is skewed). If we consider the **normal distribution** - as this is the most frequently assessed in statistics - when the data is perfectly normal, the mean, median and mode are identical. Moreover, they all represent the most typical value in the data set. However, as the data becomes skewed the mean loses its ability to provide the best central location for the data because the skewed data is dragging it away from the typical value. However, the median best retains this position and is not as strongly influenced by the skewed values.

3.8.2 Median

The median is the middle score for a set of data that has been arranged in order of magnitude. The median is less affected by outliers and skewed data. In order to calculate the median, suppose we have the data below:

65	55	89	56	35	14	56	55	87	45	92

We first need to rearrange that data into order of magnitude (smallest first):

14	35	45	55	55	56	56	65	87	89	92

Our median mark is the middle mark - in this case, 56 (highlighted in bold). It is the middle mark because there are 5 scores before it and 5 scores after it.

This works fine when you have an odd number of scores, but what happens when you have an even number of scores? What if you had only 10 scores? Well, you simply have to take the middle two scores and average the result. So, if we look at the example below:

We again rearrange that data into order of magnitude (smallest first):

Only now we have to take the 5th and 6th score in our data set and average them to get a median of 53.3.

3.8.3 Mode

The mode is the most frequent score in our data set. On a histogram it represents the highest bar in a bar chart or histogram. You can, therefore, sometimes consider the mode as being the most popular option. An example of a mode is presented below:

The **Mode** is the value that occurs most often:

Example 3.7: *Birthday Activities (continued)*

Group the numbers so we can count them:

1, 1, 1, 1, 1, 13, 13, 13, 13, 13, 13

"13" occurs 6 times, "1" occurs only 5 times, so the mode is **13**.

But Mode can be tricky, there can sometimes be more than one Mode.

Example 3.8: *What is the Mode of 3, 4, 4, 5, 6, 6, 7 ...*

Well ... 4 occurs twice but 6 also occurs twice.

So **both 4 and 6** are modes.

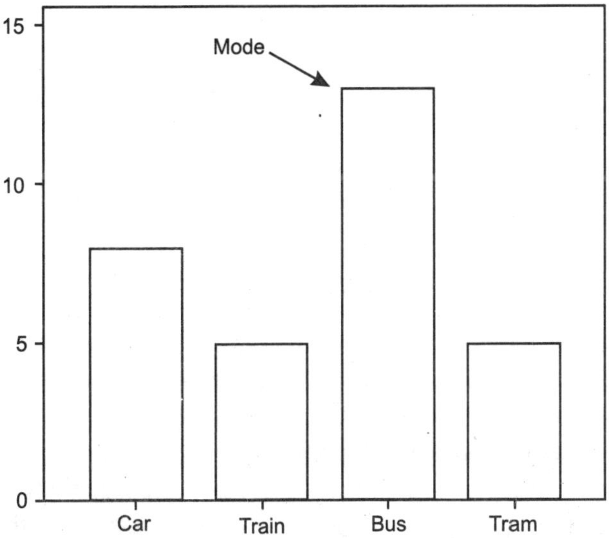

Fig. 3.5: Mode of a Populated Data

We can see above that the most common form of transport, in this particular data set, is the bus. One of the problems with the mode is that it is not **unique,** so it leaves us with problems when we have two or more values that share the highest frequency, such as below: We are now stuck as to which mode best describes the central tendency of the data. This is particularly problematic when we have continuous data because we are more likely not to have any one value that is more frequent than the other. Another problem with the mode is that it will not provide us with a very good measure of central tendency when the most common mark is far away from the rest of the data in the data set,

When there are two modes it is called "bimodal", when there are three or more modes we call it "multimodal".

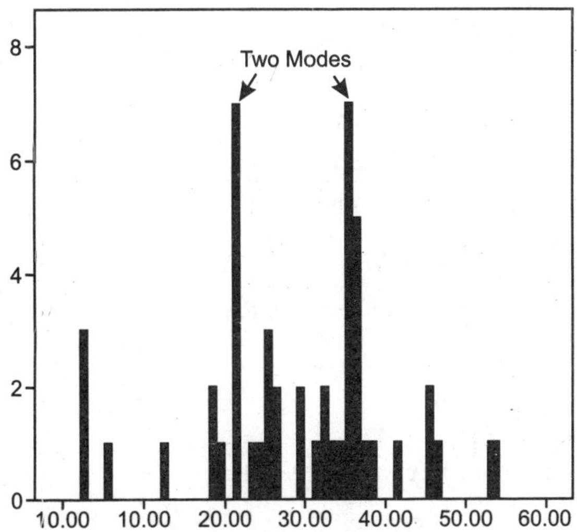

Fig. 3.6: Bi-Modal representation

3.8.4 Outliers

An outlier is an observation point that is distant from other observations. An outlier may be due to variability in the measurement or it may indicate experimental measurement error; Outliers can occur by chance in any distribution and as such are more than often excluded from the data set otherwise an outlier can cause serious problems in statistical analyses.

Causes

Outliers can have many anomalous causes. A physical apparatus for taking measurements may have suffered a transient malfunction. There may have been an error in data transmission or transcription. Outliers arise due to changes in system behaviour, fraudulent behaviour, human error, instrument error or simply through natural deviations in populations. A sample may have been contaminated with elements from outside the population being examined. Alternatively, an outlier could be the result of a flaw in the assumed theory, calling for further investigation by the researcher.

3.9 DIFFERENT TYPES OF STATISTICAL MEANS

1. The arithmetic mean,
2. geometric mean,
3. median and
4. mode

There are different kinds of statistical means or measures of central tendency for the data points. Each one has its own utility.

For example, the arithmetic mean is frequently used in scientific experimentation, the geometric mean is used in finance to calculate compounding quantities, the median is used as a robust mean in case of skewed data with many outliers and the mode is frequently used in determining the most frequently occurring data, like during an election

The arithmetic mean is perhaps the most commonly used statistical mean to measure the central tendency of data. The arithmetic mean is also called the "average". It is used in most scientific experiments.

Mathematically, the arithmetic mean is given by:

$$= \frac{\text{arithmetic mean}}{\text{Sum of all datapoints}}$$

Statisticcally we write

$$\bar{x} = \frac{1}{n}\sum_{i=1}^{n} x_i = \frac{1}{n}(x_1 + \ldots + x_n)$$

3.9.1 The Mean vs. the Median

As measures of central tendency, the mean and the median each have advantages and disadvantages. Some pros and cons of each measure are summarized below.

1. The median may be a better indicator of the most typical value if a set of scores has an **outlier**. An outlier is an extreme value that differs greatly from other values.
2. However, when the sample size is large and does not include outliers, the mean score usually provides a better measure of central tendency.

   To illustrate these points, consider the following example. Suppose we examine a sample of 10 households to estimate the typical family income. Nine of the households have incomes between \$20,000 and \$100,000; but the tenth household has an annual income of \$1,000,000,000. That tenth household is an outlier. If we choose a measure to estimate the income of a typical household, the mean will greatly over-estimate the income of a typical family (because of the outlier); while the median will not.

Is The Arithmentic Mean Misleading?

When the arithmetic mean is used to calculate this, it can be misleading because the salaries can be widely spread. Thus it may happen that 10% of the class have gotten excellent job offers while half the class is without jobs. Even in such a scenario, the mean salary can be a good number, but it hides facts behind it. The median becomes a much better measure of the salaries of the students in this case.

The Gross Domestic Product or GDP used in economics to determine the financial well being of a country is an arithmetic mean. The total value of goods and services produced in the country when averaged out over the total population gives a measure of GDP. The GDP tells us nothing about the distribution of wealth inside the country, but can be a good parameter for the country to work with in improving the economic condition of its citizens.

3.9.2 Geometric Mean

The geometric mean is relevant on certain sets of data, and is different from the arithmetic mean. Mathematically, the geometric mean is the nth root of the product of n numbers.

This can be written as:

$$\textbf{Geometric Mean} = (a_1 \times a_2 \ldots a_n)^{1/n}$$

Where:

N = Number of datapoints

a = score of a datapoint

or more complicated - the exact formula

$$\left(\prod_{i=1}^{n} a_i\right)^{1/n} = \sqrt[n]{a_1 a_2 \ldots a_n}$$

The geometric mean is relevant on those sets of data that are products or exponential in nature. This includes a variety of branches of natural sciences and social sciences.

Usages

In social sciences, we frequently encounter this in a number of ways. For example, the human population growth is expressed as a percentage, and thus when population growth needs to be averaged, it is the geometric mean that is most relevant.

In surveys and studies too, the geometric mean becomes relevant. For example, if a survey found that over the years, the economic status of a poor neighborhood is getting better, they need to quote the geometric mean of the development, averaged over the years in which the survey was conducted. The arithmetic mean will not make sense in this case either.

In economics, we see the percentage growth in interest accumulation. Thus if you are starting out with a sum of money that is compounded for interest, then the mean that you should look for is the geometric mean. Many such financial instruments like bonds yield a fixed percentage return, and while quoting their "average" return, it is the geometric mean that should be quoted.

3.10 PROBLEMS OF ESTIMATION : POPULATION OR SAMPLE

A common problem in statistics is to obtain information about the mean, μ, of a population.

For example, we might want to know

1. the mean age of people in the civilian labour force,
2. the mean cost of a wedding,
3. the mean gas mileage of a new-model car, or
4. the mean starting salary of liberal-arts graduates.

If the population is small, we can ordinarily determine μ exactly by first taking a census and then computing μ from the population data. If the population is large, however, as it often is in practice, taking a census is generally impractical, extremely expensive, or impossible.

Nonetheless, we can usually obtain sufficiently accurate information about μ by taking a sample from the population.

3.11 NORMAL DISTRIBUTION CURVE

In statistics, the theoretical curve that shows how often an experiment will produce a particular result. The curve is symmetrical and bell shaped, showing that trials will usually give a result near the average, but will occasionally deviate by large amounts. Normal distribution occurs very frequently in statistics, economics, natural and social sciences and can be used to approximate many distributions occurring in nature and in the manmade world.

For example, the height of all people of a particular race, the length of all dogs of a particular breed, IQ, memory and reading skills of people in a general population and income distribution in an economy all approximately follow the normal probability distribution shaped like a bell curve.

The theory of normal distribution also finds use in advanced sciences like astronomy, photonics and quantum mechanics.

Teacher expects most of the students get good marks. If it happens, then the cure looks like the normal curve below:

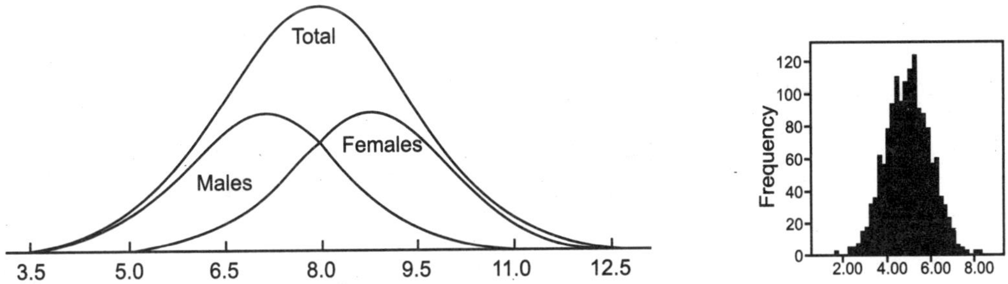

Fig. 3.7: Normal Distribution Curve

In case of perfectly symmetrical distribution the mean, median and mode are equal.

Use the following summary table to know what the best measure of central tendency is with respect to the different types of variable.

Type of Variable	Best measure of central tendency
Nominal	Mode
Ordinal	Median
Interval/Ratio (not skewed)	Mean
Interval/Ratio (skewed)	Median

3.11.1 Characteristics of Normal Distribution curve

There are four characteristics of a normal distribution. Normal distributions are:

1. Symmetric,
2. Unimodal, and
3. Asymptotic, and the
4. Mean, median, and mode are all equal.

A normal distribution is perfectly symmetrical around its center. That is, the right side of the center is a mirror image of the left side.

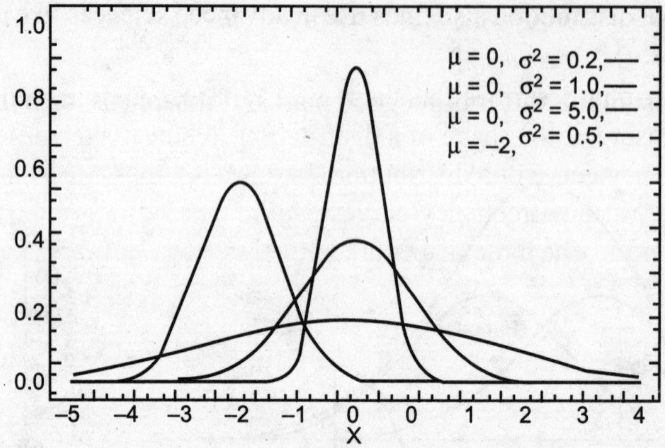

Fig. 3.8: Normal Distribution Curve with various values of μ (Mu i.e. population mean) and σ^2 is the population variance pronounced as Sigmasquare.

3.12 SKEWNESS

Skewness is a measure of symmetry, or more precisely, the lack of symmetry. A distribution, or data set, is symmetric if it looks the same to the left and right of the center point.

A fundamental task in many statistical analyses is to characterize the location and variability of a data set. A further characterization of the data includes skewness and kurtosis.Measure of Dispersion tells us about the variation of the data set. Skewness tells us about the direction of variation of the data set.

3.12.1 Types of Skewness : Positive Skewness Negative Skewness

But for some reasons (e. g., lazy students, not understanding the lectures, not attentive etc.) it is not happening. So we get another two curves.

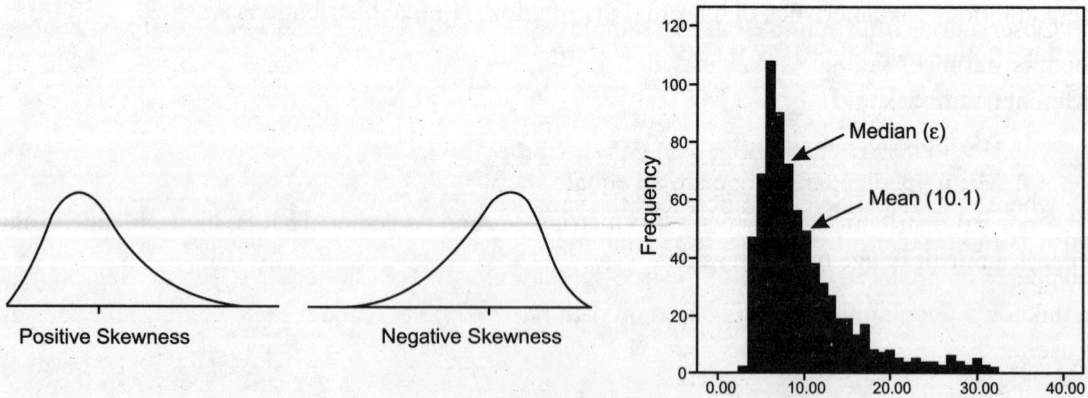

Fig. 3.9. Types of Skewness

The first one is known as positively skewed and the second one is known as negatively skewed curve.

3.13 KURTOSIS

Kurtosis is a parameter that describes the shape of a random variable's probability distribution. Kurtosis is another measure of the shape of a distribution. Whereas skewness measures the lack of symmetry of the frequency curve of a distribution, kurtosis is a measure of the relative peakedness of its frequency curve. Various frequency curves can be divided into three categories depending upon the shape of their peak. The three shapes are termed as *Leptokurtic, Mesokurtic* and *Platykurhc* as shown in Fig. 3.8

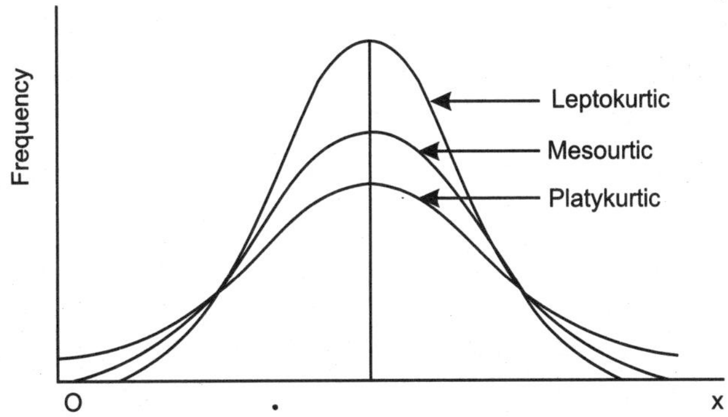

Fig. 3.10: Three types of Kurtosys

3.14 THE VARIANCE

In a population, variance is the average squared deviation from the population mean, as defined by the following formula:

$$\sigma^2 = \Sigma(X_i - \mu)^2/N$$

where σ^2 is the population variance, μ is the population mean, x_i is the *i*th element from the population, and N is the number of elements in the population.

Observations from a simple random sample can be used to estimate the variance of a population. For this purpose, sample variance is defined by slightly different formula, and uses a slightly different notation:

$$s^2 = \Sigma(x_i - \bar{x})^2/(n-1)$$

where s^2 is the sample variance, x is the sample mean, x_i is the *i*th element from the sample, and n is the number of elements in the sample. Using this formula, the sample variance can be considered an unbiased estimate of the true population variance. Therefore, if you need to estimate an unknown population variance, based on data from a simple random sample, this is the formula to use.

3.15 THE STANDARD DEVIATION

The standard deviation is the square root of the variance. Thus, the standard deviation of a population is:

$$\sigma = \sqrt{\sigma^2} = \sqrt{\frac{\Sigma(X_1 - \quad)}{N}}$$

where σ is the population standard deviation, μ is the population mean, *Xi* is the *i*th element from the population, and *N* is the number of elements in the population.

Statisticians often use simple random samples to estimate the standard deviation of a population, based on sample data. Given a simple random sample, the best estimate of the standard deviation of a population is:

$$s = \sqrt{s^2} = \sqrt{\frac{\Sigma(x_i \quad x)^2}{n \quad 1}}$$

where *s* is the sample standard deviation, x is the sample mean, xi is the ith element from the sample, and n is the number of elements in the sample.

Example 3.9 (*a*): *Calculate the standard deviation for the following sample : 2, 4, 8, 6, 10, and 12.*

Solution: Actual Mean Method

>Xi	>(Xi – μ)2
>2	>$(2 - 7)^2 = 25$
>4	>$(4 - 7)^2 = 9$
>8	>$(8 - 7)^2 = 1$
>6	>$(6 - 7)^2 = 1$
>10	>$(10 - 7)^2 = 9$
>12	>$(12 - 7)^2 = 25$
>$\Sigma X_i = 42$	>$S(Xi - \mu)^2 = 70$

$$\overline{X} = \frac{\Sigma x_i}{n} = \frac{42}{6} = 7$$

$$S = \sqrt{\frac{\Sigma(x_1 - \overline{X})^2}{n}}$$

$$S = \sqrt{\frac{70}{6}} = \sqrt{\frac{35}{3}} = 3.42$$

Second method

Taking assumed mean as zero	
>X	>$(X_i - \mu)^2$
>2	>4
>4	>16
>8	>64
>6	>36
>10	>100
>12	>144
>$\Sigma X = 42$	>$\Sigma X^2 = 364$

$$S = \sqrt{\frac{\Sigma X^2}{n} - \left(\frac{\Sigma X}{n}\right)^2}$$

$$S = \sqrt{\frac{364}{6} - \left(\frac{42}{6}\right)^2}$$

$$S = \sqrt{\frac{70}{6}} = \sqrt{\frac{35}{3}} = 3.42$$

As a simple example, consider the average daily maximum temperatures for two cities, one inland and one on the coast. It is helpful to understand that the range of daily maximum temperatures for cities near the coast is smaller than for cities inland. Thus, while these two cities may each have the same average maximum temperature, the standard deviation of the daily maximum temperature for the coastal city will be less than that of the inland city as, on any particular day, the actual maximum temperature is more likely to be farther from the average maximum temperature for the inland city than for the coastal one.

Example 3.9 (*b*): *For example, the data points 50, 51, 52, 55, 56, 57, 59 and 60 have a mean at 55 (Blue/Rhombus).*

Another data set of 12, 32, 43, 48, 64, 71, 83 and 87. This set too has a mean of 55 (Pink/ Rectangle)

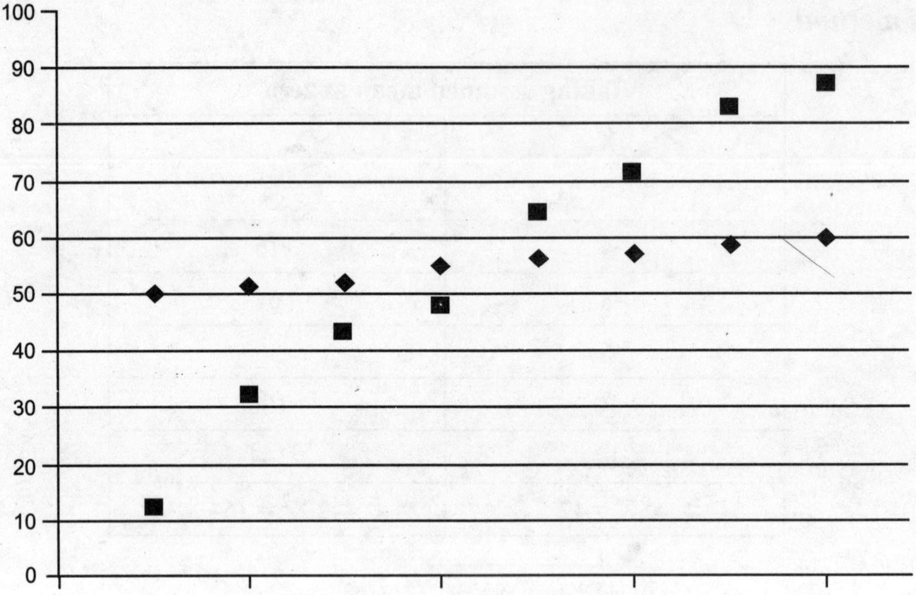

Fig. 3.11: Two different series of Data Collection

However, it can clearly be seen that the properties of these two sets are different. The first set is much more closely packed than the second one. Through standard deviation, we can measure this distribution of data about the mean.

One Standard Deviation

In a *normal distribution*, values falling within 68.2% of the mean fall within one standard deviation. This means if the mean energy consumption of various houses in a colony is 200 units with a standard deviation of 20 units, it means that 68.2% of the households consume energy between 180 to 220 units. This is assuming that the data of energy consumption is normally distributed.

If a researcher considers three standard deviations to either side of the mean, this covers 99% of the data. Thus in the previous example, 99% of the households have their energy consumption between 140 to 260 units. In most cases, this is considered as the whole *data set*, especially when the data can extend to infinity.

Usage

The measurement of uncertainty through standard deviation is used in many experiments of social sciences and finances. For example, the more risky and volatile ventures have a higher standard deviation. Also, a very high standard deviation of the results for the same survey, for example, should make one rethink about the sample size and the survey as a whole.

In physical experiments, it is important to have a measurement of uncertainty. Standard deviation provides a way to check the results. Very large values of standard deviation can mean the experiment is faulty - either there is too much noise from outside or there could be a fault in the measuring instrument

3.13 VARIABILITY

Variability refers to how spread out a group of data is. In other words, variability measures how much your scores differ from each other. Variability is also referred to as **dispersion or spread**. Data sets with similar values are said to have little variability, while data sets that have values that are spread out have high variability.

Imagine that you are teaching a Psychology course and you want to examine your students' performance on the midterm and final exams. The grades of your students are as follows:

Student	Midterm	Final
1	71	80
2	90	99
3	100	85
4	75	95
5	55	72
6	52	78
7	100	100
8	90	92
9	85	100
10	81	87
11	83	69
12	99	88
13	89	97

Notice that there are thirteen students in the class and both the midterm and final grades are listed for each student. Notice that there is only one student who received the same grade for both the midterm and the final. You now want to know if the students' scores on each exam are similar to each other, or if the scores are spread out. This is called **variability**.

How to Measure Variability in Statistics

Statisticians use summary measures to describe the amount of variability or spread in a set of data. The most common measures of variability are the range, the interquartile range (IQR), variance, and standard deviation.

The Range

The range is the difference between the largest and smallest values in a set of values.

For example, consider the following numbers: 1, 3, 4, 5, 5, 6, 7, 11. For this set of numbers, the range would be 11 - 1 or 10.

3.13.1 Measures of Variability

The **range** is the simplest measure of variability. You take the smallest number and subtract it from the largest number to calculate the range. This lets us know the spread of our data. The range is sensitive to **outliers**, or values that are significantly higher or lower than the rest of the data set, and should not be used when outliers are present. ***Data set B is wider and more spread out than data set A. This indicates that data set B has more variability***

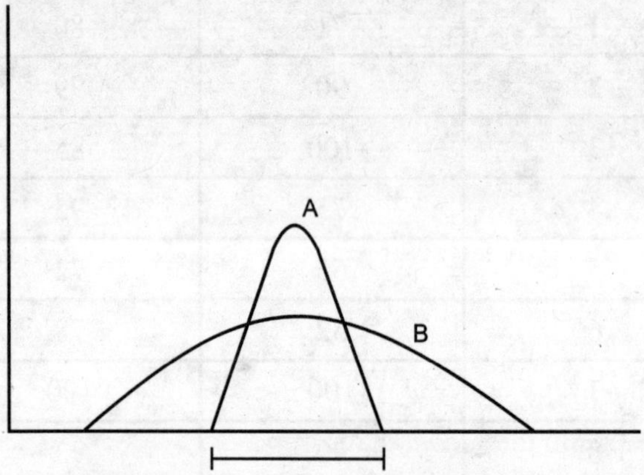

Fig. 3.12: Measures of Variability

Let's calculate the range for midterm exam grades. The midterm grades listed in numerical order are shown here. Since the range is equal to the highest midterm grade minus the lowest midterm grade, we can easily find the range for this data set. Plugging in 100 for our highest midterm grade and 52 for our lowest midterm grade, we find that the range is equal to 100 minus 52, or 48.

Range = highest midterm grade minus lowest midterm grade

Range = 100 – 52 = 48

Student	Midterm	Final
1	71	80
2	90	99
3	100	85
4	75	95
5	55	72
6	52	78

7	100	100
8	90	92
9	85	100
10	81	87
11	83	69
12	99	88
13	89	97

3.14 THE INTERQUARTILE RANGE (IQR)

The **interquartile range** (IQR) is a measure of variability, based on dividing a data set into quartiles.

Quartiles divide a rank-ordered data set into four equal parts. The values that divide each part are called the first, second, and third quartiles; and they are denoted by Q1, Q2, and Q3, respectively.

Q1 is the «middle» value in the *first* half of the rank-ordered data set.

Q2 is the median value in the set.

Q3 is the «middle» value in the *second* half of the rank-ordered data set.

The interquartile range is equal to Q3 minus Q1.

For example, consider the following numbers: 1, 3, 4, 5, 5, 6, 7, 11. Q1 is the middle value in the first half of the data set. Since there are an even number of data points in the first half of the data set, the middle value is the average of the two middle values; that is, Q1 = (3 + 4)/2 or Q1 = 3.3. Q3 is the middle value in the second half of the data set. Again, since the second half of the data set has an even number of observations, the middle value is the average of the two middle values; that is, Q3 = (6 + 7)/2 or Q3=3.3. **Interquartile range** is Q3 minus Q1, so IQR = 3.5-3.5 = 3.

An Alternative Definition for IQR

In some texts, the interquartile range is defined differently. It is defined as the difference between the largest and smallest values in the middle 50% of a set of data.

To compute an interquartile range using this definition, first remove observations from the lower quartile. Then, remove observations from the upper quartile. Then, from the remaining observations, compute the difference between the largest and smallest values.

For example, consider the following numbers: 1, 3, 4, 5, 5, 6, 7, 11. After we remove observations from the lower and upper quartiles, we are left with: 4, 5, 5, 3. The interquartile range (IQR) would be 6 – 4 = 2.

When the data set is large, the two definitions usually produce the same (or very close) results. However, when the data set is small, the definitions can produce different results.

3.15 CALCULATING VARIOUS STATISTICAL MEASURES USING R

We explain how to compute in R with examples. The tutorials are based on the previously discussed built-in data set faithful. Annexure–1 is devoted to tell how to in star and use R programming language for statistical data.

- Mean
- Median
- Quartile
- Percentile
- Range
- Interquartile Range
- Box Plot
- Variance
- Standard Deviation
- Covariance
- Correlation Coefficient
- Central Moment
- Skewness
- Kurtosis

3.15.1 Mean

The mean of an observation variable is a numerical measure of the central location of the data values. It is the sum of its data values divided by data count.

Hence, for a data sample of size n, its sample mean is defined as follows:

$$\bar{x} = \frac{1}{n}\sum_{i=1}^{n} x_i$$

Similarly, for a data population of size *N*, the population mean is:

$$\mu = \frac{1}{N}\sum_{i=1}^{n} x_i$$

Example 3.10: Find the mean eruption duration in the data set faithful.

Solution: We apply the mean function to compute the mean value of eruptions.

```
> duration = faithful$eruptions # the eruption durations
> mean(duration)                # apply the mean function
[1] 3.4878
> mean(waiting)                 # apply the mean function
[1] 3.4878
```

Answer

The mean eruption duration is 3.4878 minutes.

```
> mean (duration)           # apply the mean function
[1] 3.487783
> mean (waiting)
[1] 70.89706
> |
```

3.15.2 Median

The median of an observation variable is the value at the middle when the data is sorted in ascending order. It is an ordinal measure of the central location of the data values.

Exercise 3.11: Find the median of the eruption duration in the data set faithful.

Solution: We apply the median function to compute the median value of eruptions.

```
> duration = faithful$eruptions      # the eruption durations
> median(duration)                   # apply the median function
[1] 4
```

Answer

The median of the eruption duration is 4 minutes.

```
> mean (duration)          # apply the median function
[1] 4
> median (waiting)         # apply the median function
[1] 76
> |
```

3.15.3 Quartile

There are several quartiles of an observation variable. The first quartile, or lower quartile, is the value that cuts off the first 25% of the data when it is sorted in ascending order. The second quartile, or median, is the value that cuts off the first 50%. The third quartile, or upper quartile, is the value that cuts off the first 75%.

Exercise 3.12: Find the quartiles of the eruption durations in the data set faithful.

Solution: We apply the quantile function to compute the quartiles of eruptions.

```
> duration = faithful$eruptions     # the eruption durations
>
     0%      25%      50%      75%     100%
1.6000 2.1627 4.0000 4.4543 5.1000
```

Answer

```
> quantile (duration)              # apply the median function
      0%       25%       50%       75%      100%
1.60000 2.16275 4.00000 4.45425 5.10000
> quantile (waiting)             # apply the quantile function
  0%  25%  50%  75%  100%
  43  58   76   82   96
> |
```

The first, second and third quartiles of the eruption duration are 2.1627, 4.0000 and 4.4543 minutes respectively.

```
> mean (duration)          # apply the mean function
[1] 3.487783
> median (waiting)
[1] 70.89709
> median (duration)        # apply the median function
[1] 4
> median (waiting)         # apply the median function
[1] 76
> quantile (duration)      # apply the quantile function
     0%      25%      50%      75%     100%
1.60000  2.16275  4.00000  4.45425  5.10000
> quantile (waiting)       # apply the quantile function
  0%  25%  50% 75% 100%
  43   58   76   82   96
> quantile (duration, c(.31, .56, .95))
     31%      56%      95%
2.35017  4.11292  4.81700
```

3.15.4 Range

The range of an observation variable is the difference of its largest and smallest data values. It is a measure of how far apart the entire data spreads in value.

$$\text{Range} = \text{Largest Value} - \text{Smallest Value}$$

Exercise 3.13: Find the range of the eruption duration in the data set faithful.

Solution: We apply the max and min function to compute the largest and smallest values of eruptions, then take the difference.

```
> duration = faithful$eruptions          # the eruption durations
> max(duration) - min(duration)          # apply the max and min functions

[1] 3.5
```

Answer

The range of the eruption duration is 3.5 minutes.

3.15.5 Box Plot

The box plot of an observation variable is a graphical representation based on its quartiles, as well as its smallest and largest values. It attempts to provide a visual shape of the data distribution.

Exercise 3.14: Find the box plot of the eruption duration in the data set faithful.

Solution: We apply the boxplot function to produce the box plot of eruptions.

```
> duration = faithful$eruptions                # the eruption durations
> boxplot(duration, horizontal=TRUE)   # horizontal box plot
```

Answer

The box plot of the eruption duration is:

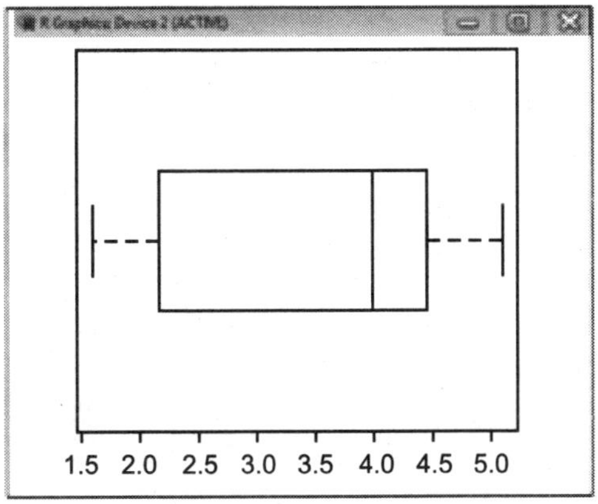

Fig. 3.13: Box Plot

3.15.6 Variance

The variance is a numerical measure of how the data values is dispersed around the mean. In particular, the sample variance is defined as:

$$s^2 = \frac{1}{n-1}\sum_{i=1}^{n}(x_i - \bar{x})^2$$

Similarly, the population variance is defined in terms of the population mean μ and population size N:

$$\sigma^2 = \frac{1}{N}\sum_{i=1}^{N}(x_i - \;)^2$$

Exercise 3.15: Find the variance of the eruption duration in the data set faithful.

Solution: We apply the var function to compute the variance of eruptions.

```
> duration = faithful$eruptions     # the eruption durations
> var(duration)                               # apply the var function
[1] 1.3027
```

Answer

The variance of the eruption duration is 1.3027.

3.15.7 Standard Deviation

The standard deviation of an observation variable is the square root of its variance.

Exercise 3.16: Find the standard deviation of the eruption duration in the data set faithful.

Solution: We apply the sd function to compute the standard deviation of eruptions.

```
> duration = faithful$eruptions     # the eruption durations
> sd(duration)                      # apply the sd function
[1] 1.1414
```

Answer

The standard deviation of the eruption duration is 1.1414.

3.15.8 Covariance

The covariance of two variables *x* and *y* in a data set measures how the two are linearly related. A positive covariance would indicate a positive linear relationship between the variables, and a negative covariance would indicate the opposite.

The sample covariance is defined in terms of the sample means as:

$$s_{xy} = \frac{1}{n-1}\sum_{i=1}^{n}(x_i - \bar{x})(y_i - \bar{y})$$

Similarly, the population covariance is defined in terms of the population mean μ_x, μ_y as:

$$\sigma_{xy} = \frac{1}{N}\sum_{i=1}^{N}(x_i - {}_x)(y_i - {}_y)$$

Exercise 3.17: Find the covariance of eruption duration and waiting time in the data set faithful. Observe if there is any linear relationship between the two variables.

Solution: We apply the cov function to compute the covariance of eruptions and waiting.

```
> duration = faithful$eruptions    # eruption durations
> waiting = faithful$waiting       # the waiting period
> cov(duration, waiting)           # apply the cov function
[1] 13.978
```

Answer

The covariance of eruption duration and waiting time is about 14. It indicates a positive linear relationship between the two variables.

3.15.9 Correlation Coefficient

The correlation coefficient of two variables in a data set equals to their covariance divided by the product of their individual standard deviations. It is a normalized measurement of how the two are linearly related.

Formally, the sample correlation coefficient is defined by the following formula, where s_x and s_y are the sample standard deviations, and s_{xy} is the sample covariance.

$$r_{xy} = \frac{s_{xy}}{s_x s_y}$$

Similarly, the population correlation coefficient is defined as follows, where σ_x and σ_y are the population standard deviations, and σ_{xy} is the population covariance.

$$\rho_{xy} = \frac{\sigma_{xy}}{\sigma_x \sigma_y}$$

If the correlation coefficient is close to 1, it would indicate that the variables are positively linearly related and the scatter plot falls almost along a straight line with positive slope. For -1, it indicates that the variables are negatively linearly related and the scatter plot almost falls along a straight line with negative slope. And for zero, it would indicate a weak linear relationship between the variables.

Exercise 3.13: Find the correlation coefficient of eruption duration and waiting time in the data set faithful. Observe if there is any linear relationship between the variables.

Solution: We apply the cor function to compute the correlation coefficient of eruptions and waiting.

```
> duration = faithful$eruptions     # eruption durations
> waiting = faithful$waiting        # the waiting period
> cor(duration, waiting)            # apply the cor function
[1] 0.90081
```

Answer

The correlation coefficient of eruption duration and waiting time is 0.90081. Since it is rather close to 1, we can conclude that the variables are positively linearly related.

3.15.10 Central Moment

The kth central moment (or moment about the mean) of a data population is:

$$\mu_k = \frac{1}{N}\sum_{i=1}^{N}(x_i - \quad)^k$$

Similarly, the kth central moment of a data sample is:

$$m_k = \frac{1}{n}\sum_{i=1}^{n}(x_i - \bar{x})^k$$

In particular, the second central moment of a population is its variance.

Exercise 3.19: Find the third central moment of eruption duration in the data set faithful.

Solution: We apply the function moment from the e1071 package. As it is not in the core R library, the package has to be installed and loaded into the R workspace.

```
> library(e1071)                          # load e1071
> duration = faithful$eruptions           # eruption durations
> moment(duration, order=3, center=TRUE)
[1] -0.6149
```

Answer

The third central moment of eruption duration is -0.6149.

3.15.11 Skewness

The skewness of a data population is defined by the following formula, where μ_2 and μ_3 are the second and third central moments.

$$\gamma_1 = \mu_3/\mu_2^{3/2}$$

Intuitively, the skewness is a measure of symmetry. As a rule, negative skewness indicates that the mean of the data values is less than the median, and the data distribution is *left-skewed*. Positive skewness would indicate that the mean of the data values is larger than the median, and the data distribution is *right-skewed*.

Exercise 3.20: Find the skewness of eruption duration in the data set faithful.

Solution: We apply the function skewness from the e1071 package to compute the skewness coefficient of eruptions. As the package is not in the core R library, it has to be installed and loaded into the R workspace.

```
> library(e1071)                          # load e1071
> duration = faithful$eruptions           # eruption durations
>skewness(duration)                       # apply the skewness function
[1] -0.41355
```

Answer

The skewness of eruption duration is -0.41355. It indicates that the eruption duration distribution is skewed towards the left.

3.15.12 Kurtosis

The kurtosis of a univariate population is defined by the following formula, where μ_2 and μ_4 are respectively the second and fourth central moments.

$$\gamma_2 = \mu_4/\mu_2^2 - 3$$

Intuitively, the *kurtosis* describes the *tail shape* of the data distribution. The normal distribution has zero kurtosis and thus the standard tail shape. It is said to be mesokurtic. Negative kurtosis would indicate a *thin-tailed* data distribution, and is said to be platykurtic. Positive kurtosis would indicate a *fat-tailed* distribution, and is said to be leptokurtic.

Exercise 3.21: Find the kurtosis of eruption duration in the data set faithful.

Solution: We apply the function kurtosis from the e1071 package to compute the kurtosis of eruptions. As the package is not in the core R library, it has to be installed and loaded into the R workspace.

```
> library(e1071)                        # load e1071
> duration = faithful$eruptions         # eruption durations
> kurtosis(duration)                    # apply the kurtosis function
[1] -1.5116
```

Answer

The kurtosis of eruption duration is -1.5116, which indicates that eruption duration distribution is platykurtic. This is consistent with the fact that its histogram is not bell-shaped.

Note : The default algorithm of the function kurtosis is based on the formula $g_2 = m_4/s^4 - 3$, where m_4 and s are the fourth central moment and sample standard deviation respectively.

```
> library(e1071)                        # load e1071
> help(kurtosis)
```

3.16 EXAMINING THE DISTRIBUTION OF A SET OF DATA

Given a (univariate) set of data we can examine its distribution in a large number of ways. The simplest is to examine the numbers. Two slightly different summaries are given by summary and fivenum and a display of the numbers by stem (a "stem and leaf" plot).

```
> attach (faithful)
> summary (eruptions)
```

Summary will be displayed on console. Now enter

```
> fivenum(eruptions)
[1] 1.6000 2.1585 4.0000 4.4585 5.1000
```

If you enter

```
> stem(eruptions)
```

Following shall be displayed on console.

```
> attach (faithful)
> summary (eruptions)
  Min.  1st Qu.  Median   Mean  3rd Qu.  Max.
 1.600   2.163    4.000  3.488   4.454 5.100
> stem (eruptions)
```

```
The decimal point is 1 digit(s) to the left of the |

16 | 070355555588

18 | 000022233333335577777777888822335777888

20 | 00002223378800035778

22 | 0002335578023578

24 | 00228

26 | 23

28 | 080

30 | 7

32 | 2337

34 | 250077

36 | 0000823577

38 | 2333335582225577

40 | 0000003357788888002233555577778

42 | 03335555778800233333555577778

44 | 02222335557780000000023333357777888

46 | 0000233357700000023578

48 | 00000022335800333
```

A stem-and-leaf plot is like a histogram, and R has a function hist to plot histograms. Enter

```
> hist(eruptions)
# make the bins smaller,
```

We can write the remarks in our program after entering ##. To make make a plot of density

```
> hist(eruptions, seq(1.6, 5.2, 0.2), prob=TRUE)
```

A histogram shall appear in a separate window as shown below:

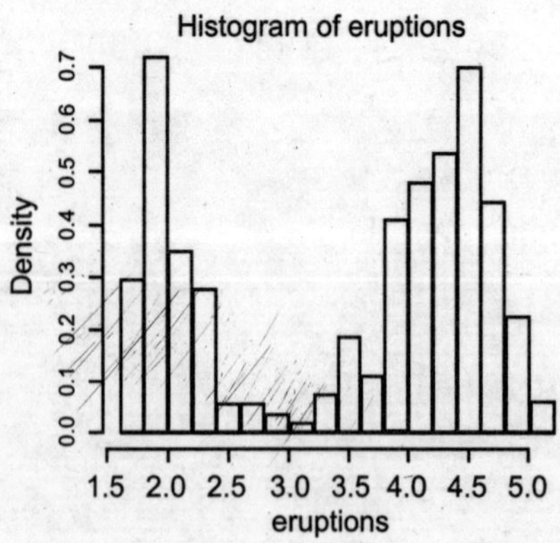


```
> lines(density(eruptions, bw=0.1))
```

Another histogram shall appear in a separate window showing the density lines linearly as below :

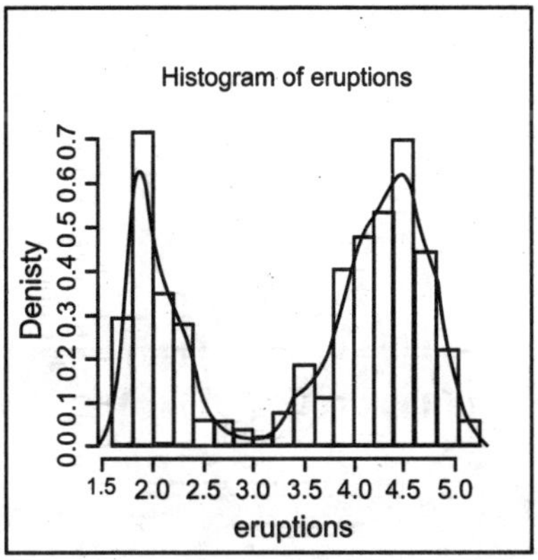


```
> rug(eruptions)
# show the actual data points
```

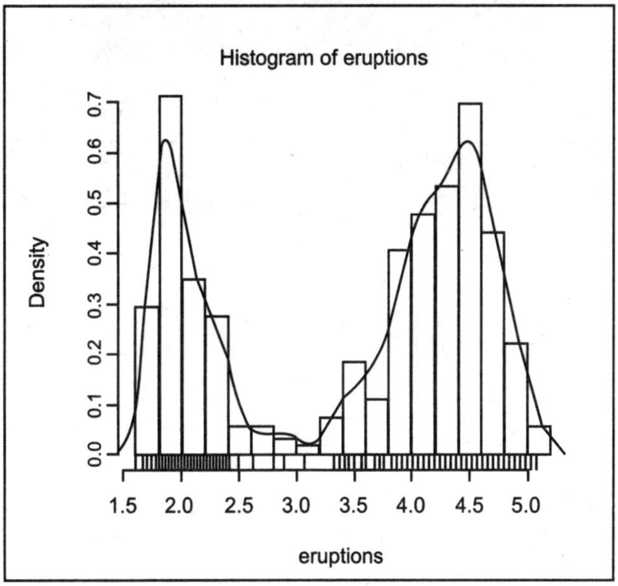

Fig. 3.14: Hisogram Plot

3.16.1 Quantitative data

Quantitative data, also known as continuous data, consists of numeric data that support arithmetic operations. This is in contrast with qualitative data, whose values belong to pre-defined classes with no arithmetic operation allowed. We will explain how to apply some of the R tools for quantitative data analysis with examples.

The examples in this section are based on a built-in data frame named **faithful**. It consists of a collection of observations of the Old Faithful geyser in the USA Yellowstone National Park .

The Great Fountain Geyser is a fountain-type geyser located in the Firehole Lake area of Lower Geyser Basin of Yellowstone National Park, Wyoming. It is the only predictable geyser in the Lower Geyser Basin.The geyser erupts every 9 to 15 hours. Great Fountain's maximum height ranges from about 23 m (75 feet) to over 67 m (220 feet). Its duration is usually about one hour but durations of over two hours have been seen. The duration of an eruption affects the interval that will elapse before the next eruption, so that if the duration of an eruption is recorded, the time of the following eruption can be predicted to a precision of about two hours. The prediction can be refined, to plus or minus 15 minutes or so, through observation of overflow from the crater during the period between eruptions.

Fig. 3.15: Photograph of Old Faithful geyser in the USA Yellowstone National Park

The following is a preview via the head function

Enter following at the command prompt in the R console to see the preview of head function of faithful dataframe :

```
> head(faithful)
```

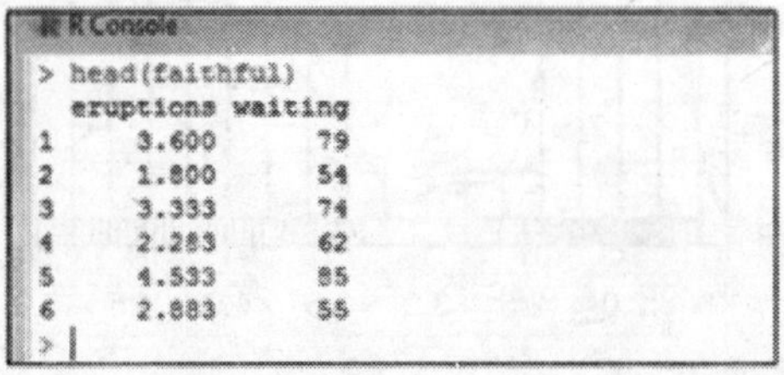

```
R Console
> head(faithful)
  eruptions waiting
1     3.600      79
2     1.800      54
3     3.333      74
4     2.283      62
5     4.533      85
6     2.883      55
>
```

3.16.2 Scatter Plot

A scatter plot pairs up values of two quantitative variables in a data set and display them as geometric points inside a Cartesian diagram.

Example 3.15

In the data set faithful, we pair up the eruptions and waiting values in the same observation as (x, y) coordinates. Then we plot the points in the Cartesian plane.

Problem

Find the scatter plot of the eruption durations and waiting intervals in faithful. Does it reveal any relationship between the variables?

Solution

We apply the plot function to compute the scatter plot of eruptions and waiting.Enter following code snipett at command prompt :

```
> duration = faithful$eruptions      # the eruption durations
> waiting = faithful$waiting         # the waiting interval
> plot(duration, waiting,            # plot the variables
+    xlab="Eruption duration",       # x-axis label
+    ylab="Time waited")             # y-axis label
```

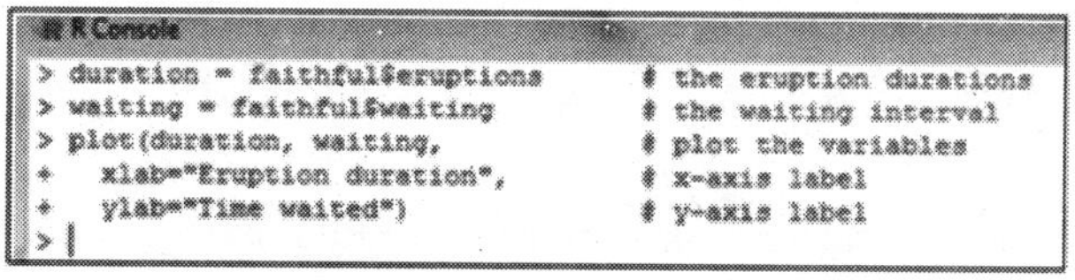

The scatter data plot of Figure 3.12 shall appear in the separate window. It reveals a positive linear relationship between them.

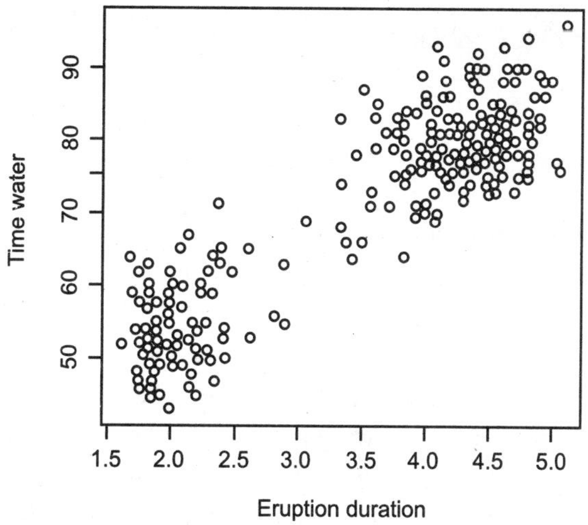

Fig. 3.16: Scatter data plot of Eruption of geyser in the USA Yellowstone National Park

Enhanced Solution

We can generate a linear regression model of the two variables with the lm function, and then draw a trend line with abline.

```
> abline(lm(waiting ~ duration))
```

3.16.3 Existing Local Data

R has a function dedicated to reading comma-separated files. To import a local CSV file named filename.txt and store the data into one R variable named mydata, the syntax would be:

```
mydata <- read.csv(«filename.txt»)
```

(Aside: What›s that <- where you expect to see an equals sign? It›s the R assignment operator. I said R syntax was a bit quirky.

And if you›re wondering what kind of object is created with this command, mydata is an extremely handy data type called a data frame — basically a table of data. A data frame is organized with rows and columns, similar to a spreadsheet or database table.

The read.csv function assumes that your file has a header row, so row 1 is the name of each column. If that's *not* the case, you can add `header=FALSE` to the command:

```
mydata <- read.csv("filename.txt", header=FALSE)
```

In this case, R will read the first line as data, not column headers (and assigns default column header names you can change later).

If your data use another character to separate the fields, not a comma, R also has the more general read.table function. So if your separator is a tab, for instance, this would work:

```
mydata <- read.table(«filename.txt», sep=»\t», header=TRUE)
```

The command above also indicates there›s a header row in the file with header=TRUE.

If, say, your separator is a character such as | you would change the separator part of the command to sep=»|»

3.17 CRITIQUE OF STATISTICAL SAMPLING METHODS

Mark Twain famously quipped that there were three ways to avoid telling the truth: lies, damned lies, and statistics. The joke works because statistics frequently seem like a black box—it can be difficult to understand how statistical theorems make it possible to draw conclusions from data that, on their face, defy easy analysis.

Peter Flom, Independent statistical consultant for researchers in behavioral, social and medical science suggested that although height and weight are often cited as examples, they are not exactly normally distributed. Weight, in particular, is somewhat right skewed. The average American man weighs about 190 pounds. There are some men who weigh well over 380 but none who weigh even close to 0.

IQ is sometimes cited as an example, but it has fatter tails than the normal. No physical variable is exactly normally distributed.

3.18 QUANTITATIVE APPLICATIONS IN THE SOCIAL SCIENCES

It is a process or collection of rules or set to complete a task. It is one of the primary concept in, or building blocks of, computer science: the basis of the design of elegant and efficient code, data processing and preparation, and software engineering.

In data science there are mainly three algorithms are used:

1. Data preparation, munging, and process algorithms
2. Optimization algorithms for parameter estimation which includes Stochastic Gradient Descent, Least Squares, Newton's Method
3. Machine learning algorithms

3.19 MACHINE LEARNING ALGORITHMS

Machine learning is used to predict, categorize, classify, finding polarity, etc from the given datasets and concerned with minimizing the error. Machine Learning is always algorithm based and basic machine learning algorithms can be classified as given in Figure 3.17.

	Unsupervised	Supervised
Continuous	• Clusterin and Dimensionality Reduction ○ SVD ○ PCA ○ K-means	• Regression ○ Linear ○ Polynomial • Decision Trees • Random Forests
Categorical	• Association Analysis ○ Apriori ○ FP-Growth • Hidden markov Model	• Classification ○ KNN ○ Trees ○ Logistic Regression ○ Naive-Bayes ○ SVM

Fig. 3.17: Variety of Machine Learning Algorithms

Machine learning is a term closely associated with data science. It uses training data for artificial intelligence. Since there are many algorithms like SVM, Bayes algorithm, logistic regression, etc. which will use training data to match with input data and then it will provide conclusion with maximum accuracy.

It refers to a broad class of methods that revolve around data modelling to

1. Algorithmically make predictions, and
2. Algorithmically decipher patterns in data.

This wide-ranging breadth of machine learning techniques comprise an important part of the data science toolbox. It is up to the data scientist to figure out which tool to use in different circumstances (as well as how to use the tool correctly) in order to solve analytically open-ended problems.

3.19.1 Supervised Learning

It is used for structured dataset. It analyzes the training data and generates function which will be used for other datasets. It is *Machine learning for making predictions* — Core concept is to use tagged data to train predictive models. *Tagged data* means observations where ground truth is already known. *Training models* means automatically characterizing tagged data in ways to predict tags for unknown data points. For example a credit card fraud detection model can be trained using a historical record of tagged fraud purchases. The resultant model estimates the likelihood that any new purchase is fraudulent. Common methods for training models range from basic regressions to complex neural nets. All follow the same paradigm known as *supervised learning*.

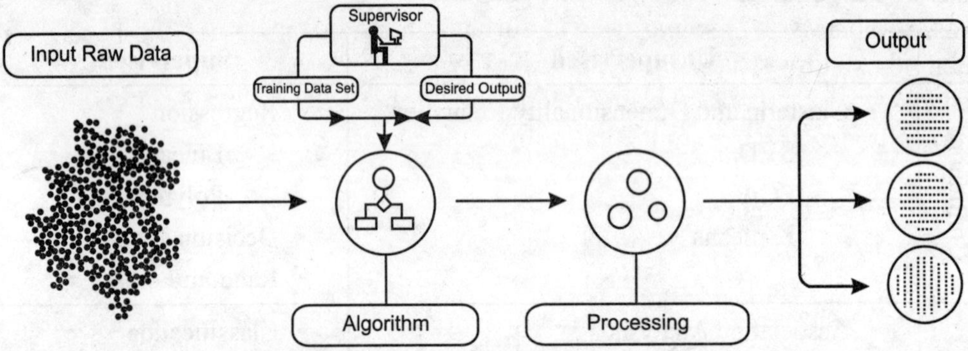

Fig. 3.18: Supervised Learning Process

Before we go into the technical details regarding supervised learning, it is imperative to give a brief and simplistic overview that can be understood by all readers, regardless of their experience in this growing field.

With supervised learning, you feed the output of your algorithm into the system.[10] This means that in supervised learning, the machine already knows the output of the algorithm before it starts working on it or learning it. A basic example of this concept would be a student learning a course from an instructor. The student knows what he/she is learning from the course.

With the output of the algorithm known, all that a system needs to do is to work out the steps or process needed to reach from the input to the output. The algorithm is being taught through a training data set that guides the machine. If the process goes haywire and the algorithms come up with results completely different than what should be expected, then the training data does its part to guide the algorithm back towards the right path.

Supervised Machine Learning currently makes up most of the ML that is being used by systems across the world. The input variable (x) is used to connect with the output variable (y) through the use of an algorithm. All of the input, the output, the algorithm, and the scenario are being provided by humans. We can understand supervised learning in an even better way by looking at it through two types of problems.

1. **Classification:** Classification problems categorize all the variables that form the output. Examples of these categories formed through classification would include demographic data such as marital status, sex, or age. The most common model used for this type of

service status is the support vector machine. The support vector machines set forth to define the linear decision boundaries.

2. **Regression:** Problems that can be classified as regression problems include types where the output variables are set as a real number. The format for this problem often follows a linear format.

3.19.2 Unsupervised Learning

It is used for raw datasets. Its main task is to convert raw data to structured data. In today's world there is a huge amount of raw data in ever field. Even the computer generates log files which are in the form of raw data. Therefore it's the most important part of machine learning. It consists of **machine learning for pattern discovery** — Another modeling paradigm known as *unsupervised learning* tries to surface underlying patterns and associations in data when no existing ground truth is known (i.e. no observations are tagged). Within this broad category of methods, the most commonly used are clustering techniques, which algorithmically detect what are the natural groupings that exist in a data set. For example, clustering can be used to programmatically learn the natural customer segments in a company›s user base. Other unsupervised methods for mining underlying characteristics include: principal component analysis, hidden markov models, topic models, and more.

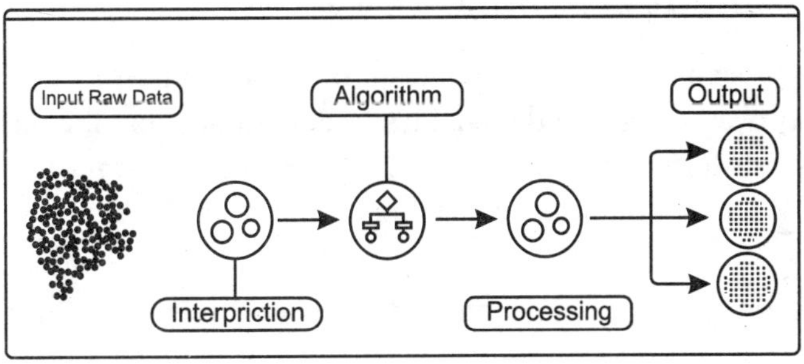

Fig. 3.19: UnSupervised Learning Process

The concept of unsupervised learning is not as widespread and frequently used as supervised learning. In fact, the concept has been put to use in only a limited amount of applications as of yet.

During the process of unsupervised learning, the system does not have concrete data sets, and the outcomes to most of the problems are largely unknown. In simple terminology, the AI system and the ML objective is blinded when it goes into the operation. The system has its faultless and immense logical operations to guide it along the way, but the lack of proper input and output algorithms makes the process even more challenging. Incredible as the whole process may sound, unsupervised learning has the ability to interpret and find solutions to a limitless amount of data, through the input data and the binary logic mechanism present in all computer systems. The system has no reference data at all.

Since we expect readers to have a basic imagery of unsupervised learning by now, it would be pertinent to make the understanding even simpler through the use of an example. Just consider that we have a digital image that has a variety of colored geometric shapes on it. These geometric shapes needed to be matched into groups according to color and other classification features. For a system that follows supervised learning, this whole process is a bit too simple. The procedure is extremely straightforward, as you just have to teach the computer all the details pertaining to the figures. You can let the system know that all shapes with four sides are known as squares, and others with eight sides are known as octagons, etc. We can also teach the system to interpret the colors and see how the light being given out is classified.

However, in unsupervised learning, the whole process becomes a little trickier. The algorithm for an unsupervised learning system has the same input data as the one for its supervised counterpart (in our case, digital images showing shapes in different colors).

Once it has the input data, the system learns all it can from the information at hand. In fact, the system works by itself to recognize the problem of classification and also the difference in shapes and colors. With information related to the problem at hand, the unsupervised learning system will then recognize all similar objects, and group them together. The labels that it will give to these objects will be designed by the machine itself. Technically, there are bound to be wrong answers, since there is a certain degree of probability. However, just like how we humans work, the strength of machine learning lies in its ability to recognize mistakes, learn from them, and to eventually make better estimations next time around.

3.19.3 Reinforcement Learning

Reinforcement Learning spurs off from the concept of Unsupervised Learning, and gives a high sphere of control to software agents and machines to determine what the ideal behavior within a context can be. This link is formed to maximize the performance of the machine in a way that helps it to grow. Simple feedback that informs the machine about its progress is required here to help the machine learn its behavior.

Reinforcement Learning is not simple, and is tackled by a plethora of different algorithms. As a matter of fact, in Reinforcement Learning an agent decides the best action based on the current state of the results.

The growth in Reinforcement Learning has led to the production of a wide variety of algorithms that help machines learn the outcome of what they are doing. Since we have a basic understanding of Reinforcement Learning by now, we can get a better grasp by forming a comparative analysis between Reinforcement Learning and the concepts of Supervised and Unsupervised Learning that we have studied in detail before.

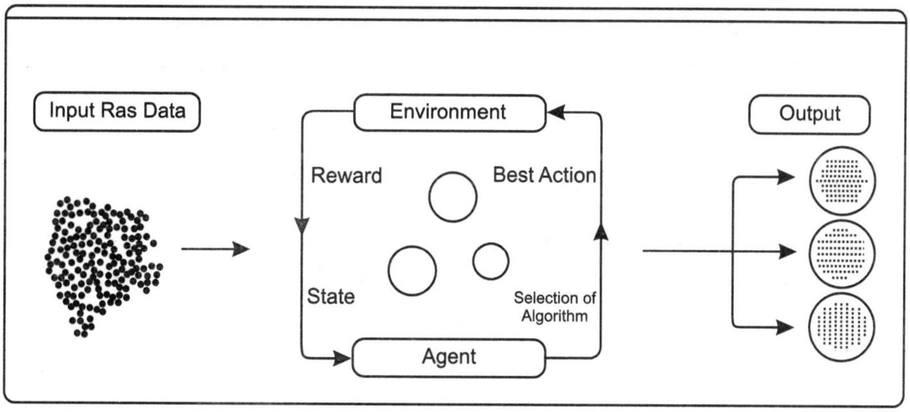

Fig. 3.20: Reinforcement Learning Process

Not all machine learning methods fit neatly into the above three categories. For example, collaborative filtering is a type of recommendations algorithm with elements related to both supervised and unsupervised learning. Contextual bandits are a twist on supervised learning where predictions get adaptively modified on-the-fly using live feedback.

3.20 LINEAR REGRESSION

It is the most well known and popular algorithm in machine learning and statistics. This model will assume a linear relationship between the input and the output variable. It is represented in the form of linear equation which has a set of inputs and a predictive output. Then it will estimate the values of coefficient used in the representation.

The overall idea of regression is to examine two things:

1. does a set of predictor variables do a good job in predicting an outcome (dependent) variable?
2. Which variables in particular are significant predictors of the outcome variable, and in what way do they–indicated by the magnitude and sign of the beta estimates–impact the outcome variable?

These regression estimates are used to explain the relationship between one dependent variable and one or more independent variables. The simplest form of the regression equation with one dependent and one independent variable is defined by the formula $y = c + b*x$, where y = estimated dependent variable score, c = constant, b = regression coefficient, and x = score on the independent variable.

Simple linear regression is a statistical method that allows us to summarize and study relationships between two continuous (quantitative) variables:

One variable, denoted x, is regarded as the predictor, explanatory, or independent variable.

The other variable, denoted y, is regarded as the response, outcome, or dependent variable.

Because the other terms are used less frequently today, we'll use the "predictor" and "response" terms to refer to the variables encountered in this course. The other terms are mentioned only to make you aware of them should you encounter them in other arenas. Simple linear regression gets its adjective "simple," because it concerns the study of only one predictor variable. In contrast, multiple linear regression, which we study later in this course, gets its adjective "multiple," because it concerns the study of two or more predictor variables.

3.20.1 Types of Relationships

Before proceeding, we must clarify what types of relationships we won't study in this course, namely, deterministic (or functional) relationships. Here is an example of a deterministic relationship.[11]

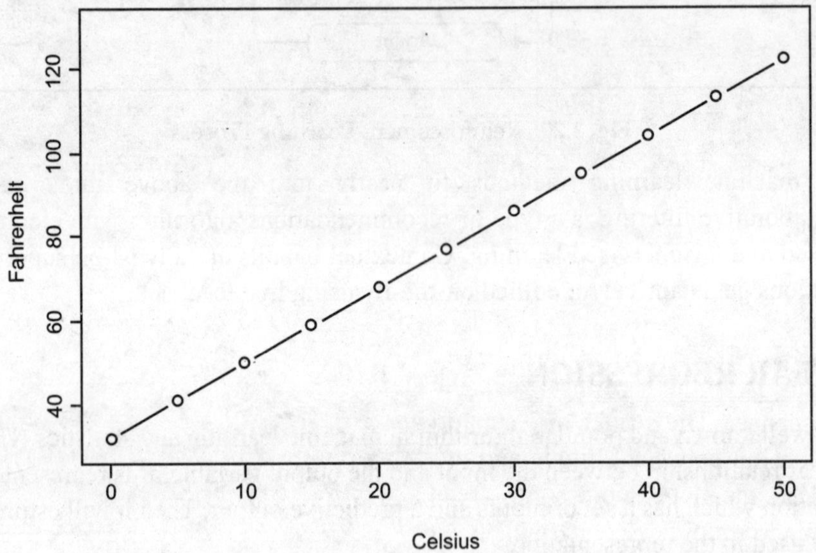

Fig. 3.21: Linear Regression between Fahrenheit vs Celsius plot

Note that the observed (*x, y*) data points fall directly on a line. As you may remember, the relationship between degrees Fahrenheit and degrees Celsius is known to be:

$$Fahr = 1.8\ Cels + 32$$

That is, if you know the temperature in degrees Celsius, you can use this equation to determine the temperature in degrees Fahrenheit exactly.

Here are some examples of other deterministic relationships that students from previous semesters have shared:

1. ***Circumference*** $= \pi \times$ ***diameter***
2. Hooke's Law: $Y = \alpha + \beta X$, where Y = amount of stretch in a spring, and X = applied weight.
3. Ohm's Law: $I = V/r$, where V = voltage applied, r = resistance, and I = current.
4. Boyle's Law: For a constant temperature, $P = \alpha/V$, where P = pressure, α = constant for each gas, and V = volume of gas.

For each of these deterministic relationships, the equation exactly describes the relationship between the two variables. This course does not examine deterministic relationships. Instead, we are interested in statistical relationships, in which the relationship between the variables is not perfect.

Here is an example of a statistical relationship. The response variable y is the mortality due to skin cancer (number of deaths per 10 million people) and the predictor variable x is the latitude (degrees North) at the center of each of 49 states in the U.S. (skincancer.txt) (The data were compiled in the 1950s, so Alaska and Hawaii were not yet states. And, Washington, D.C. is included in the data set even though it is not technically a state.)

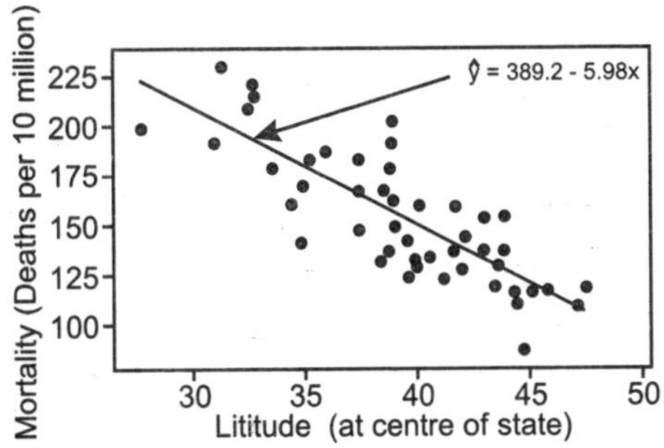

Fig. 3.22: Skin Cancer Vs State Latitude Plot

You might anticipate that if you lived in the higher latitudes of the northern U.S., the less exposed you'd be to the harmful rays of the sun, and therefore, the less risk you'd have of death due to skin cancer. The scatter plot supports such a hypothesis. There appears to be a negative linear relationship between latitude and mortality due to skin cancer, but the relationship is not perfect. Indeed, the plot exhibits some "trend," but it also exhibits some "scatter." Therefore, it is a statistical relationship, not a deterministic one.

3.20.2 Best Fitting Line

Since we are interested in summarizing the trend between two quantitative variables, the natural question arises — "what is the best fitting line?" At some point in your education, you were probably shown a scatter plot of (x, y) data and were asked to draw the "most appropriate" line through the data. Even if you weren't, you can try it now on a set of heights (x) and weights (y) of 10 students as given below as a sample. Looking at the plot below, which line — the solid line or the dashed line — do you think best summarizes the trend between height and weight?

Ht (inches)	wt (pounds)	Ht (inches)	wt (pounds)
63	127	71	156
64	121	71	169
66	142	72	165
69	157	73	181
69	162	75	208

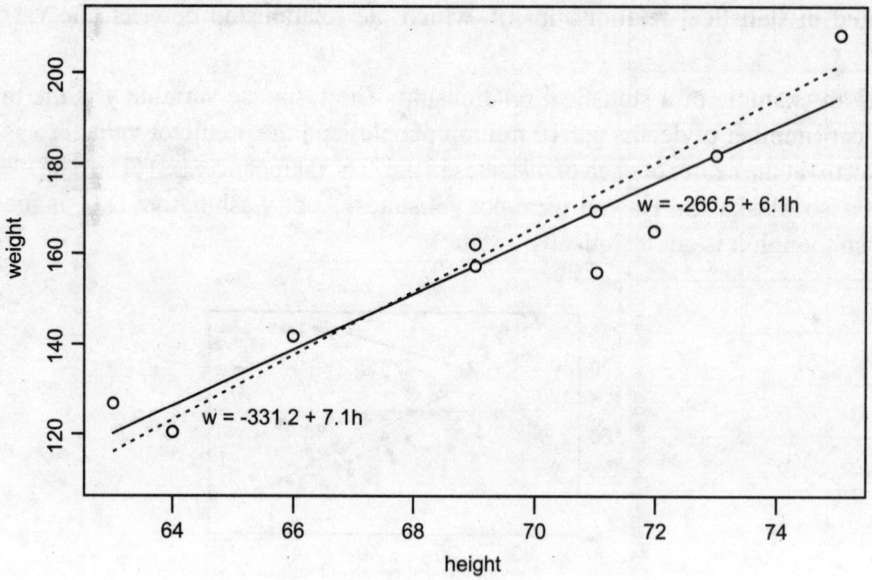

Fig. 3.23: Trying to plot best fitted line

Let us consider the equation for best Fitting line:

The equation for the best fitting line is:

$$y_1 = b_0 + b_1 x_1$$

Where

y_1 denotes the observed response for experimental unit i

x_1 denotes the predictor value for experimental unit i

y_1 is the predicted response (or fitted value) for experimental unit i

Then,

incidentally, recall that an "**experimental unit**" is the object or person on which the measurement is made. in out height and weight example, the experimental units are students.

Let's try out the notation on our example with the trend summarized by the line $w = -266.53 + 6.1376\, h$. (Note that this line is just a more precise version fo the above solid line, $w = -266.5 + 6.1\, h$). The first data point in the list indicates that student 1 is 63 inches tall and weights 127 pounds. That is $x_1 = 63$ and $y_1 = 127$. Do you see this point on the plot? If we know this student's beight but not his or her weight, we could use the equation of the line to predict his or her weight. We'd predict the student's weight to be –266.53 + 6.1376(63) or 120.1 pounds. That is $y_1 = 120.1$. Clearly, oru prediction wouldn't be perfectly correct — it has some "prediction error" (or "**residual error**"). In fact, the size of its prediction error is 127–120.1 or 6.9 pounds.

i	x_i	y_i	y_i
1	63	127	120.1
2	64	121	126.3
3	66	142	138.5
4	69	157	157.0
5	69	162	157.0
6	71	156	169.2
7	71	169	169.2
8	72	165	175.4
9	73	181	181.5
10	75	208	193.8

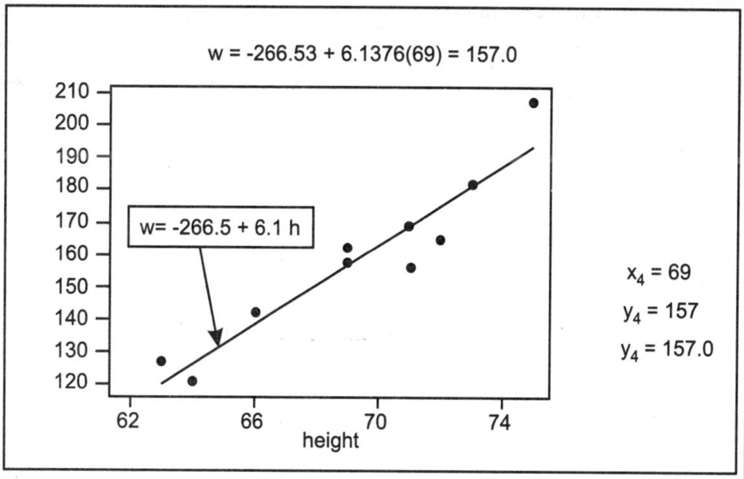

Fig. 3.24: Prediction Error

From above we can realise that the size of the prediction error depends on the data point. If we didn't know the weight of student 5, the equation of the line would predict *his or her* weight to be -266.53 + 6.1376(69) or 157 pounds. The size of the prediction error here is 162-157, or 5 pounds.

3.20.3 Least Squares Criterion

In general, when we use $y_i = b_0 + b_1 x_i$ to predict the actual response y_i, we make a prediction error (or residual error) of size:

$$e_i = y_i - y_i$$

A line that fits the data "**best**" will be one for which the ***n* prediction errors**—one for each observed data point—**are as small as possible in some overall sense**. One way to achieve this goal is to invoke the "**least squares criterion**" which says to "minimize the sum of squared prediction errors". That is:

$$Q = \sum_{i=1}^{n} (y_i - y_i)^2$$

Here's hwo you might think about this quantity Q:

- The quantity $e_i = y_i - y_i$ is the prediction error for data point i.
- We just need to find the values b_0 and b_1 that make the sum of the squared prediction errors the smallest it can be.
- That is, we need to find the values b_0 and b_1 that minimize:

Incidentally, if we didn't square the prediction error $e_i = y_i - y_i$ to get $e_i^2 = (y_i - y_i)^2$, the positive and negative prediction errors would cancel each other out when summed, always yielding 0.

Now, being familiar with the least squares criterion, let's take a fresh look at out plot again. In light of the least squares criterion, which line do you now think is the best fitting line?

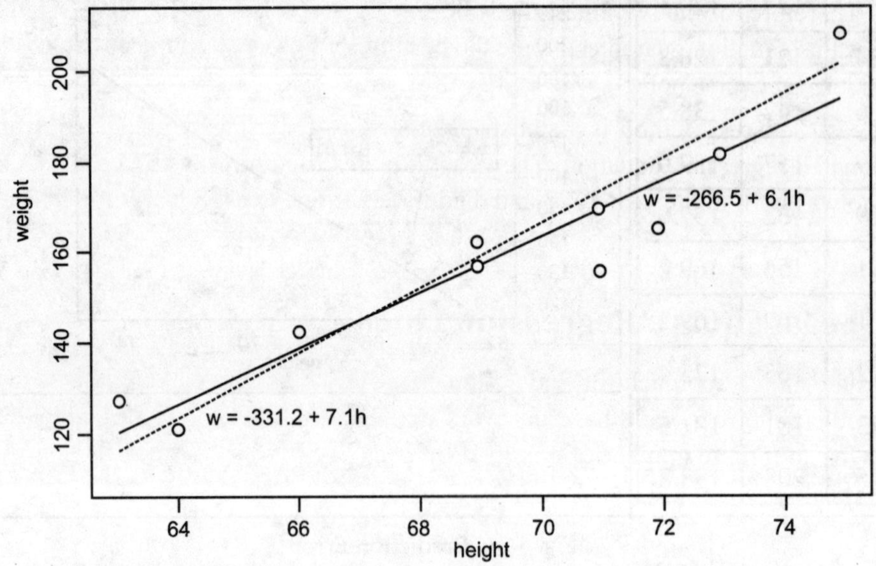

Fig. 3.25: Finding out bestfitting Line with Least Squares Criterion

3.20.4 Implementation of Least Squares Criterion

Let explore how we did! The following two side-by-side tables illustrate the implementation of the least squares criterion for the two lines up for consideration — the dashed line and the solid line.

$w = -331.2 + 7.1\,h$ (the dashed line)					
i	x_i	y_i	$\hat{y}_i$	$(y_i - \hat{y}_i)$	$(y_i - \hat{y}_i)^2$
1	63	127	116.1	10.9	118.81
2	64	121	123.2	–2.2	4.84
3	66	142	137.4	4.6	21.16
4	69	157	158.7	–1.7	2.89
5	69	162	158.7	3.3	10.89
6	71	156	172.9	–16.9	285.61
7	71	169	172.9	–3.9	15.21
8	72	165	180.0	–15.0	225.00
9	73	181	187.1	–6.1	37.21
10	75	208	201.3	6.7	44.89
					766.5

$w = -266.53 + 6.1376\,h$ (the solid line)					
i	x_i	y_i	$\hat{y}_i$	$(y_i - \hat{y}_i)$	$(y_i - \hat{y}_i)^2$
1	63	127	120.139	6.8612	47.076
2	64	121	126.276	–5.2764	27.840
3	66	142	138.552	3.4484	11.891
4	69	157	156.964	0.0356	0.001
5	69	162	156.964	5.0356	25.357
6	71	156	169.240	–13.2396	175.287
7	71	169	169.240	–0.2396	0.057
8	72	165	175.377	–10.3772	107.686
9	73	181	181.515	–0.5148	0.265
10	75	208	193.790	14.2100	201.924
					597.4

Let us find out based on the least squares criterion, which equation best summarizes the data? The sum of the squared prediction errors is 766.5 for the dashed line, while it is only 597.4 for the solid line. Therefore, of the two lines, the solid line, w = -266.53 + 6.1376h, best summarizes the data. But, is this equation guaranteed to be the best fitting line of all of the possible lines we didn›t even consider? Of course not!

The Least Squares Method is a statistical procedure for using sample data to find the value of the estimated regression equation. The Least Squares Method was proposed by Carl Friedrich Gauss, who was born in the year 1777 and died in 1855. The Least Squares Method is still widely used.

3.20.5 Least Square Regression Line

If we used the above approach for finding the equation of the line that minimizes the sum of the squared prediction errors, we'd have our work cut out for us. We'd have to implement the above procedure for an infinite number of possible lines that is clearly, an impossible task! Fortunately, somebody has done some dirty work for us by figuring out formulas for the **intercept** b_0 and the **slope** b_1 for the equation of the line that minimizes the sum of the squared prediction errors.

The formulas are determined using methods of calculus. We minimize the equation for the sum of the squared prediction errors:

The formulas are determined using methods of calculus. We minimize the equation for the sum of the squared prediction errors:

$$Q = \sum_{i=1}^{n}(y_i - (b_0 + b_1 x_i))^2$$

(that is, take the derivative with respect to b_0 and b_1, set to 0, and solve for b_0 and b_1) and get the "**least squares estimates**" for b_0 and b_1:

$$b_0 = \bar{y} - b_1\bar{x} \text{ and:}$$

$$b_1 = \frac{\sum_{i=1}^{n}(x_i - \bar{x})(y_i - \bar{y})}{\sum_{i=1}^{n}(x_i - \bar{x})^2}$$

Because the formulas for b_0 and b_1 are derived using the least squares criterion, the resulting equation — $\hat{y}_i = b_0 + b_1 x_i$ — is often referred to as the "**least squares regression line**," or simply the "**least squares line.**" It is also sometimes called the "**estimated regression equation.**" Incidentally, note that in derving the above formulas, we made no assumptions about the data other than that they follow some sort of linear trend.

We can see from these formulas that the least squares line passes through the point $(\bar{x}, \bar{y})$,

since when $x = \bar{x}$, then

$$y = b_0 + b_1\bar{x} = \bar{y} - b_1\bar{x} + b_1\bar{x} = \bar{y}.$$

In practice, you won't really need to worry about the formulas for b_0 and b_1. Instead, you are going to let statistical software, such as Minitab, find least squares lines for you. But, we can still learn something from the formulas — for b_1 in particular.

If you study the formula for the slope b_1:

$$b_1 = \frac{\sum_{i=1}^{n}(x_i - \bar{x})(y_i - \bar{y})}{\sum_{i=1}^{n}(x_i - \bar{x})^2}$$

you see that the denominator is necessarily positive since it only involves summing positive terms. Therefore, the sign of the slope b_1 is solely determine by the numerator. The numerator tells us, for each data point, to sum up the product of two distances — the distance of the x-value from the mean of all of the x-values and the distance of the y-value from the mean of all of the y-values.

3.20.6 Uses of *Linear Regression*

Three major uses for regression analysis are

1. Determining the strength of predictors,
2. Forecasting an effect, and
3. Trend forecasting.

First, the regression might be used to identify the strength of the effect that the independent variable(s) have on a dependent variable. Typical questions are what is the strength of relationship between dose and effect, sales and marketing spending, or age and income.

Second, it can be used to forecast effects or impact of changes. That is, the regression analysis helps us to understand how much the dependent variable changes with a change in one or more independent variables. A typical question is, "how much additional sales income do I get for each additional $1000 spent on marketing?"

Third, regression analysis predicts trends and future values. The regression analysis can be used to get point estimates. A typical question is, "what will the price of gold be in 6 months?"

3.20.7 Linear Regression Models

Linear regression models are used to show or predict the relationship between two variables or factors. The factor that is being predicted (the factor that the equation solves for) is called the dependent variable. The factors that are used to predict the value of the dependent variable are called the independent variables.

Good data does not always tell the complete story. Regression analysis is commonly used in research as it establishes that a correlation exists between variables. In simple linear regression, each observation consists of two values. One value is for the dependent variable and one value is for the independent variable.

3.20.8 Multiple Regression Analysis

When two or more independent variables are used in regression analysis, the model is no longer a simple linear one.

(*a*) Simple Linear Regression Model

The simple linear regression equation is represented like this:

$$E(y) = (\beta_0 + \beta_1 x)$$

Where

Parameter **β0** is the *y* intercept of the regression line.

And **β1** is the slope.

E*(*y*)** is the mean or expected value of ***y for a given value of ***x***.

Needless to say that the simple linear regression equation is graphed as a straight line.

A regression line can show a positive linear relationship, a negative linear relationship, or no relationship. If the graphed line in a simple linear regression is flat (not sloped), there is no relationship between the two variables. If the regression line slopes upward with the lower end of the line at the y intercept (axis) of the graph, and the upper end of line extending upward into the graph field, away from the x intercept (axis) a positive linear relationship exists. If the regression line slopes downward with the upper end of the line at the y intercept (axis) of the graph, and the lower end of line extending downward into the graph field, toward the x intercept (axis) a negative linear relationship exists.

The graph of the estimated simple regression equation is called the ***estimated regression line***.

Important Note: Regression analysis is not used to interpret cause-and-effect relationships between variables. Regression analysis can, however, indicate how variables are related or to what extent variables are associated with each other.

In so doing, regression analysis tends to make salient relationships that warrant a knowledgeable researcher taking a closer look.

There are several types of linear regression analyses available to researchers.

1. **Simple linear regression:** 1 dependent variable (interval or ratio), 1 independent variable (interval or ratio or dichotomous)
2. **Multiple linear regression:** 1 dependent variable (interval or ratio) , 2+ independent variables (interval or ratio or dichotomous)
3. **Logistic regression:** 1 dependent variable (dichotomous), 2+ independent variable(s) (interval or ratio or dichotomous)
4. Ordinal regression 1 dependent variable (ordinal), 1+ independent variable(s) (nominal or dichotomous)
5. **Multinominal regression:** 1 dependent variable (nominal), 1+ independent variable(s) (interval or ratio or dichotomous)
6. **Discriminant analysis:** 1 dependent variable (nominal), 1+ independent variable(s) (interval or ratio)

When selecting the model for the analysis, an important consideration is model fitting. Adding independent variables to a linear regression model will always increase the explained variance of the model (typically expressed as R^2). However, overfitting can occur by adding too many variables to the model, which reduces model generalizability. Occam's razor describes the problem extremely well – a simple model is usually preferable to a more complex model. Statistically, if a model includes a large number of variables, some of the variables will be statistically significant due to chance alone

3.21 SUPPORT VECTOR MACHINE (SVM)

SVM is a supervised machine learning algorithm which can be used for both **classification** or **regression** challenges. However, it is mostly used in classification problems. In this *algorithm*, we plot each data item as a point in *n-dimensional space* (where n is number of features you have) with the value of each feature being the value of a particular coordinate. Then, we perform *classification* by finding the *hyper-plane* (in two dimensional space it is a classifier line ,mostly strait) that differentiate the two classes (groups of data) very well (vide Figure 3.26).

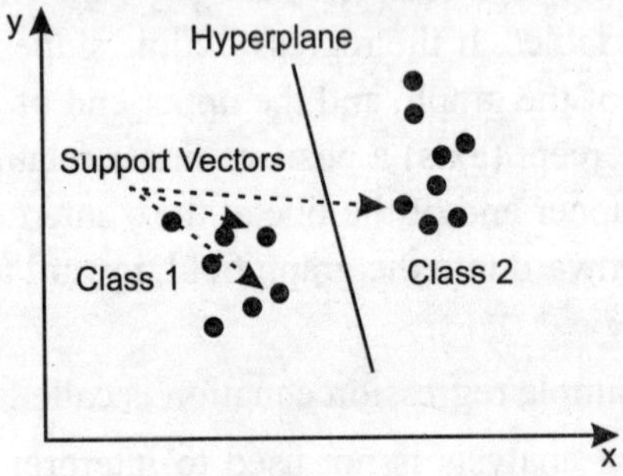

Fig. 3.26: Support Vectors

Support Vectors are simply the co-ordinates of individual observation. Support Vector Machine is a frontier which best segregates the two classes (hyper-plane/ line).

Fig. 3.20 describes the process of segregating the two classes with a hyper-plane.

3.21.1 Determining the right hyper-plane[12]

Case-1: Here, we have three hyper-planes (A, B and C) segregation two distinct data groups to classification star and circle.

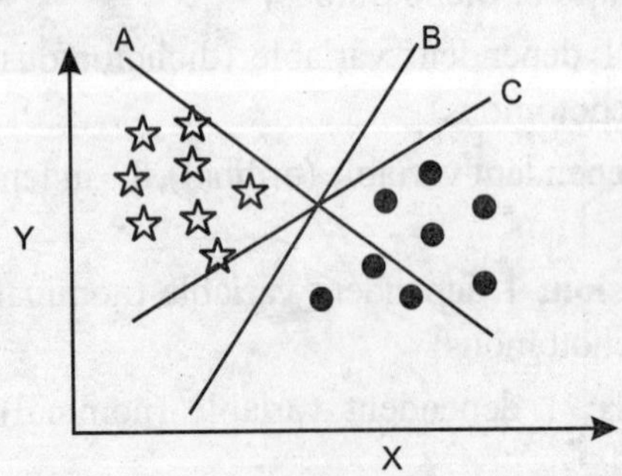

Fig. 3.27: Determining nearest correct Hyperplane

Select the hyper-plane which segregates the two classes better. In this scenario, hyper-plane "B" is best option among the three.

Case-2: In this case three hyper-planes (A, B and C) are seemingly segregating the classes well, and we have to identify the right hyper-plane?

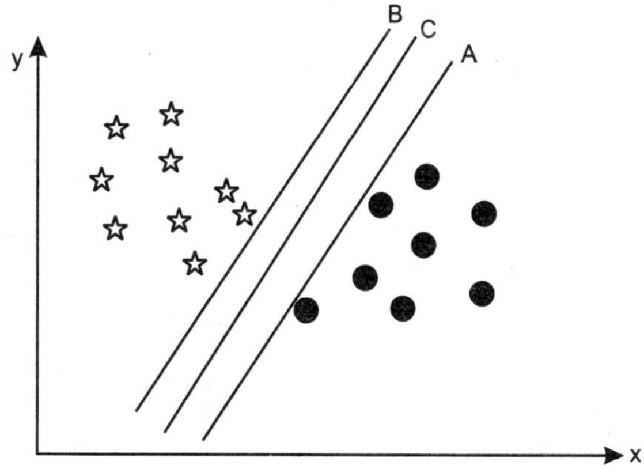

Fig. 3.28: Determining best among bettert Hyperplanes

We have to use technique of optimizing the distances between group of points of either of the class and classifier hyperplane This distance is called as **Margin**. Let's look at Figure 3.29.

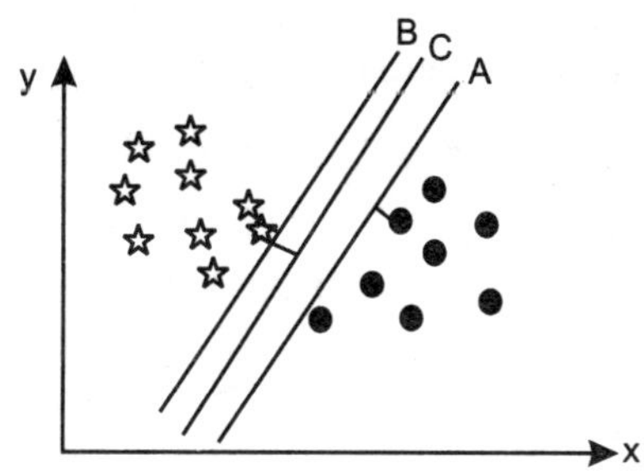

Fig. 3.29: Margin between a point (i.e. a data instance)Desired Hyperplane

From figure 3.29 we can realise that you the margin for hyper-plane C is high as compared to both A and B. Hence, the right hyper-plane is C. Another lightning reason for selecting the hyper-plane with higher margin is *robustness*. If we select a hyper-plane having low margin then there is high chance of miss-classification.

Case-3: Figure 3.30

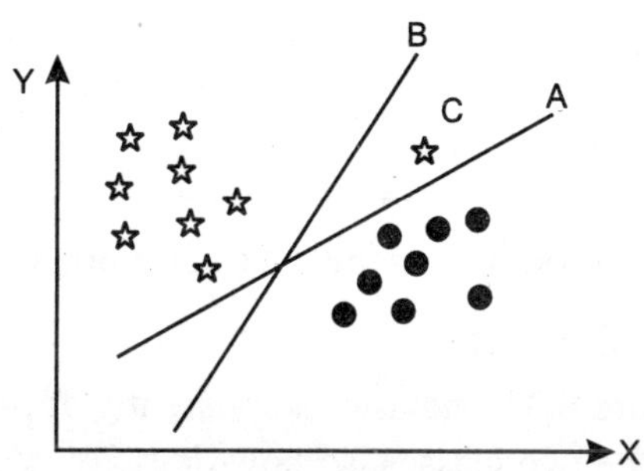

Fig. 3.30: Choosing the Hyperplane after correct data group classification

Adopt the procedure as earlier but carefully to identify the right hyper-plane Some of us may tend to select the hyper-plane **B** as it has higher margin compared to **A.** But, here is the catch, SVM selects the hyper-plane which classifies the classes accurately prior to maximizing *margin*. Here, hyper-plane B has a classification error as it forgot to include point C, and A has classified all correctly. Therefore, the right hyper-plane is **A. But keep in mind that some times the point C may be *outlier* also.**

Case-4: Example with outlier

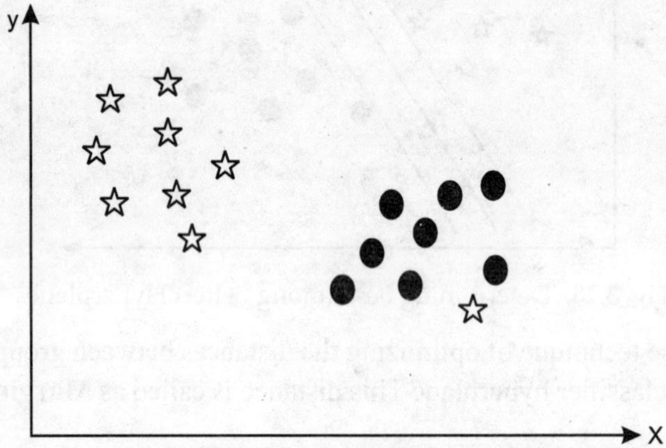

Fig. 3.31: Case with an outlier posing problem of misclassification

In Figure 3.31 the programmer may be unable to segregate the two classes using a straight line, as one of star lies in the territory of other(circle) class as an *outlier*.

One star at other end is like an outlier for star class. SVM has a feature to ignore outliers and find the hyper-plane that has maximum margin. AS such we can say, SVM is robust to outliers.

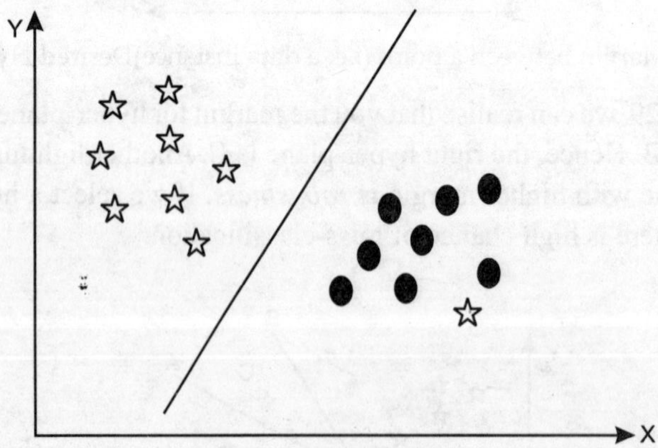

Fig. 3.32: SVM rejects the outlierand finds the appropriate hyperplane classifier

Case-5: Inter mixing classes of Data Set

In the scenario of Figure 3.33, the user is apparently at problem in putting up the linear hyper-plane between the two classes, so how does SVM classify these two classes? Till now, we have only looked at the linear hyper-plane.

Classifying data is a common task in machine learning. Suppose some given data points each belong to one of two classes, and the goal is to decide which class a new Data point will be in. In the case of support vector machines, a data point is viewed as a *p*-dimensional vector (a list of *p* numbers), and we want to know whether we can separate such points with *(p-1)*-dimensional hyperplane. This is called a **linear classifier.**

There are many hyperplanes that might classify the data. One reasonable choice as the best hyperplane is the one that represents the largest separation, or margin, between the two classes. So we choose the hyperplane so that the distance from it to the nearest data point on each side is maximized. If such a hyperplane exists, it is known as the maximum-margin hyperplane and the linear classifier it defines is known as a maximum margin classifier; or equivalently, the perceptron of optimal stability.

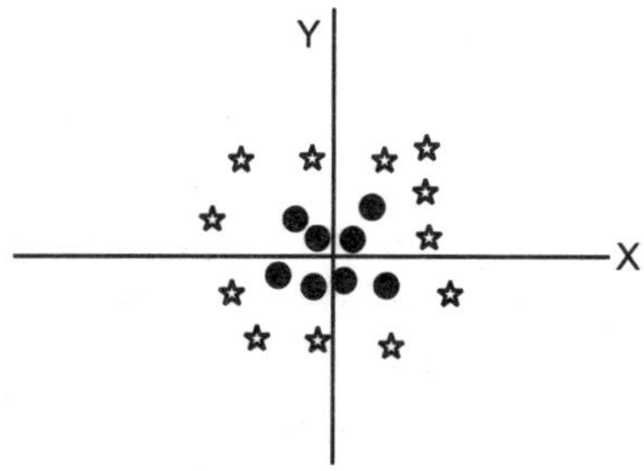

Fig. 3.33: Intermixing Classification

SVM is provided with an algorithm to solve this problem by introducing additional feature. Here, we will add a new feature $z = x^2 + y^2$. Now, let's plot the data points on axis x and z:

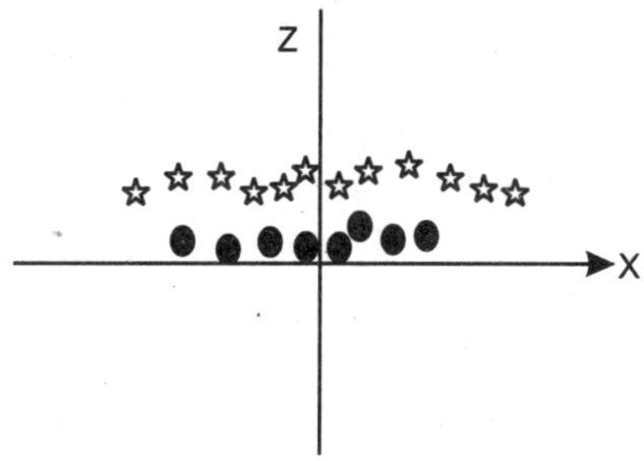

Fig. 3.34: Z-Plane method with square values

In above plot, points to consider are:

1. All values for z would be positive always because z is the squared sum of both x and y
2. In the original plot, red circles appear close to the origin of x and y axes, leading to lower value of z and star relatively away from the origin result to higher value of z.

In SVM, it is easy to have a linear hyper-plane between these two classes. SVM has a technique called the kernel **trick**. These are functions which takes low dimensional input space and transform it to a higher dimensional space i.e. it converts not separable problem to separable problem, these functions are called kernels. It is mostly useful in non-linear separation problem. Simply put, it does some extremely complex data transformations, then find out the process to separate the data based on the labels or outputs you've defined.

When we look at the hyper-plane in original input space it looks like a circle:

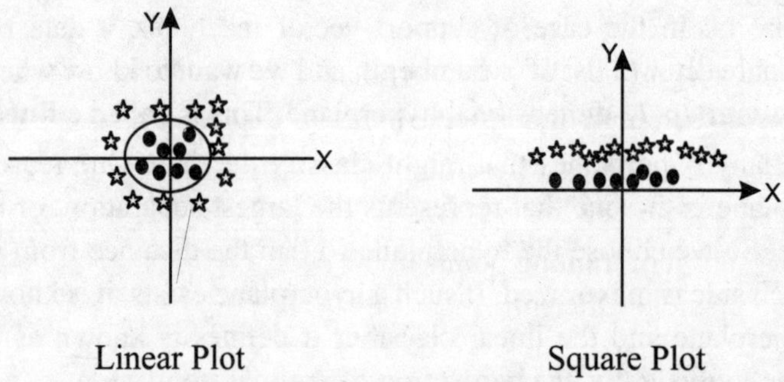

Fig. 3.34: Comparing Z-Plane method with square values

Now, let's look at the methods to apply SVM algorithm in a data science challenge.

Support Vector Machines (SVMs, as a part of machine learning, also support vector networks) are supervised learning models with associated learning algorithms that analyze data used for classification and regression analysis. Given a set of training examples say a cluster of data of one group, each marked as belonging to one or the other of two categories, an SVM training algorithm builds a model that assigns new examples to one category or the other, making it a non-probabilistic binary linear classifier.

3.21.2 Applications

SVMs can be used to solve various real world problems:

SVMs are helpful in text and hypertext categorization as their application can significantly reduce the need for labelled training instances in both the standard inductive and transductive settings.

Classification of images can also be performed using SVMs. Experimental results show that SVMs achieve significantly higher search accuracy than traditional query refinement schemes after just three to four rounds of relevance feedback. This is also true of image segmentation systems, including those using a modified version SVM that uses the privileged approach as suggested by Vapnik.[13.14]

Hand-written characters can be recognized using SVM[15].

The SVM algorithm has been widely applied in the biological and other sciences. They have been used to classify proteins with up to 90% of the compounds classified correctly. Permutation tests based on SVM weights have been suggested as a mechanism for interpretation of SVM models.[16][17] Support vector machine weights have also been used to interpret SVM models in the past.[18] Posthoc interpretation of support vector machine models in order to identify features used by the model to make predictions is a relatively new area of research with special significance in the biological sciences.

3.21.3 Pros and Cons associated with SVM

- **Pros:**
  1. It works really well with clear margin of separation
  2. It is effective in high dimensional spaces.
  3. It is effective in cases where number of dimensions is greater than the number of samples.
  4. It uses a subset of training points in the decision function (called support vectors), so it is also memory efficient.
- **Cons:**
  1. It doesn't perform well, when we have large data set because the required training time is higher
  2. It also doesn't perform very well, when the data set has more noise i.e. target classes are overlapping
  3. SVM doesn't directly provide probability estimates, these are calculated using an expensive five-fold cross-validation. It is related SVC method of Python scikit-learn library.

3.21.4 Issues with SVM

Potential drawbacks of the SVM include the following aspects:

1. Requires full labeling of input data
2. Uncalibrated class membership probabilities – SVM stems from Vapnik's theory which avoids estimating probabilities on finite data
3. The SVM is only directly applicable for two-class tasks. Therefore, algorithms that reduce the multi-class task to several binary problems have to be applied; see the multi-class SVM section.
4. Parameters of a solved model are difficult to interpret.

3.22 NAIVE BAYES

Naive Bayes is a simple technique for constructing classifiers: models that assign class labels to problem instances, represented as vectors of feature values, where the class labels are drawn from some finite set. It is not a single algorithm for training such classifiers, but a family of algorithms based on a common principle: all naive Bayes classifiers assume that the value of a particular feature is independent of the value of any other feature, given the class variable. For example, a fruit may be considered to be an apple if it is red, round, and about 10 cm in diameter. A naive Bayes classifier considers each of these features to contribute independently to the probability that this fruit is an apple, regardless of any possible correlations between the color, roundness, and diameter features.

What makes a naive Bayes classifier naive is its assumption that all attributes of a data point under consideration are independent of each other. A classifier sorting fruits into apples and oranges would know that apples are red, round and are a certain size, but would not assume all these things at once. Oranges are round too, after all.

For some types of probability models, naive Bayes classifiers can be trained very efficiently in a supervised learning setting. In many practical applications, parameter estimation for naive Bayes models uses the method of maximum likelihood; in other words, one can work with the naive Bayes model without accepting Bayesian probability or using any Bayesian methods.

Despite their naive design and apparently oversimplified assumptions, naive Bayes classifiers have worked quite well in many complex real-world situations. In 2004, an analysis of the Bayesian classification problem showed that there are sound theoretical reasons for the apparently implausible efficacy of naive Bayes classifiers.[19]Still, a comprehensive comparison with other classification algorithms in 2006 showed that Bayes classification is outperformed by other approaches, such as boosted trees or random forests.[20]

An advantage of naive Bayes is that it only requires a small number of training data to estimate the parameters necessary for classification.

A naive Bayes classifier uses probability theory to classify data. Naive Bayes classifier algorithms make use of Bayes' theorem. The key insight of Bayes' theorem is that the probability of an event can be adjusted as new data is introduced.

A naive Bayes classifier is not a single algorithm, but a family of machine learning algorithms that make uses of statistical independence. These algorithms are relatively easy to write and run more efficiently than more complex Bayes algorithms.

The most popular application is spam filters. A spam filter looks at email messages for certain key words and puts them in a spam folder if they match.Despite the name, the more data it gets, the more accurate a naive Bayes classifier becomes, such as from a user flagging email messages in an inbox for spam.

It is a classification technique based on Bayes' Theorem with an assumption of independence among predictors. In simple terms, a Naive Bayes classifier assumes that the presence of a particular feature in a class is unrelated to the presence of any other feature. For example, a fruit may be considered to be an apple if it is red, round, and about 7.5 Centimeter (3 inches) in diameter. Even if these features depend on each other or upon the existence of the other features, all of these properties independently contribute to the probability that this fruit is an apple and that is why it is known as 'Naive'.

Naive Bayes model is easy to build and particularly useful for very large data sets. Along with simplicity, Naive Bayes is known to outperform even highly sophisticated classification methods.

3.22.1 Bayes Theorem

Bayes theorem provides a way of calculating posterior probability $P(c|x)$ from $P(c)$, $P(x)$ and $P(x|c)$. Look at the equation below:

Likelihood   Class Prior Probability

$$P(c \mid x) = \frac{P(x \mid c)P(c)}{P(x)}$$

Posterior Probability   Predictor Prior Probability

In above equation:

1. $P(c|x)$ is the posterior probability of *class* (c, *target*) given *predictor* (x, *attributes*).
2. $P(c)$ is the prior probability of *class*.
3. $P(x|c)$ is the likelihood which is the probability of *predictor* given *class*.
4. $P(x)$ is the prior probability of *predictor*.

3.22.2 How Naive Bayes algorithm works?

Let's presume a training data set of weather and corresponding target variable 'Play' (suggesting possibilities of playing). Now, we need to classify whether players will play or not, based on weather condition. Let's follow the below steps to perform it.

Step 1: Convert the data set into a frequency table

Step 2: Create Likelihood table by finding the probabilities like Overcast probability = 0.29 and probability of playing is 0.64.

Weather	Play
Sunny	No
Overcast	Yes
Rainy	Yes
Sunny	yes
Sunny	Yes
Overcast	yes
Rainy	No
Rainy	No
Sunny	Yes
Rainy	Yes
Sunny	No
Overcast	Yes
Overcast	yes
Rainy	No

Frequency Table		
Weather	No	Yes
Overcast		4
Rainy	3	2
Sunny	2	3
Grand Total	65	9

Likelihood table				
Weather	No	Yes		
Overcast		4	=4/14	0.29
Rainy	3	2	=5/14	0.36
Sunny	2	3	=5/14	0.36
All	5	9		
	=5/14	=9/14		
	0.36	0.64		

Step 3: Now, use Naive Bayesian equation to calculate the posterior probability for each class. The class with the highest posterior probability is the outcome of prediction.

Example 3.16: To find out whetherkollowing statement is true "Players will play if weather is sun.?

We can solve it using above discussed method of posterior probability.

P(Yes | Sunny) = P(Sunny | Yes) * P(Yes) / P (Sunny)

Here we have *P (Sunny |Yes) = 3/9 = 0.33, P(Sunny) = 5/14 = 0.36, P(Yes)= 9/14 = 0.64*

Now, P *(Yes | Sunny) = 0.33 * 0.64 / 0.36 = 0.60*, which has higher probability.

Naive Bayes uses a similar method to predict the probability of different class based on various *attributes*. This algorithm is mostly used in text classification and with problems having multiple classes.

3.22.3 Pros and Cons of Naive Bayes?

Pros:

1. It is easy and fast to predict class of test data set. It also perform well in multi class prediction
2. When assumption of independence holds, a Naive Bayes classifier performs better compare to other models like logistic regression and you need less training data.
3. It perform well in case of categorical input variables compared to numerical variable(s). For numerical variable, normal distribution is assumed (bell curve, which is a strong assumption).

Cons:

1. If categorical variable has a category (in test data set), which was not observed in training data set, then model will assign a 0 (zero) probability and will be unable to make a prediction. This is often known as "*Zero Frequency*". To solve this, we can use the smoothing technique. One of the simplest smoothing techniques is called Laplace estimation.
2. On the other side naive Bayes is also known as a bad estimator, so the probability outputs from predict_*proba* are not to be taken too seriously.
3. Another limitation of Naive Bayes is the assumption of independent predictors. In real life, it is almost impossible that we get a set of predictors which are completely independent.

3.22.4 Applications of Naive Bayes Algorithms

(*a*) Frequentist and Bayesian Methods

There are at least two different ways of considering uncertainty, resulting in two different classes of methods for inference, decision, and other statistical questions. These are called frequentist and Bayesian methods. Some people prefer frequentist methods, while others prefer Bayesian methods.

Frequentists interpret a probability as a statistical average across many independent realizations (law of large numbers). Bayesians interpret it as a degree of belief (no need for many realizations). The Bayesian interpretation is very useful when only a single trial is considered. In addition, Bayesian theory takes into account our prior knowledge about a random process. This prior probability distribution is updated into a posterior distribution as we get more and more data.

Both frequentist and Bayesian methods have their advantages and disadvantages. For instance, one could say that frequentist methods might be easier to apply than Bayesian methods, but more difficult to interpret.

(*b*) Real time Prediction

Naive Bayes is an eager learning classifier and it is sure fast. Thus, it could be used for making predictions in real time.

1. **Multi class Prediction:** This algorithm is also well known for multi class prediction feature. Here we can predict the probability of multiple classes of target variable.
2. **Text classification/ Spam Filtering/ Sentiment Analysis:** Naive Bayes classifiers mostly used in text classification (due to better result in multi class problems and independence rule) have higher success rate as compared to other algorithms. As a result, it is widely used in Spam filtering (identify spam e-mail) and Sentiment Analysis (in social media analysis, to identify positive and negative customer sentiments)
3. **Recommendation System:** Naive Bayes Classifier and Collaborative Filteringtogether builds a Recommendation System that uses machine learning and data mining techniques to filter unseen information and predict whether a user would like a given resource or not

3.22.5 Building a Basic Model using Naive Bayes in Python

Again, scikit learn (python library) will help here to build a Naive Bayes model in Python. There are three types of Naive Bayes model under scikit learn library:

- **Gaussian:** It is used in classification and it assumes that features follow a normal distribution.
- **Multinomial:** It is used for discrete counts. For example, let's say, we have a text classification problem. Here we can consider bernoulli trials which is one step further and instead of "word occurring in the document", we have "count how often word occurs in the document", you can think of it as "number of times outcome number x_i is observed over the n trials".
- **Bernoulli:** The binomial model is useful if your feature vectors are binary (i.e. zeros and ones). One application would be text classification with 'bag of words' model where the 1s & 0s are "word occurs in the document" and "word does not occur in the document" respectively.

Based on your data set, you can choose any of above discussed model. Below is the example of Gaussian model.

***(a)* Python Code**

```
#Import Library of Gaussian Naive Bayes model from sklearn.
naive_bayes import GaussianNB
import numpy as np
#assigning predictor and target variables
x= np.array([[-3,7],[1,5], [1,2], [-2,0], [2,3], [-4,0],
[-1,1], [1,1], [-2,2], [2,7], [-4,1], [-2,7]])
Y = np.array([3, 3, 3, 3, 4, 3, 3, 4, 3, 4, 4, 4])
#Create a Gaussian Classifier
model = GaussianNB()
# Train the model using the training sets
model.fit(x, y)
#Predict Output
predicted= model.predict([[1,2],[3,4]])
print predicted
```

Output: ([3,4])

***(b)* R Code:**

```
require(e1071) #Holds the Naive Bayes Classifier
Train <- read.csv(file.choose())
Test <- read.csv(file.choose())
#Make sure the target variable is of a two-class classification
problem only
levels(Train$Item_Fat_Content)
model <- naiveBayes(Item_Fat_Content~., data = Train)
class(model)
pred <- predict(model,Test)
table(pred)
```

Above, we looked at the basic Naive Bayes model, you can improve the power of this basic model by tuning parameters and handle assumption intelligently. Let's look at the methods to improve the performance of Naive Bayes Model. I'd recommend you to go through this document for more details on Text classification using Naive Bayes.

3.22.6 Improving the Power of Naive Bayes Model

Here are some tips for improving power of Naive Bayes Model:

1. If continuous features do not have normal distribution, we should use transformation or different methods to convert it in normal distribution.

2. If test data set has zero frequency issue, apply smoothing techniques "Laplace Correction" to predict the class of test data set.
3. Remove correlated features, as the highly correlated features are voted twice in the model and it can lead to over inflating importance.
4. Naive Bayes classifiers has limited options for parameter tuning like alpha=1 for smoothing, fit_prior=[True|False] to learn class prior probabilities or not and some other options .
5. You might think to apply some *classifier combination technique like* ensembling, bagging and boosting but these methods would not help. Actually, "ensembling, boosting, bagging" won't help since their purpose is to reduce variance. Naive Bayes has no variance to minimize.

References

1. James Huddleston in Business 2 community web site article "5 Types of Big Data Analytics and How They Help Customer Success"
2. "Data collection". SearchCIO. TechTarget. Retrieved 20 December 2016.
3. "Which Data Collection Method Should I Choose?". B2B International. Retrieved 20 December 2016.
4. "How and Why Data Will Save Small Business". Small Business Trends Small Business Trends. LLC. Retrieved 20 December 2016.
5. "FAQ: Data Collection Requirements for Broker-Dealers". FINRA.org. Financial Industry Regulatory Authority, Inc. on behalf of the U.S. Securities and Exchange Commission (SEC). Retrieved 4 February 2017.
6. Data Collection and Analysis By Dr. Roger Sapsford, Victor Jupp ISBN 0-7619-5046-X
7. Glossary of statistical terms: Population». Statistics.com. Retrieved 22 February 2016.
8. Weisstein, Eric W. «Statistical population». MathWorld.
9. Weisberg H.F (1992) Central Tendency and Variability, Sage University Paper Series on Quantitative Applications in the Social Sciences, ISBN 0-8039-4007-6 p.2
10. Ronald van Loon, Director Adversitement Machine Learning Explained: Understanding Supervised, Unsupervised, and Reinforcement Learning,Published on Published onJanuary 15, 2018
11. Anderson, D. R., Sweeney, D. J., and Williams, T. A. (2003). Essentials of Statistics for Business and Economics (3rd ed.) Mason, Ohio: Southwestern, Thompson Learning.
12. Sunil Ray , September 13, 2017 article " Understanding Support Vector Machine algorithm from examples (along with code)" available in www.analyticsvidhya.com/blog/2017/09/understaing-support-vector-machine-example-code/
13. Vapnik, Vladimir N.: Invited Speaker. IPMU Information Processing and Management 2014)
14. Barghout, Lauren. Spatial-Taxon Information Granules as Used in Iterative Fuzzy-Decision-Making for Image Segmentation." Granular Computing and Decision-Making. Springer International Publishing, 2015. 285-318.

15. DeCoste, Dennis (2002). "Training Invariant Support Vector Machines" (PDF). Machine Learning. 46: 161–190.
16. Gaonkar, Bilwaj; Davatzikos, Christos; "Analytic estimation of statistical significance maps for support vector machine based multi-variate image analysis and classification"
17. Cuingnet, Rémi; Rosso, Charlotte; Chupin, Marie; Lehéricy, Stéphane; Dormont, Didier; Benali, Habib; Samson, Yves; and Colliot, Olivier; "Spatial regularization of SVM for the detection of diffusion alterations associated with stroke outcome", *Medical Image Analysis*, 2011, 15 (5): 729–737
18. Statnikov, Alexander; Hardin, Douglas; & Aliferis, Constantin; (2006); "Using SVM weight-based methods to identify causally relevant and non-causally relevant variables", *Sign*, 1, 4
19. Zhang, Harry. The Optimality of Naive Bayes (PDF). FLAIRS2004 conference.
20. Caruana, R.; Niculescu-Mizil, A. (2006). An empirical comparison of supervised learning algorithms. Proc. 23rd International Conference on Machine Learning. CiteSeerX 10.1.1.122.5901

Chapter 4

DATA VISUALISATION

☞ Learning Objectives and Outcomes

In this unit we shall learn about

- ☞ What is Data Visualisation and its importance
- ☞ Types of Data Visualisation
- ☞ Data Encodings,
- ☞ Visual Perception and Retinal variables,
- ☞ Mapping Variables to Encodings,
- ☞ Visual Encodings

4.1 DATA VISUALIZATION

Data visualization is a general term that describes any effort to help people understand the significance of data by placing it in a visual context. Patterns, trends and correlations that might go undetected in text-based data can be exposed and recognized easier with data visualization software. Data visualization is the presentation of data in a pictorial or graphical format. It enables decision makers to see analytics presented visually, so they can grasp difficult concepts or identify new patterns. With interactive visualization, you can take the concept a step further by using technology to drill down into charts and graphs for more detail, interactively changing what data you see and how it's processed.

Data visualization is both an art and a science.[1] It is viewed as a branch of descriptive statistics by some, but also as a grounded theory development tool by others. Increased amounts of data created by Internet activity and an expanding number of sensors in the environment are referred to as "big data" or Internet of things. Processing, analyzing and communicating this data present ethical and analytical challenges for data visualization. Various data visualisation tools are discussed in sction 6.2 of this book.

4.2 Data Attributes

When it comes to data attributes, there are two categories: quantitative data and qualitative data. Quantitative data is exactly what it sounds like: a numerical value placed on an ascending scale (i.e. I am 61 years of age, I drank two bottles of water today). Qualitative data refers to values that cannot be measured numerically, but can be described through language (i.e. I came in 3rd place at the swim meet, since I'm always on the run I prefer a laptop over a desktop). Within these two categories are a total of four subcategories as well:

4.2.1 Quantitative Data

Quantitative Data can take shape as:

1. Ratio (cost $10, $20, $30 or age 10 years old, 20 years old, 30 years old)
2. Data you can perform arithmetic operations on (add, divide, etc)
3. Intervals (temperature -5°, 10°, 25° or time 1am, 5am, 9am)
4. Data with a set value that you cannot perform all arithmetic operations on

Example: You cannot calculate the sum of temperature during a week but you can calculate the average temperature per day and the high/low for each day.

Other data types for Visualisation

Author Stephen Few described eight types of quantitative messages that users may attempt to understand or communicate from a set of data and the associated graphs used to help communicate the message:

Time-series: A single variable is captured over a period of time, such as the unemployment rate over a 10-year period. A line chart may be used to demonstrate the trend.

Ranking: Categorical subdivisions are ranked in ascending or descending order, such as a ranking of sales performance (the measure) by sales persons (the category, with each sales person a categorical subdivision) during a single period. A bar chart may be used to show the comparison across the sales persons.

Part-to-whole: Categorical subdivisions are measured as a ratio to the whole (i.e., a percentage out of 100%). A pie chart or bar chart can show the comparison of ratios, such as the market share represented by competitors in a market.

Deviation: Categorical subdivisions are compared against a reference, such as a comparison of actual vs. budget expenses for several departments of a business for a given time period. A bar chart can show comparison of the actual versus the reference amount.

Frequency distribution: Shows the number of observations of a particular variable for given interval, such as the number of years in which the stock market return is between intervals such as 0-10%, 11-20%, etc. A histogram, a type of bar chart, may be used for this analysis. A boxplot helps visualize key statistics about the distribution, such as median, quartiles, outliers, etc.

Correlation: Comparison between observations represented by two variables (X,Y) to determine if they tend to move in the same or opposite directions. For example, plotting unemployment (X) and inflation (Y) for a sample of months. A scatter plot is typically used for this message.

Nominal comparison: Comparing categorical subdivisions in no particular order, such as the sales volume by product code. A bar chart may be used for this comparison.

Geographic or geospatial: Comparison of a variable across a map or layout, such as the unemployment rate by state or the number of persons on the various floors of a building. A cartogram is a typical graphic used.

4.2.2 Qualitative Data

Ordinal (size small, medium, large or position 1st place, 2nd place, 3rd place)

Data with a fixed ranking with indeterminate distance between the values

Example: A large elephant in India is very different from a large elephant in the Africa, but I don't know exactly how much larger.

(*a*) Nominal (sports NFL football vs. English football or computers laptop vs. desktop)

Data where you can distinguish between values, but not order them

Based on these classifications, the methods for aggregation and visualization of the data needs to adjust accordingly. For example, if you were to map car manufacturing data like the image below, and your data set included year-to-year manufacturing figures – it makes more sense to stick to an annual order. If you try to sort the values by highest value, your readers will have trouble following the order of the years (1978, 1979, 1980, etc). Ideally, ordinal data should be sorted by its order as opposed to the alphabetical sorting of the names in the values (if you were mapping month-by-month for example).

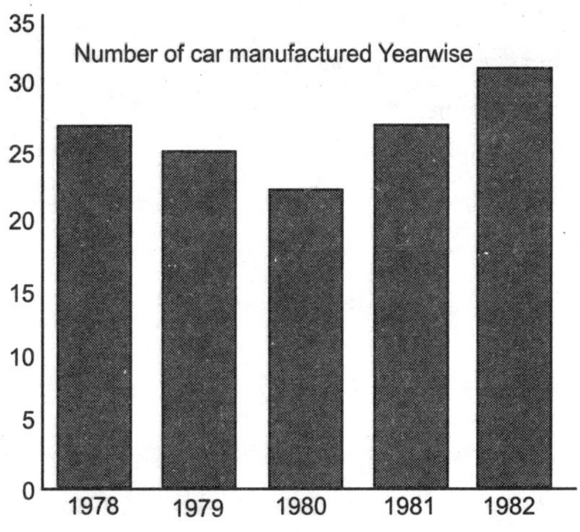

Fig. 4.1 Example of wrong graphical representation for sorting purpose

4.3 IMPORTANCE OF DATA VISUALIZATION

A primary goal of data visualization is to communicate information clearly and efficiently via statistical graphics, plots and information graphics. Numerical data may be encoded using dots, lines, or bars, to visually communicate a quantitative message.[2] Effective visualization helps users analyze and reason about data and evidence. It makes complex data more accessible, understandable and usable.

Because of the way the human brain processes information, using charts or graphs to visualize large amounts of complex data is easier than poring over spreadsheets or reports. Data visualization is a quick, easy way to convey concepts in a universal manner – and you can experiment with different scenarios by making slight adjustments.This subject is further discussed in section 6.2.1 of this book.

Data visualization can also:

1. Identify areas that need attention or improvement.
2. Clarify which factors influence customer behavior.
3. Help you understand which products to place where.
4. Predict sales volumes.
5. Data visualization solutions were initially developed as a business tool for enterprises
6. that could afford to hire business analysts, citizen data scientists and BI experts capable
7. of performing sophisticated discovery and data analysis. Often, these experts functioned
8. (and still do) as internal consulting groups. This model is too expensive, slow and
9. clumsy for midsize businesses, and it should be avoided.

Graphical displays should:

1. show the data
2. induce the viewer to think about the substance rather than about methodology, graphic design, the technology of graphic production or something else
3. avoid distorting what the data has to say
4. present many numbers in a small space
5. make large data sets coherent
6. encourage the eye to compare different pieces of data
7. reveal the data at several levels of detail, from a broad overview to the fine structure
8. serve a reasonably clear purpose: description, exploration, tabulation or decoration
9. be closely integrated with the statistical and verbal descriptions of a data set.

4.4 CONVENTIONAL DATA VISUALIZATION METHODS

Many conventional data visualization methods are often used. They are: table, histogram, scatter plot, line chart, bar chart, pie chart, area chart, flow chart, bubble chart, multiple data series or combination of charts, time line, Venn diagram, data flow diagram, and entity relationship diagram, etc. In addition, some data visualization methods have been used although they are less known compared the above methods. Theseare described in detail in section 5.6.1 of this book.

The additional methods are: parallel coordinates, treemap, cone tree, and semantic network, etc.[3].

Parallel coordinates is used to plot individual data elements across many dimensions. Parallel coordinate is very useful when to display multidimensional data. Fig. 4.2 shows parallel coordinates. Treemap is an effective method for visualizing hierarchies. The size of each sub-rectangle represents one measure, while color is often used to represent another measure of data. Figure 4.3 shows a treemap of a collection of choices for streaming music and video tracks in a social network community. Cone tree is another method displaying hierarchical data such as organizational body in three dimensions. The branches grow in the form of cone. A semantic network is a graphical representation of logical relationship between different concepts. It generates directed graph, the combination of nodes or vertices, edges or arcs, and label over each edge [3].

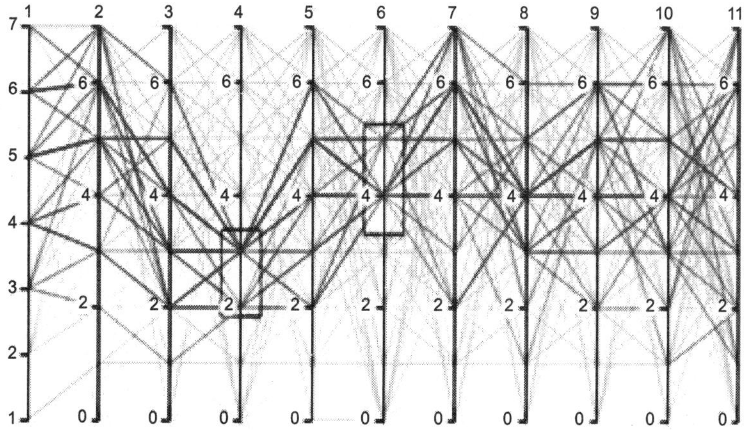

Fig. 4.2. Parallel coordinates [4]

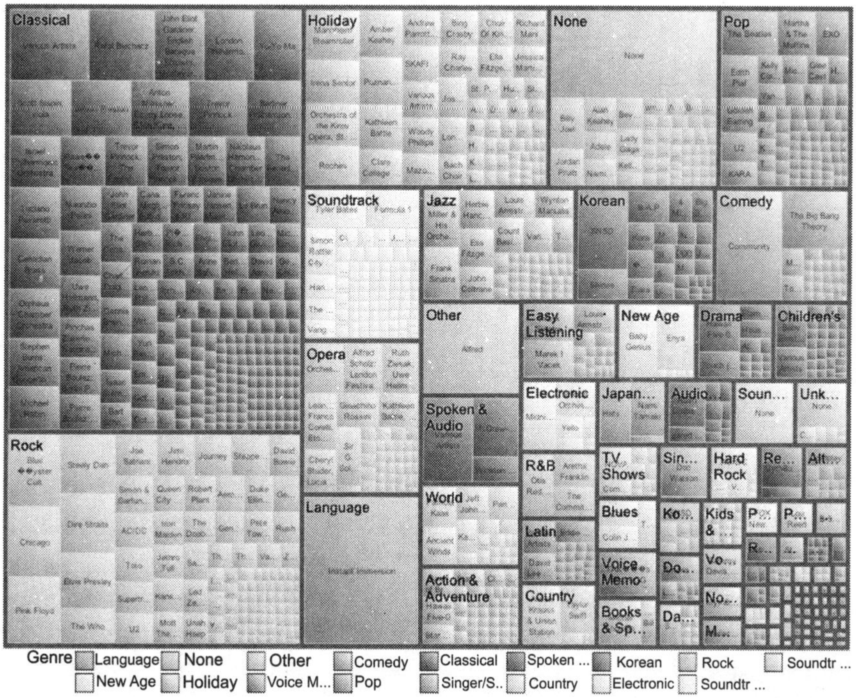

Fig. 4.3. Treemap view of a social network's track selections from a streaming media service [5]

4.4.1 Visual Perception and Data Visualization

A human can distinguish differences in line length, shape, orientation, and colour (hue) readily without significant processing effort; these are referred to as "pre-attentive attributes". For example, it may require significant time and effort ("attentive processing") to identify the number of times the digit "5" appears in a series of numbers; but if that digit is different in size, orientation, or color, instances of the digit can be noted quickly through pre-attentive processing.

Pattern	Example	Pattern	Example
High, low and in between		Non-intersecting and intersecting	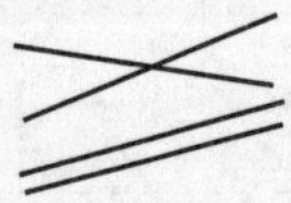
Going up, going down and remaining flat	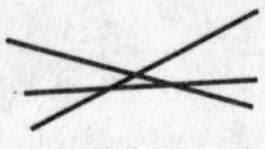	Symmetrical and skewed	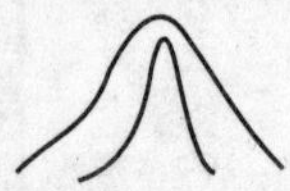
Steep and gradual		Wide and narrow	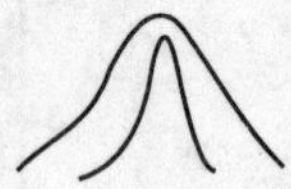
Steady and fluctuating		Clusters and gaps	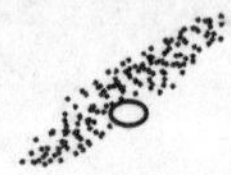
Random and repeating	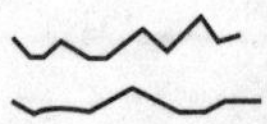	Tightly and loosely distributed	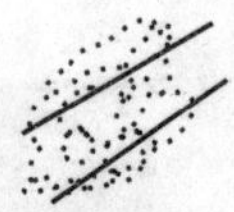
Straight and curved		Normal and abnormal	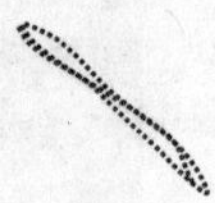

Visualizations are not only static; they can be interactive. Interactive visualization can be performed through approaches such as zooming (zoom in and zoom out), overview and detail, zoom and pan, and focus and context or fish eye[6]. The steps for interactive visualization are as follows [3]:

1. **Selecting:** Interactive selection of data entities or subset or part of whole data or whole data set according to the user interest.
2. **Linking:** It is useful for relating information among multiple views.
3. **Filtering:** It helps users adjust the amount of information for display. It decreases information quantity and focuses on information of interest.
4. **Rearranging or Remapping:** Because the spatial layout is the most important visual mapping, rearranging the spatial layout of the information is very effective in producing different insights.

We have already identified a process to determine what data type it is you have (nominal, ordinal, interval, ratio) and the axis to map it on. Now we need to figure out how to best visually display that data using colours, shapes, sizes and position.

For proper perspective on the subject, in 1984 William S. Cleveland and Robert McGill published a landmark piece of research on graphical perception that articulated the standards that many data visualizations abide by today. Their research, which was published in the Journal of American

Statistical Association, concluded that everyone has different perceptions of visualizations but there are a few simple steps that everyone can follow. Cleveland and McGill tested a series of visual encoding theories through experimentation and established a series of guidelines based on which visual marker is more accurate vs. less accurate.

4.4.2 Mapping of Data visualisation

For all data to be mapped to a visualization, these are your basic options of display:

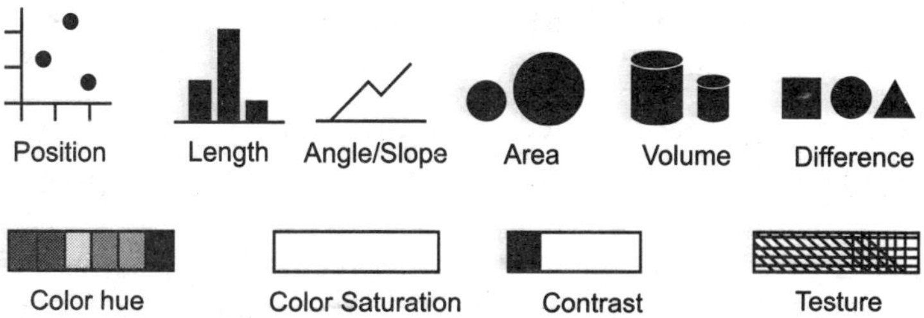

Fig. 4.4: Data Mapping : Basic Options of Dispaly

4.5 RETINAL VARIABLES

Simone GarlandiniSara Irina Fabrikant in their article "Evaluating the Effectiveness and Efficiency of Visual Variables for Geographic Information Visualization" (typically multivariate) spatial data into a two-, three- or four-dimensional visuospatial display. This process is typically performed by applying scientific (i.e., Systematic, Transparent, and Reproducible) cartographic design methods, as well as aesthetic expressivity visual means. He lists seven basic visual variables and presents effects of varying the perceptual properties of the visual variables in order to derive meaningful representations.

4.5.1 Seven Variables for Visulisation

1. two planar variables
2. five so-called "retinal"

- There are two planar variables (the x and y position on the map plane).

Five "Retinal" Variables

1. Size,
2. Color value,
3. Color hue,
4. Shape, and
5. Orientation,

Which we (and perhaps vision researchers) would probably translate as "pre-attentive" (Bertin, 1967/83). Although Bertin (1967/83) lists these variables individually, effective map representables.

4.5.2 Types of visual Variables

A visual variable can be categorised in three different categories :

1. Selective (e.g., colour hue)
2. Associative (e.g., shape)
3. Ordered

A visual variable is selective (e.g., colour hue) and therefore fundamental for symbolization of data, if all symbols can be easily isolated (perceptually selected) to form a group of similar symbols based on this variable (e.g., where are the red signs compared to the green signs). Bertin contends that shape (for points, lines and areas) and orientation (only when applied to areas) are not selective.

Conversely, a visual variable is called associative (e.g., shape) if it allows to perceptually group all categories or instances of symbols based on that particular visual characteristic (signs of the same shape with different sizes vs. signs of different sizes with the same shape). Only the visual variables size and color value are said to have perceptual dissociative characteristics (Bertin, 1967/83). With dissociative visual variables (e.g., size) it is easier to detect visual variations among the signs themselves, than to visually form groups of similar symbols across other visual variables. Dissociative variables can be ordered or quantitative.

A visual variable is defined ordered if it is possible to perceptually rank symbols based on one particular visually varying characteristic (e.g., lighter vs. assessing the effectiveness and efficiency of longstanding cartographic design principles applied to 2D map displays. The approach includes bottom-up visual saliency models that are compared with eye-movement data collected in human-subject experiments on map stimuli embedded in the so-called flicker paradigm. The proposed methods are applied to the assessment of four commonly used visual variables for designing 2D maps:

1. size,
2. color value,
3. color hue, and
4. orientation.

The empirical results suggest that the visual variable size is the most efficient (fastest) and most effective (accurate) visual variable to detect change under flicker conditions. The visual variable orientation proved to be the least efficient and effective of the tested visual variables.

4.5.3 Effectiveness of Mappings

Mapping from (filtered) data to renderable representation

- Most important part of visualization
- Possible visual representations:
  1. Position
  2. Size
  3. Orientation
  4. Shape
  5. Brightness
  6. Color (hue, saturation)

Effectiveness of Mappings

- Efficiency and effectiveness depends on input data:
  1. Nominal
  2. Ordinal

– Quantitative

- Good visual design – Based on psychology and psychophysics
- Psychological investigations to evaluate the appropriateness of mapping approaches

4.6 MAPPING VARIABLES TO ENCODINGS

This is just one example, but if you have other types of data, you will need a guide in order to determine which visual encoding method is best for you. Take a look at the image below, it provides a neat priority guideline by which your data should be mapped.

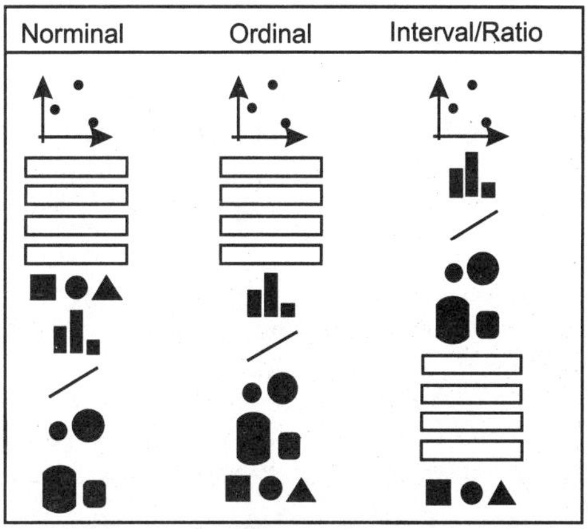

Fig. 4.5: Priority Guideline for Data to be Mapped

Across the board, any time you can use positional data it is in your best interest. However, positional data must not be taken lightly as you can see in the example below. In the first chart, we see a visualization trying to indicate cars being sold across various countries, but there is a problem. In this case, a nominal attribute (country) being mapped by length, which does not help us understand the data very well. Let's try mapping this data another way.

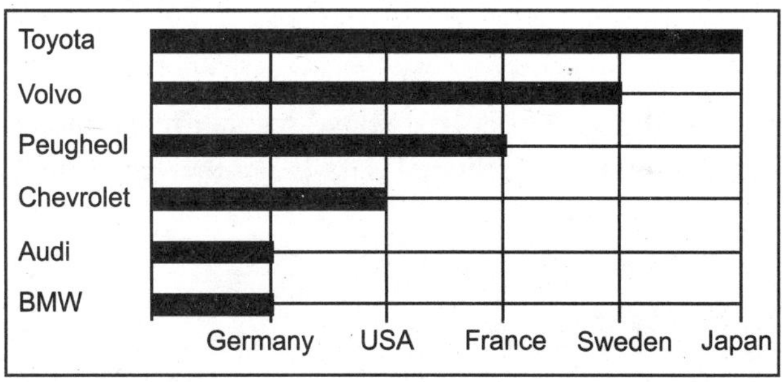

Fig. 4.6: An inappropriate Encoding where a nominal attribute (country) has been mapped to length

Below, you can see that both attributes have been mapped by position, which allows us to learn more about the data. This is much better. It also allows the reader to interpret new possibilities, unlike our previous example, which is always a good thing.

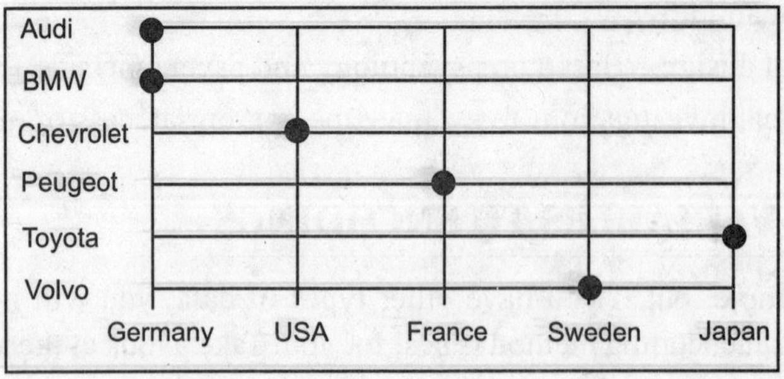

Fig. 4.7: A more appropriate Encoding where both attributes (country and brand) have been mapped to position

One other asset you may be familiar with is our guide to choosing the right visualization from my first blog post. For a popular chart like a scatterplot, if you were to map data this way, it would make more sense (using the data guide you see three images above) to utilize the size of the dots over multiple colors when looking at interval/ratio data. There are many more other factors to consider, but you will be in good shape if you remember the following:

For Nominal data: No one value is more important than the next: while position is best, circles and squares will can be helpful to display your data.

For Ordinal data: Because you are trying to map data with an inherent ranking, the light and dark tones of shading will further emphasize your data's importance.

For Interval/Ratio data: You are looking to map numerical values, therefore the best way to measure those values is through position or length.

4.6.1 Choosing Appropriate Visual Encodings

As we discussed in Data, once you know the "shape" of your data, you can encode its various dimensions with appropriate visual properties. Different visual properties vary—or may be modified—in different ways, which makes them good for encoding different types of data. Two key factors are whether a visual property is naturally ordered, and how many distinct values of this property the reader can easily differentiate. Natural ordering and number of distinct values will indicate whether a visual property is best suited to one of the main data types: quantitative, ordinal, categorical, or relational data. (Spatial data is another common data type, and is usually best represented with some kind of map.)

4.6.2 Natural Ordering

Whether a visual property has a natural ordering is determined by whether the mechanics of our visual system and the "software" in our brains automatically—unintentionally—assign an order, or ranking, to different values of that property. The "software" that makes these judgments is deeply embedded in our brains and evaluates relative order independent of language, culture, convention, or other learned factors; it's not optional and you can't design around it.

For example, position has a natural ordering; shape doesn't. Length has a natural ordering; texture doesn't (but pattern density does). Line thickness or weight has a natural ordering; line style (solid, dotted, dashed) doesn't. Depending on the specifics of the visual property, its natural ordering may be well suited to representing quantitative differences or ordinal differences (small, medium, large, enormous).

Natural orderings are not to be confused with properties for which we have learned or social conventions about their ordering. Social conventions are powerful, and you should be aware of them, but you cannot depend on them to be interpreted in the same way as naturally-ordered properties—which are not social and not learned, and the interpretation of which is not optional.

Color is not ordered

Here's a tricky one: Colour (hue) is not naturally ordered in our brains. Brightness lightness or luminance, sometimes called tint) and intensity (saturation) are, but colour itself is not. We have strong social conventions about color, and there is an ordering by wavelength in the physical world, but colour does not have a non-negotiable natural ordering built into the brain. You can't depend on everyone to agree that yellow follows purple in the way that you can depend on them to agree that four follows three.

The misuse of color to imply order is rampant; don't fall into this common trap. In contexts where you're tempted to use "ordered colour" (elevation, heat maps, etc.), consider varying brightness along one, or perhaps two, axes. For example, elevation can be represented by increasing the darkness of browns, rather than cycling through the rainbow (see Figure 4.8 [7] .

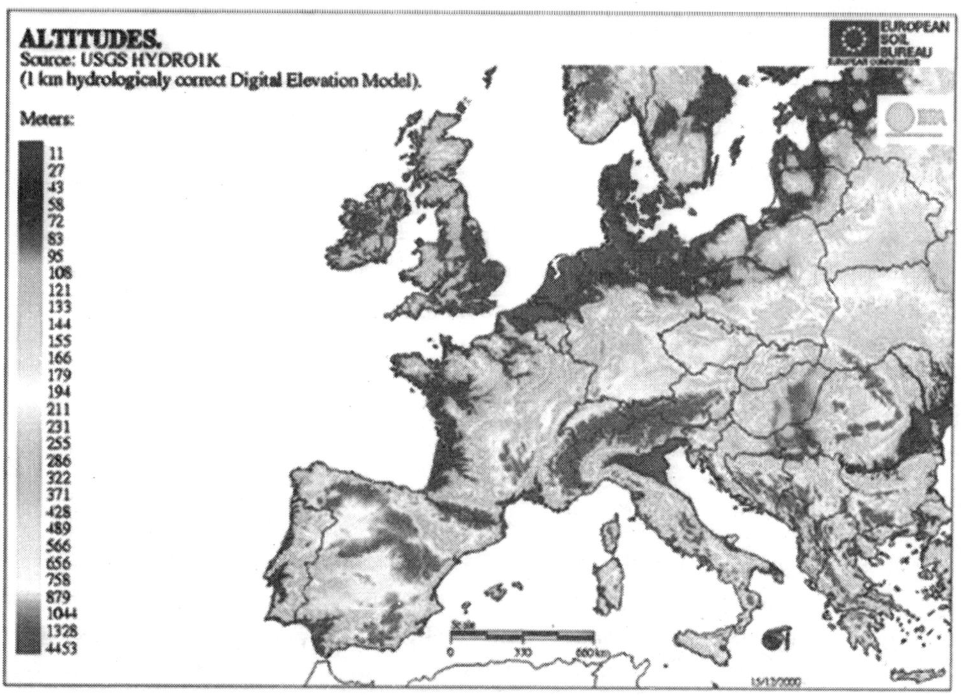

Fig. 4.8: A rainbow encoding leads to a map that is very difficult to understand. Does red mean the Alps are hotter than the rest of Europe?

4.6.3 Distinct Values

The second main factor to consider when choosing a visual property is how many distinct values it has that your reader will be able to perceive, differentiate, and possibly remember. For example, there are a lot of colors in the world, but we can't tell them apart if they're too similar. We can more easily differentiate a large number of shapes, a huge number of positions, and an infinite number of numbers. When choosing a visual property, select one that has a number of useful differentiable values and an ordering similar to that of your data (see Figure 4.9).

Example	Encoding	Ordered	Useful values	Quantit-ative	Ordinal	Catego-rical	Relati-onal
	Position Placement	Yes	Infinite	Good	Good	Good	Good
1, 2, 3, A, B, C	text labels	optional alpha or num	Infinite	Good	Good	Good	Good
	length	yes	many	Good	Good		
	size, atea	yes	many	Good	Good		
	angle	yes	medium	Good	Good		
	patxrn density	yes	few	Good	Good		
	weight, boldness	yes	few		Good		
	saturation, brightness	yes	few		Good		
	color	no	few (>20)			Good	
	shape, icon	no	medium			Good	
	pattern texture	no	medium			Good	
	endosure, connection	no	infinite			Good	Good
	line pattern	no	few				Good
	line endings	no	few				Good
	line weight	yes	few		Good		

Fig. 4.9: Use this table of common visual properties to help you select an appropriate encoding for your data type.

Figure 4.10 shows another way to think about visual properties, depending on what kind of data you need to encode. As you can see, many visual properties may be used to encode multiple data types. Position and placement, as well as text, can be used to encode any type of data—which is why every visualization you design needs to begin with careful consideration of how you'll use them.

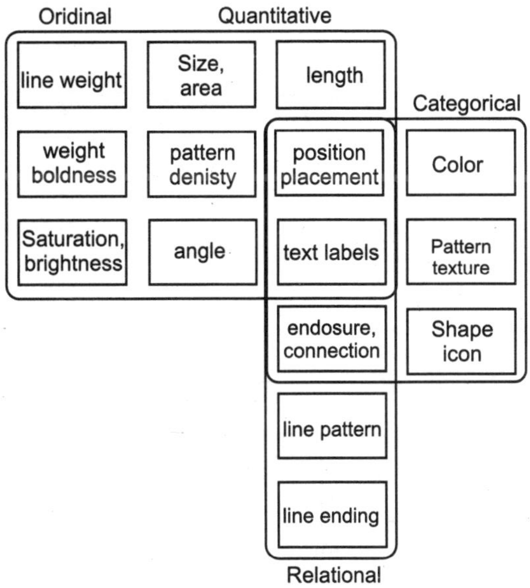

Fig. 4.10. Visual properties grouped by the types of data they can be used to encode.

Just as we don't write PhD dissertations in sonnet form, or thank-you notes like legal briefs complete with footnote citations, it's important that the structure of your visualization be appropriate to your data.

The structure of a visualization should reveal something about the underlying data.

4.6.4 Mapping of data types according to Mackinlay

Mackinlay[6] prepared a chart showing the quality of mapping of data types is shown in fig 4.11.

	Nominal	Ordinal	Quantitative
Position	Good	Good	Good
Size	Good	Good	Good
(Grey) Value	Good	Good	OK
Texture	Good	OK	Bad
Color	Good	Bad	Bad
Orientation	Good	Bad	Bad
Shape	Good	Bad	Bad

Fig. 4.11: Quality of mapping of data types

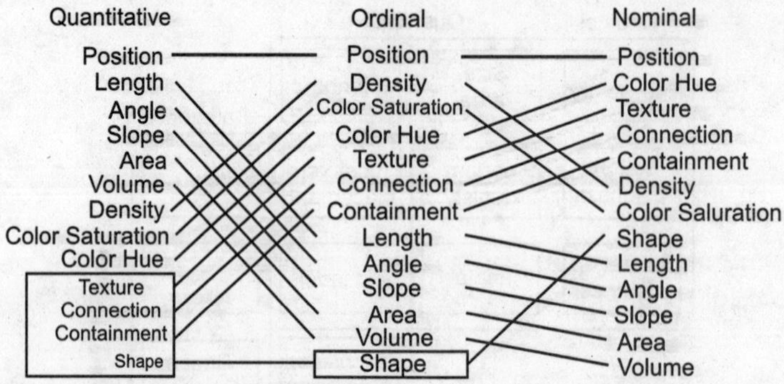

Fig. 4.12 Ranking of perceptual Tasks (Mackinlay)

The tasks shown in grey boxes (Fig. 4.12) are not relevant to these types of data. To be totally accurate, in Figure 4.12, adding colour more strongly defined the groupings that weren't strongly defined before, but those groups are a subset of the information already provided by position. For that reason, in this case colour adds slightly more informational value beyond mere redundancy. A few years ago Dr. Andrew Abela published a good Diagram helping to decide about which chart are a better fit for a given data and problem at hand Dr. Abela also published interesting thoughts about visualization taxonomies. (Fig. 4.13)

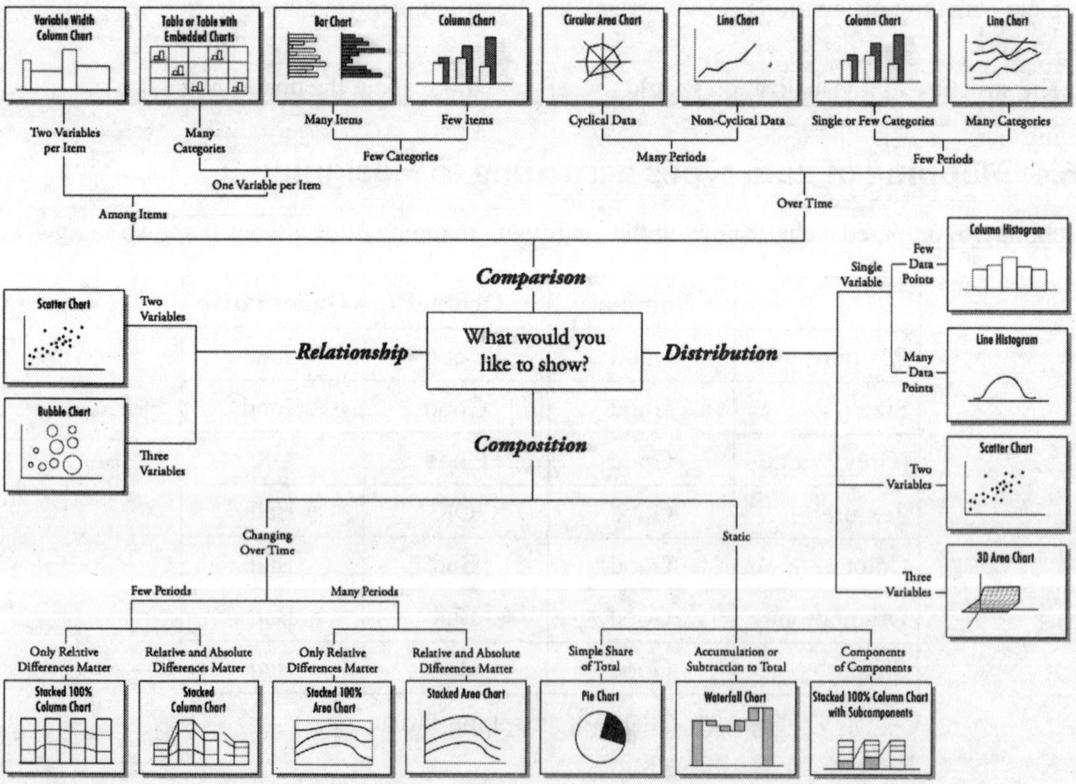

Fig. 4.13: A type of graphics selection chart suggested by Dr. Abela.

4.7 CASE STUDY

In current Air Traffic Control (ATC) environments, air traffic controllers use numerous visualization systems like radar views, timelines, electronic strips, meteorological views or supervision systems. Each of these visualizations is rich and dynamic: it displays numerous visual entities that move and evolve over time. Among its different tasks, the most important activity of the controller is the monitoring of conflicts; this refers to the process to detect a loss of safe separation between aircrafts. Conflict resolution requires quick decisions that are sometimes performed under a high uncertainty. Conflicts resolutions generate psychological stress; consequently, the ATC activity may strongly load the cognitive system. The objective of our work is a first step to evaluate the matching between the Bertin[9] classification of visual properties and the effectiveness of these visual properties in the ATC context.

Furthermore, Bertin introduced seven visual variables (Position, Size, Shape, Orientation, Color, and Texture). Subsequently, Cleveland[10], and then Mackinlay[11] built scales of expressivity and effectiveness for Bertin's visual variables (dependent on the human perceptual capabilities). This scale depends on Bertin's data type. The quantitative data type ranking has been experimentally verified by Cleveland. This ranking was built for statistical graphs; nevertheless, this approach might be applied in many other visualization fields.

The psychophysiological measurements provide objective measures of the state of operators, precious clues on the impact generated by a given task. In mental workload literature[12], as well as in human machine interface studies[13, 14], psychophysiological data are commonly used as an index of the level of cognitive demand generated by a task (e.g. increased temporal demand, memory loading etc.). This level is characterized by physiological changes, in particular the catabolic activity within the autonomous nervous system (ANS) and is associated with energy mobilization and the investment of mental effort to copy with a task The analysis of psychophysiological responses like the eye movements or the pupil diameter has been also successfully used in ATC, for instance to assess the workload generates by a dynamic forecast tool compared to a static one[15].

REFERENCES

1. Michael Friendly (2008). "Milestones in the history of thematic cartography, statistical graphics, and data visualization".
2. Stephen Few-Perceptual Edge-Selecting the Right Graph for Your Message-2004
3. M. Khan, S.S. Khan, Data and Information Visualization Methods and Interactive Mechanisms: A Survey, International Journal of Computer Applications, 34(1), 2011, pp. 1-14.
4. B. Porter, Visualizing Big Data in Drupal: Using Data Visualizations to Drive Knowledge Discovery, Report, University of Washington, October 2012, pp. 1-38.
5. T. A. Keahey, Using visualization to understand big data, Technical Report, IBM Corporation, 2013, pp. 1-16
6. Z. Liu, B. Jiangz and J. Heer, imMens: Real-time Visual Querying of Big Data, Eurographics Conference on Visualization (EuroVis) 2013, 32(3), 2013, pp. 421-430.

7. European Soil Bureau. Copyright © 1995–2011, European Union. Used with stated authorization to reproduce, with acknowledgment. http://eusoils.jrc.ec.europa.eu/
8. J.Mackinlay: Automating the design of raphical presentations of relational information. ACM Transactions on Graphics. 5(2). 110–141. 19861
9. Bertin J. "Graphics and Graphic Information Processing" deGruyter Press, Berlin (1977).
10. Cleveland, W.S., McGill, R., Graphical Perception: Theory, Experimentation, and Application to the Development of Graphical Methods. Journal of the American Statistical Association 79 (1984).
11. Mackinlay, J.Applying a theory of graphical presentation to the graphic design of user interfaces. UIST (1988).
12. Gaillard, A.W.K. Stress, workload, and fatigue as three biobehavioural states: a general overview. In: Hancock, P.A., Desmond, P.A. (Eds.), Stress, Workload, and Fatigue. Erlbaum, Mahweh, NJ, pp. 623– 639 (2001).
13. Gevins, A., Smith, M.E. Neurophysiological measures of cognitive workload during human–computer interaction. Theoretical Issues in Ergonomic Science 4 (1–2), 113– 121 (2003).
14. Iqbal, S., Adamczyk, P., Zheng, X., Bailey, B. Towards an index of opportunity: understanding changes in mental workload during task execution, Proceedings of the SIGCHI conference on Human factors in computing systems, Portland, Oregon, USA (2005).
15. Ahlstrom, U., & Friedman-Berg, F. J. Using eye movement activity as a correlate of cognitive workload. International Journal of Industrial Ergonomics, 36(7), 623-636 (2006).

Chapter 5

APPLICATIONS OF DATA SCIENCE, TECHNOLOGIES FOR VISUALISATION AND BOKEH (PYTHON)

☞ Learning Objectives and Outcomes

In this unit we will learn about

- ☞ Applications of Data Science,
- ☞ Technologies for visualisation,
- ☞ Programming with Python
- ☞ Visualisation Data types through Python Matplotlib
- ☞ Vissalisation with Bokeh (Python)

5.1 APPLICATIONS OF DATA SCIENCE TECHNOLOGIES FOR VISUALISATION

Data visualization has become the de facto standard for modern business intelligence (BI). The success of the two leading vendors in the BI space, Tableau and Qlik -- both of which heavily emphasize visualization–has moved other vendors toward a more visual approach in their software. Virtually all BI software has strong data visualization functionality.

Data visualization tools have been important in democratizing data and analytics and making data-driven insights available to workers throughout an organization. They are typically easier to operate than traditional statistical analysis software or earlier versions of BI software. This has led to a rise in lines of business implementing data visualization tools on their own, without support from IT.

Overall, data scientists should have a working knowledge of statistical programming languages for constructing data processing systems, databases, and visualization tools. Many in the field also deem a knowledge of programming an integral part of data science; however, not all data scientist students study programming, so it is helpful to be aware of tools that circumvent programming and include a user-friendly graphical interface so that data scientists' knowledge of algorithms is enough to help them build predictive models

Data visualization software also plays an important role in big data and advanced analytics projects. As businesses accumulated massive troves of data during the early years of the big data trend, they needed a way to quickly and easily get an overview of their data. Visualization tools were a natural fit.

Visualization is central to advanced analytics for similar reasons. When a data scientist is writing advanced predictive analytics or machine learning algorithms, it becomes important to visualize the outputs to monitor results and ensure that models are performing as intended. This is because visualizations of complex algorithms are generally easier to interpret than numerical outputs.

Examples of data visualization

Data visualization tools can be used in a variety of ways. The most common use today is as a BI reporting tool. Users can set up visualization tools to generate automatic dashboards that track company performance across key performance indicators and visually interpret the results.

Many business departments implement data visualization software to track their own initiatives. For example, a marketing team might implement the software to monitor the performance of an email campaign, tracking metrics like open rate.

The Census Bureau is working to increase our use of visualization in making data available to the public,

5.2 INTRODUCTION TO PYTHON

Firstly, Python is a general purpose programming language and it's not only for Data Science. This means, that you don't have to learn every part of it to be a great data scientist. At the same time, if you learn the basics well, you will understand other programming languages too – which is always very handy, if you work in IT.[1]

Secondly, Python is a high-level language. It means, that in terms of CPU-time it's not the most effective language on the planet. But on the other hand it was made to be simple, "user-friendly" and easy-to-interpret. Thus what you might lose on CPU-time, you might win back on engineering time.

The popularity of it comes from at least following characteristics :

1. Python is fairly easy to interpret and learn.
2. Python handles different data structures very well.
3. Python has very powerful statistical and data visualization libraries.
4. It's easy and fun.
5. It has many packages, that suits solving simpler Analytics projects (eg. segmentation, cohort analysis, explorative analytics, etc.) just as much as advanced Data Science projects (eg. building machine learning models)

When it comes to learn data coding, one has to focus on these four languages:

1. SQL
2. Python
3. R
4. Bash

It s somebody's fortune if having time to learn all four. But if the programmer are newer on this field, you have to pick one or two first. Using first two languages, you will cover the 99% of the data science and analytics problem you have to deal with in the future.

5.2.1 Python 2 vs Python 3-which one to learn for Data Science?

(*a*) Why Python 2.7?

1 Awesome community support! This is something you'd need in your early days. Python 2 was released in late 2000 and has been in use for more than 15 years.
2. Plethora of third-party libraries! Though many libraries have provided 3.x support but still a large number of modules work only on 2.x versions. If you plan to use Python for specific applications like web-development with high reliance on external modules, you might be better off with 2.7.
3. Some of the features of 3.x versions have backward compatibility and can work with 2.7 version.

(*b*) Why Python 3.4?

1. Cleaner and faster! Python developers have fixed some inherent glitches and minor drawbacks in order to set a stronger foundation for the future. These might not be very relevant initially, but will matter eventually.
2. It is the future! 2.7 is the last release for the 2.x family and eventually everyone has to shift to 3.x versions. Python 3 has released stable versions for past 5 years and will continue the same.

Python 3 is around since 2008 – and 95% of the data science related features and libraries have been migrated already. On the other hand Python 2 won't be supported after 2020. So learning Python 2 at this point is like learning Latin – it's useful in some cases, but the future is for Python 3.

5.2.2 Choosing a Development Environment

Once you have installed Python, there are various options for choosing an environment. Here are the 3 most common options:

- Terminal / Shell based
- IDLE (default environment)
- iPython notebook – similar to markdown in R

When you run a Python program through the Python shell, through hitting "play" in IDLE, or by running python3 in the command line, what you are doing is telling the interpreter to start translating.

How does this relate to Python 2 and Python 3? Well, Python 2 and Python 3 are the same language, but they rely on slightly different interpreters to translate. For example, a syntax difference between Python 2 and 3 is how you print something to the screen. In Python 2 you do print "VK Jain" but in Python 3 you do print("VK Jain"). The meaning is the same but the way you write it is different. The syntax for Python 2 is not understood by the Python 3 interpreter, and vice versa.

The other kind of difference is an interpretation difference - the syntax is the same, but the meaning is different. An example is division, which we will discuss below. Both kinds of differences cause errors in your program, and you must be aware of it.

5.2.3 Starting with Python

Starting Python in conversational mode The programming here makes heavy use of Python's conversational mode. When you start Python in this way, you will see an initial greeting message, followed by the prompt ">>>".

On a any workstation in Windows, from the Start menu, select All Programs → Python 2.7 → IDLE (Python GUI).

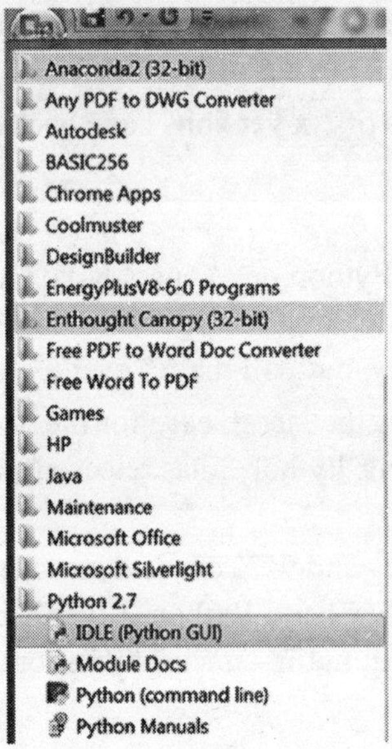

When clicked over IDLE (Python GUI),you will see something like this:

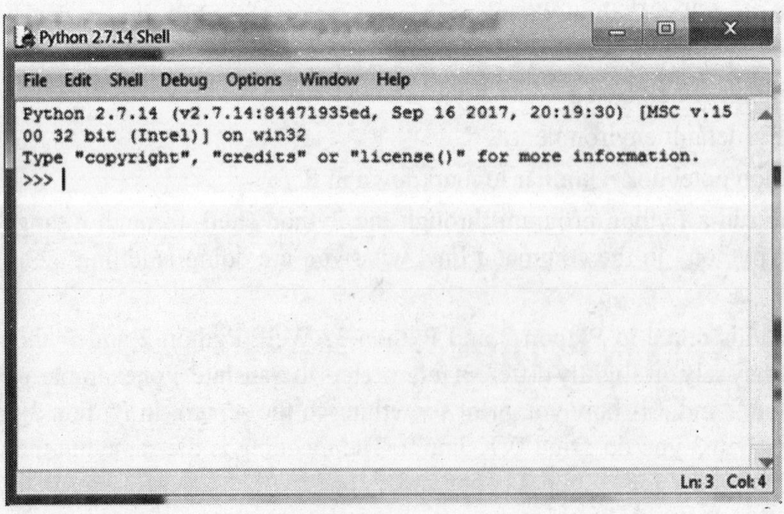

When you see the ">>>" prompt, you can type a Python expression, and Python will show you the result of that expression. This makes Python useful as a deskcalculator. (That's why we sometimes refer to conversational mode as "calculator mode".) For example:

```
Python 2.7.14 Shell
File Edit Shell Debug Options Window Help
Python 2.7.14 (v2.7.14:84471935ed, Sep 16 2017, 20:19:30) [MSC v.15
00 32 bit (Intel)] on win32
Type "copyright", "credits" or "license()" for more information.
>>> 101*101
10201
>>> |
```

5.3 BASIC NUMERIC OPERATIONS

To do numeric calculations in Python, you can write expressions that look more or less like algebraic expressions in many other common languages. The "+" operator is addition; "-" is subtraction; use "*" to multiply; and use "/" to divide. Here are some examples:

```
Python 2.7.14 Shell
File Edit Shell Debug Options Window Help
Python 2.7.14 (v2.7.14:84471935ed, Sep 16 2017, 20:19:30) [MSC v.1500
32 bit (Intel)] on win32
Type "copyright", "credits" or "license()" for more information.
>>> 101*101
10201
>>> 100-199
-99
>>> 79*5
395
>>> 12^^2
SyntaxError: invalid syntax
>>> 12**2
144
>>> 144**.5
12.0
>>> 144/12
12
>>> 155/0

Traceback (most recent call last):
  File "<pyshell#7>", line 1, in <module>
    155/0
ZeroDivisionError: integer division or modulo by zero
>>> |
```

5.4 DATA TYPES IN PYTHON

Python supports various data types, these data types defines the operations possible on the variables and the storage method.

All of standard data types available in Python are discussed below:

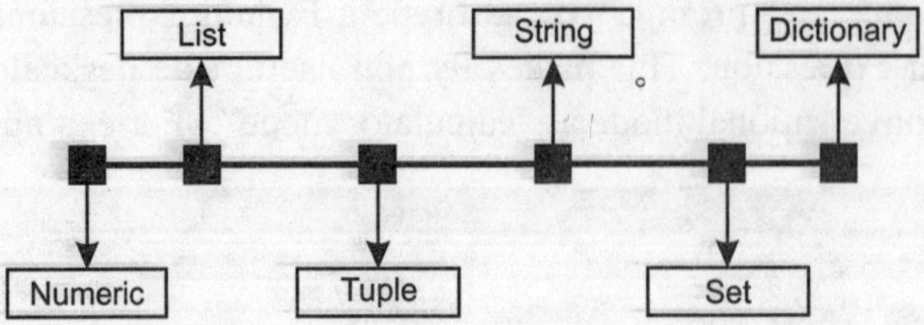

5.4.1 Numeric:

Just as expected Numeric data types store numeric values.

They are immutable data types, this means that, you cannot change it's value.

Python supports three different Numeric data types:

Integer type: It holds all the integer values i.e. all the positive and negative whole numbers, example – 10.

Float type: It holds the real numbers and are represented by decimal and sometimes even scientific notations with E or e indicating the power of 10 (2.5e2 = 2.5 x 102 = 250), example – 10.24.

Complex type: These are of the form a + bj, where a and b are floats and J represents the square root of -1 (which is an imaginary number), example – 10+6j.

Now you can even perform type conversion. For example you can convert the integer value to a float value and vice-versa. Type following at the interpreters command prompt >>>. The integers 1, 2,3,4 in above code lines have added by me, actually they will not be shown in your interpreter.

```
1 A = 10
2 # Convert it into float type
3 B = float (A)
4 print (B)
```

Press Enter key to see following :

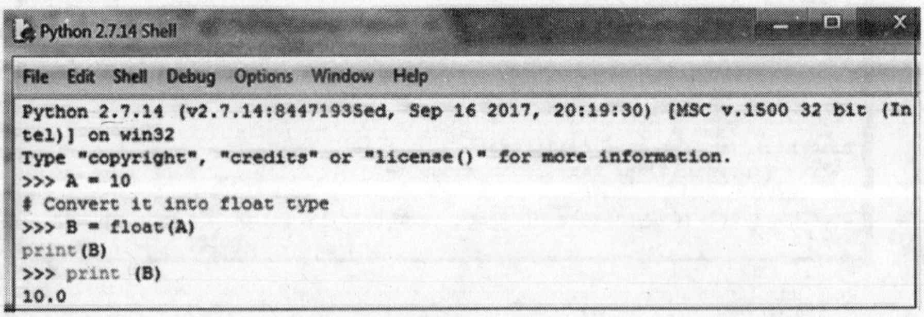

Type following at the interpreters command prompt >>> for converting from floating to inter type.

```
1 A = 10.76
2 # Convert it into int type
```

```
B = int (A)
print (B)
```

Following shall be output on screen:

```
>> A = 10.76
# Covert it into int type
B = into (A)
>>> print (B)
10.0
>>>
```

5.4.2 List Data Type

You can consider the Lists as Arrays in C, but in List you can store elements of different types, but in Array all the elements should of the same type.

List is the most versatile datatype available in Python which can be written as a list of comma-separated values (items) between square brackets. Consider the example below. Type following at the interpreters command prompt >>>

```
Subjects = ['Physics', 'Chemistry', 'Maths', 2]
print(Subjects)
```

Following shall be output on screen:

```
>>> Subjects = ['Physices', 'Chemistry', 'Maths', 2]
>>> print (Subjects)
['Physics', 'Chemistry, 'Maths', 2]
>>>
```

List Operations:

The table below contains the operations possible with Lists:

Syntax	Result	Description
Subjects [0]	Physics	This will give the index 0 value from the Subjects List.
Subjects [0 : 2]	Physics, Chemistry	This will give the index values from 0 till 2, bu won't include 2 the Subjects List.
Subjects [3] = 'Biology'	['Physics', 'Chemistry', 'Maths' 'Biology']	It will updata the List and add 'Biology' at ind 3 and remove 2.
del Subjects [2]	['Physics', 'Chemistry', 2]	This will delete the index value 2 from Subject list.

len (Subjects)	['Physics', 'Chemistry', 'Maths', 2, 1, 2, 3]	This will return the length of the list
Subjects * 2	['Physics', 'Chemistry' 'Maths', 2] ['Physics', 'Chemistry', 'Maths', 2]	This will repeat the Subjects list twice.
Subject [::-1]	[2, 'Maths', 'Chemistry', 'Physics']	This will reverse the Subjects list

Notice that the Subjects List contains both words as well as numbers. Now, let's perform some operations on our Subjects List.

5.4.3 String Data Type

Strings are amongst the most popular types in Python. We can create them simply by enclosing characters in quotes. Python treats single and double quotes in exactly the same fashion. Consider the example below:

```
A = "Welcome To Python Tutorial"
B = 'That is great'
```

Following shall be output on screen:

```
>>> A = " Welcome To Phython Tutorial"
>>> print (A)
Welcome To Python Tutorial
>>> B = 'That is great'
>>> print (B)
That isgreat
>>>
```

Let's look at few operations that you can perform with Strings.

Syntax	Operation
print (len (String_Name))	String Length
print (String_Name. index ("Char"))	Locate a character in String
print (String_Name.count "Char"))	Count the number of times a character is repeated in a String
print (String_Name [Start:Stop]	Slicing
print (String_Name [::-1]	Reverse a String
print (String_Name.upper())	Covert the letters in a String to upper-case
print (string_Name.lower())	Convert the letters in a String to lower-case

Examples

```
>>> A = "GoD"
>>> print (A[::-1])
GoD
>>>
>>> A = 'upper case'
>>> print (A. upper())
UPPER CASE
>>> A = 'UPPER CASE'
>>> A = 'LOWER CASE'
>>> print (A. lower ())
lower case
>>>
```

5.4.4 Set Data Type

A set is an unordered collection of items. Every element is unique.

A set is created by placing all the items (elements) inside curly braces {}, separated by comma. Consider the example below:

```
Set_1 = {1, 2, 3}
```

In Sets every element has to be unique. Try printing the below code:

```
Set_2 = {1, 2, 3, 3}
```

Here 3 is repeated twice, but it will print it only once.

Let's look at some Set operations:

(*a*) **Union:** Union of A and B is a set of all elements from both sets. Union is performed using | operator. Consider the below example:

```
A = {1, 2, 3, 4}
B = {3, 4, 5, 6}
print ( A | B)
```

Output shall be:

```
set ([1, 2, 3, 4, 5, 6])
```

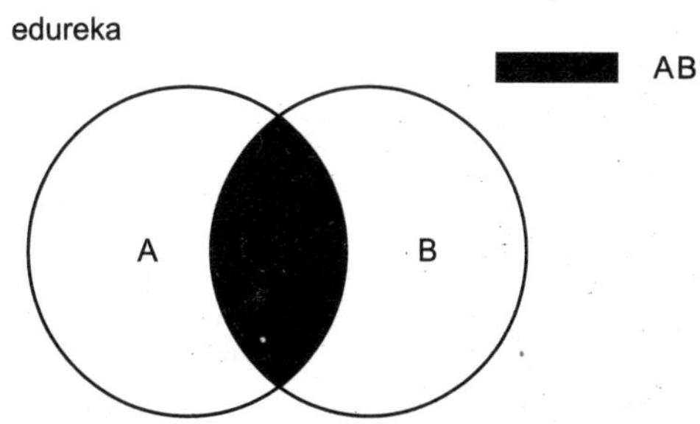

(*b*) **Intersection:** Intersection of A and B is a set of elements that are common in both sets. Intersection is performed using & operator. Consider the example below:

```
A = {1, 2, 3, 4}
B = {3, 4, 5, 6}
print ( A & B )
```

When you enter above code line by line you will get following output:

Output shall be:

```
set ([3, 4])
```

5.4.5 Dictionary Data Type

Let us take example of Aadhar card Adhaar Card.which is a unique ID which has been given to all Indian citizen. So for every Adhaar number there is a name and few other details attached. Now you can consider the Adhaar number as a Key and the person's detail as the Value attached to that Key.

In Python Dictionarry data type contains these Key Value pairs enclosed within curly braces and Keys and values are separated with ':'. Type following at the interpreters command prompt >>>

```
Dict = {'Name' : 'Jyotsna', 'Age' : 44}
```

We will go through various Dictionary operations.

Dictionary Operations:

(*a*) Access elements from a dictionary:

```
Dict = {'Name' : 'Jyotsna', 'Age' : 44}
print(Dict['Name'])
```

See the output below after (b)

(*b*) Changing elements in a Dictionary:

Type following at the interpreters command prompt >>>

```
Dict = { 'Name' : 'Jyotsna', 'Age' : 44}
Dict['Age'] = 32
Dict['Address'] = 'D-55 sector 20 Noida'
```

Following shall appear on screen:

```
>>> Dict = { 'Name' : Jyotsna'''''''', Age' : 44}
>>> print (Dict ['Name'])
Jyotsna
>>> Dict ['Age'] = 32
>>> Dict ['Address'] = 'D-55 sector 20 Noida'
>>> print (Dict ['Name', 'Age', 'Address'])
>>> print (Dict ['Age'])
32
>>> print (Dict ['Address'])
D-55 sector 20 Noida
>>>
```

5.4.6 Loops in Python

In Python, there are three types of loops:

- While
- For
- Nested

(a) While Loop: Here, first the condition is checked and if it's true, control will move inside the loop and execute the statements inside the loop until the condition becomes false. We use this loop when we are not sure how many times we need to execute a group of statements or you can say that when we are unsure about the number of iterations.

Type following at the interpreters command prompt >>>

```
count = 0
while (count < 9):
   print 'The cunt is :', count
   count = count + 1
print "Good bye!"
```

```
   The count is : 0
   The count is : 1
   The count is : 2
   The count is : 3
   The count is : 4
   The count is : 5
   The count is : 6
   The count is : 7
   The count is : 8
   Good by!
```

(b) For Loop: Like the While loop, the For loop also allows a code block to be repeated certain number of times. The difference is, in For loop we know the amount of iterations required unlike While loop, where iterations depends on the condition. You will get a better idea about the difference between the two by looking at the syntax:

1. for variable in Sequence:
2. statements

Notice here, we have specified the range, that means we know the number of times the code block will be executed.

Type following at the interpreters command prompt >>>

```
fruits = ['Mango', 'Apple',  'Grapes']
for index in range(len(fruits)):
   print (fruits[index])
```

```
Mango
Apple
Grapes
```

(*c*) **Nested Loops:** It basically means a loop inside a loop. It can be a For loop inside a While loop and vice-versa. Even a For loop can be inside a For loop or a While loop inside a While loop.

Type following at the interpreters command prompt >>>

```
count = 1
for i in range(8):
print (str(i) * i)
for j in range(0, i):
count = count +1
```

The output shall be :

```
1
22
333
4444
55555
666666
7777777
```

5.5 MODULES

A module allows you to logically organize your Python code. Grouping related code into a module makes the code easier to understand and use. A module is a Python object with arbitrarily named attributes that you can bind and reference.

Simply, a module is a file consisting of Python code. A module can define functions, classes and variables. A module can also include runnable code.

Example 5.1 Getting Calendar For A Month

The calendar module gives a wide range of methods to play with yearly and monthly calendars. Here, we print a calendar for a given month (Jan 2018) :

```
#!/usr/bin/python
import calendar
cal = calendar.month(2018, 1)
print "Here is the calendar:"
print cal
```

This would produce the following result :

Here is the calender: January 2018						
Mo	Tu	We	Th	Fr	Sa	Su
1	2	3	4	5	6	7
8	9	10	11	12	13	14
15	16	17	18	19	20	21
22	23	24	25	26	27	28
29	30	31				

The Python code for a module named aname normally resides in a file named aname.py. Here's an example of a simple module, support.py

```
def print_func( par ):
   print "Hello : ", par
   return
```

5.5.1 The import Statement

You can use any Python source file as a module by executing an import statement in some other Python source file. The import has the following syntax –

```
import module1[, module2[,... moduleN]
```

When the interpreter encounters an import statement, it imports the module if the module is present in the search path. A search path is a list of directories that the interpreter searches before importing a module. For example, to import the module support.py, you need to put the following command at the top of the script –

```
#!/usr/bin/python
# Import module support
import support
# Now you can call defined function that module as follows
support.print_func("Zara")
```

When the above code is executed, it produces the following result –

```
Hello : Zara
```

A module is loaded only once, regardless of the number of times it is imported. This prevents the module execution from happening over and over again if multiple imports occur.

5.5.2 The from...import Statement

Python's from statement lets you import specific attributes from a module into the current namespace. The from...import has the following syntax –

```
from modname import name1[, name2[, ... nameN]]
```

For example, to import the function fibonacci from the module fib, use the following statement–

```
from fib import fibonacci
```

This statement does not import the entire module fib into the current namespace; it just introduces the item fibonacci from the module fib into the global symbol table of the importing module.

5.5.3 The from...import * Statement

It is also possible to import all names from a module into the current namespace by using the following import statement –

```
from modname import *
```

This provides an easy way to import all the items from a module into the current namespace; however, this statement should be used sparingly.

5.5.4 Locating Modules

When you import a module, the Python interpreter searches for the module in the following sequences –

The current directory.

If the module isn't found, Python then searches each directory in the shell variable PYTHONPATH.

If all else fails, Python checks the default path. On UNIX, this default path is normally /usr/local/lib/python/.

The module search path is stored in the system module sys as the sys.pathvariable. The sys.path variable contains the current directory, PYTHONPATH, and the installation-dependent default.

The PYTHONPATH Variable

The PYTHONPATH is an environment variable, consisting of a list of directories. The syntax of PYTHONPATH is the same as that of the shell variable PATH.

Here is a typical PYTHONPATH from a Windows system –

```
set PYTHONPATH = c:\python20\lib;
```

And here is a typical PYTHONPATH from a UNIX system –

```
set PYTHONPATH = /usr/local/lib/python
```

5.5.5 Namespaces and Scoping

Variables are names (identifiers) that map to objects. A namespace is a dictionary of variable names (keys) and their corresponding objects (values).

A Python statement can access variables in a local namespace and in the global namespace. If a local and a global variable have the same name, the local variable shadows the global variable.

Each function has its own local namespace. Class methods follow the same scoping rule as ordinary functions.

Python makes educated guesses on whether variables are local or global. It assumes that any variable assigned a value in a function is local.

Therefore, in order to assign a value to a global variable within a function, you must first use the global statement.

The statement global VarName tells Python that VarName is a global variable. Python stops searching the local namespace for the variable.

For example, we define a variable Money in the global namespace. Within the function Money, we assign Money a value, therefore Python assumes Moneyas a local variable. However, we accessed the value of the local variable Money before setting it, so an UnboundLocalError is the result. Uncommenting the global statement fixes the problem.

```
#!/usr/bin/python
Money = 2000
def AddMoney():
        # Uncomment the following line to fix the code:
        # global Money
         Money = Money + 1
print Money
AddMoney()
print Money
```

The dir () Function

The dir() built-in function returns a sorted list of strings containing the names defined by a module.

The list contains the names of all the modules, variables and functions that are defined in a module. Following is a simple example :

```
#!/usr/bin/python
# Import built-in module math
import math
content = dir(math)
print content
```

When the above code is executed, it produces the following result –

```
['__doc__', '__name__', '__package__', 'acos', 'acosh', 'asin', 'asinh', 'atan',
'atan2', 'atanh', 'ceil', 'copysign', 'cos', 'cosh', 'degrees', 'e', 'erf', 'erfc',
'exp', 'expm1', 'fabs', 'factorial', 'floor', 'fmod', 'frexp', 'fsum', 'gamma',
'hypot', 'isinf', 'isnan', 'ldexp', 'lgamma', 'log', 'log10', 'log1p', 'modf', 'pi',
'pow', 'radians', 'sin', 'sinh', 'sqrt', 'tan', 'tanh', 'trunc']
```

Here, the special string variable __name__ is the module's name, and __file__is the filename from which the module was loaded.

5.6 LIBRARY

Following are a list of libraries, you will need for any scientific computations and data analysis[2]:

- **NumPy** stands for Numerical Python. The most powerful feature of NumPy is n-dimensional array. This library also contains basic linear algebra functions, Fourier transforms, advanced random number capabilities and tools for integration with other low level languages like Fortran, C and C++. Numpy/Scipy is used for Data Wrangling/ Representation.NumPy is a library for the Python programming language, adding support for large, multi-dimensional arrays and matrices, along with a large collection of high-level mathematical functions to operate on these arrays. NumPy is open-source software and has many contributors.
- **SciPy** stands for Scientific Python. SciPy is built on NumPy. It is one of the most useful library for variety of high level science and engineering modules like discrete Fourier transform, Linear Algebra, Optimization and Sparse matrices.
- **Matplotlib** for plotting vast variety of graphs, starting from histograms to line plots to heat plots.. You can use Pylab feature in ipython notebook (ipython notebook –pylab = inline) to use these plotting features inline. If you ignore the inline option, then pylab converts ipython environment to an environment, very similar to Matlab. You can also use Latex commands to add math to your plot.
- **Pandas** for structured data operations and manipulations, Data Munging and Wrangling It is extensively used for data munging and preparation. pandas is a software library written for the Python programming language for data manipulation and analysis. In particular, it offers data structures and operations for manipulating numerical tables and time series. It is free software released under the three-clause BSD license.The name is derived from the term "panel data", an econometrics term for multidimensional, structured data sets. Pandas were added relatively recently to Python and have been instrumental in boosting Python's usage in data scientist community. Pandas objects to add informative labels), but full customization will require changing attributes on the matplotlib objects directly. The combination of seaborn's high-level interface and matplotlib's customizability and wide range of backends makes it easy to generate publication-quality figures.
- **Scikit** Learn for machine learning. Built on NumPy, SciPy and matplotlib, this library contains a lot of effiecient tools for machine learning and statistical modeling including classification, regression, clustering and dimensionality reduction. Machine Learning library Scikit-learn (formerly scikits.learn) is a free software machine learning library for the Python programming language. It features various classification, regression and clustering algorithms including support vector machines, random forests, gradient boosting, k-means and DBSCAN, and is designed to interoperate with the Python numerical and scientific libraries NumPy and SciPy.
- **Statsmodels** for statistical modeling. Statsmodels is a Python module that allows users to

explore data, estimate statistical models, and perform statistical tests. An extensive list of descriptive statistics, statistical tests, plotting functions, and result statistics are available for different types of data and each estimator.

- **Seaborn** for statistical data visualization. Seaborn is a library for making attractive and informative statistical graphics in Python. It is based on matplotlib. Seaborn aims to make visualization a central part of exploring and understanding data. Below are the list of packages which are great for data science applications. Seaborn is a Python visualization library based on matplotlib. It provides a high-level interface for drawing attractive statistical graphics. Seaborn is a library for making attractive and informative statistical graphics in Python. It is built on top of matplotlib and tightly integrated with the PyData stack, including support for numpy and pandas data structures and statistical routines from scipy and statsmodels.
- **Bokeh** for creating interactive plots, dashboards and data applications on modern web-browsers. It empowers the user to generate elegant and concise graphics in the style of D3.js. Moreover, it has the capability of high-performance interactivity over very large or streaming datasets.
- **Blaze** for extending the capability of Numpy and Pandas to distributed and streaming datasets. It can be used to access data from a multitude of sources including Bcolz, MongoDB, SQLAlchemy, Apache Spark, PyTables, etc. Together with Bokeh, Blaze can act as a very powerful tool for creating effective visualizations and dashboards on huge chunks of data.
- **Scrapy** for web crawling. It is a very useful framework for getting specific patterns of data. It has the capability to start at a website home url and then dig through web-pages within the website to gather information.
- **SymPy** for symbolic computation. It has wide-ranging capabilities from basic symbolic arithmetic to calculus, algebra, discrete mathematics and quantum physics. Another useful feature is the capability of formatting the result of the computations as LaTeX code.
- **Requests** for accessing the web. It works similar to the the standard python library urllib2 but is much easier to code. You will find subtle differences with urllib2 but for beginners, Requests might be more convenient.

5.6.1 Python Matplotlib

Matplotlib is a plotting library used for 2D graphics in python programming language. It can be used in python scripts, shell, web application servers and other graphical user interface toolkits.

There are several toolkits which are available that extend python matplotlib functionality. Some of them are separate downloads, others can be shipped with the matplotlib source code but have external dependencies.

1. **Basemap:** It is a map plotting toolkit with various map projections, coastlines and political boundaries.
2. **Cartopy:** It is a mapping library featuring object-oriented map projection definitions, and arbitrary point, line, polygon and image transformation capabilities.

3. **Excel tools:** Matplotlib provides utilities for exchanging data with Microsoft Excel.
4. **Mplot3d:** It is used for 3-D plots.
5. **Natgrid:** It is an interface to the natgrid library for irregular gridding of the spaced data.

Matplotlib tries to make easy things easy and hard things possible. You can generate plots, histograms, power spectra, bar charts, errorcharts, scatterplots, etc., with just a few lines of code

Here you'll find a host of example plots with the code that generated them.

5.6.2 Bar Charts

Use the **bar()** function to make bar charts, which includes customizations such as error bars:

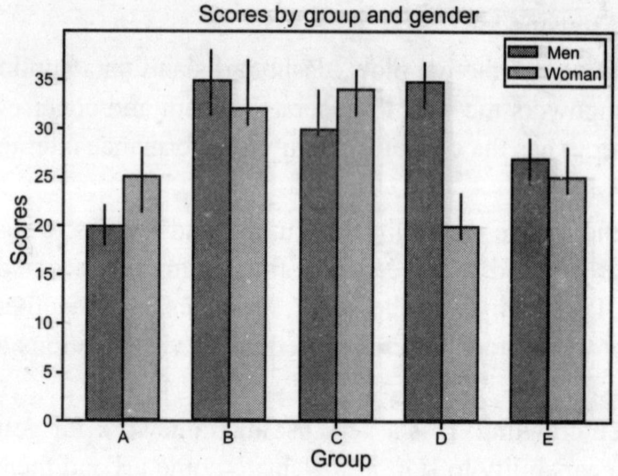

Barchart

You can also create stacked bars (bar_stacked.py), or horizontal bar charts (barh.py).

5.6.3 Pie Charts

The **pie()** function allows you to create pie charts. Optional features include auto-labeling the percentage of area, exploding one or more wedges from the center of the pie, and a shadow effect. Take a close look at the attached code, which generates this figure in just a few lines of code.

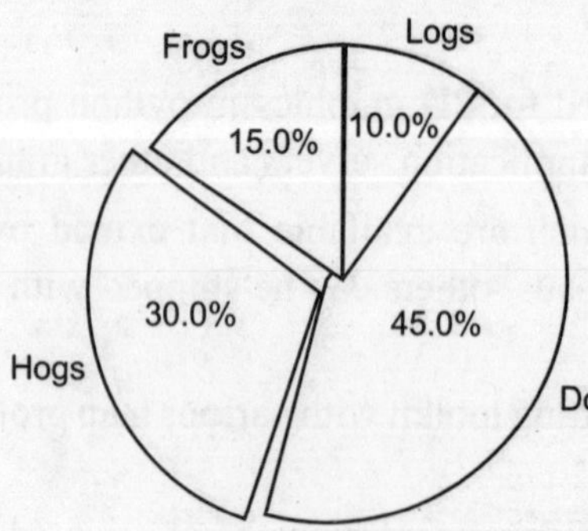

Pie Features

5.6.4 Scatter Plots

The **scatter()** function makes a scatter plot with (optional) size and color arguments. This example plots changes in Google's stock price, with marker sizes reflecting the trading volume and colors varying with time. Here, the alpha attribute is used to make semitransparent circle markers.

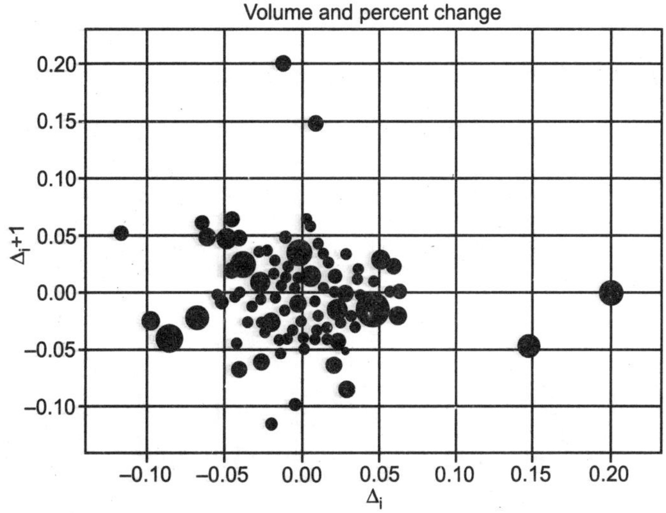

Scatter Chart

5.6.5 Histograms

The **hist()** function automatically generates histograms and returns the bin counts or probabilities:

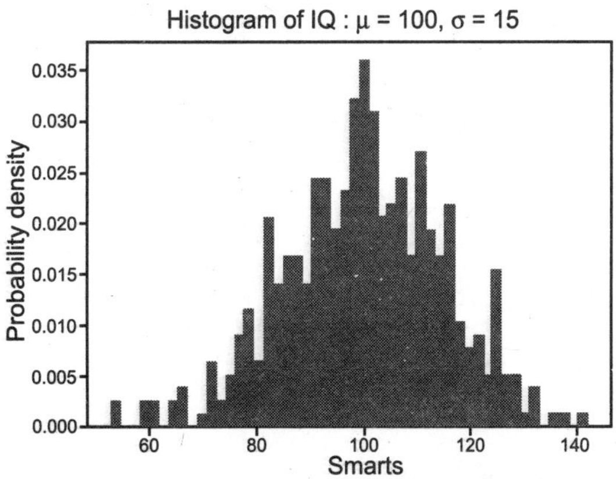

Histogram Features

5.6.6 Line Plot

Here's how to create a line plot with text labels using **plot()**.

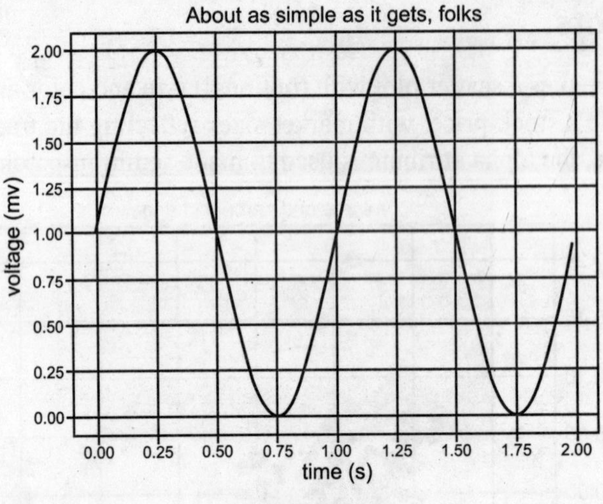

Simple Plot

5.6.7 Multiple subplots in one figure

Multiple axes (i.e. subplots) are created with the subplot() function:

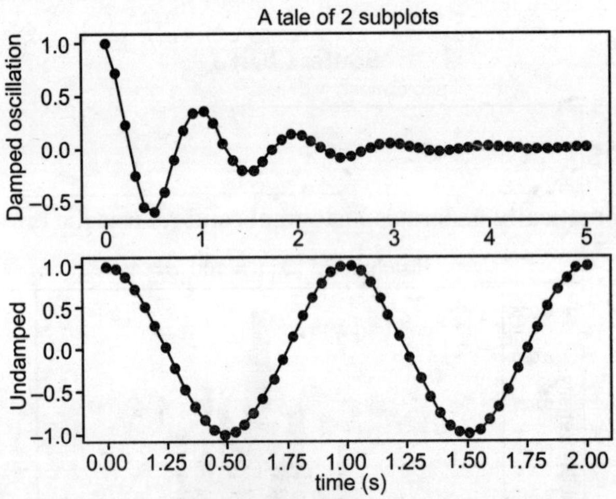

Subplot

5.6.8 Images

Matplotlib can display images (assuming equally spaced horizontal dimensions) using the imshow() function.

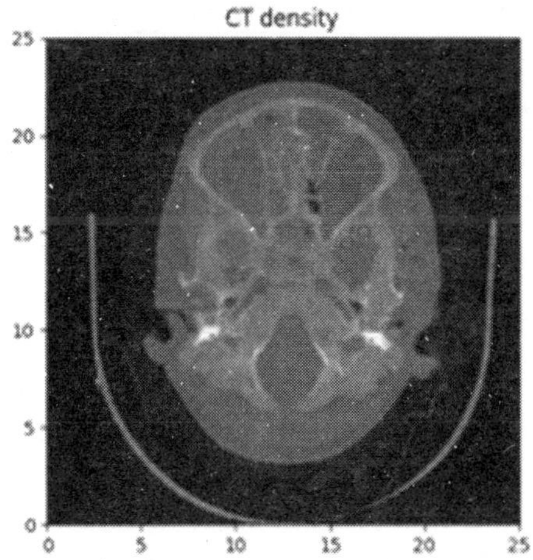

Example of using imshow() to display a CT scan

5.6.9 Contouring and pseudocolor

The **pcolormesh()** function can make a coloured representation of a two-dimensional array, even if the horizontal dimensions are unevenly spaced. The contour() function is another way to represent the same data:

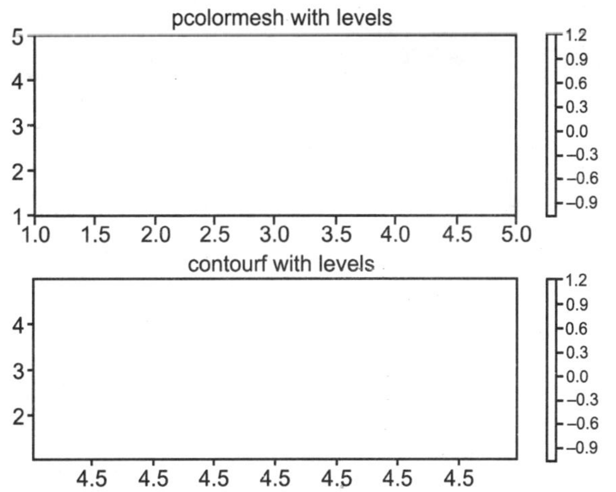

Example comparing pcolormesh() and contour() for plotting two-dimensional data

5.6.10 Paths

You can add arbitrary paths in Matplotlib using the matplotlib.path module:

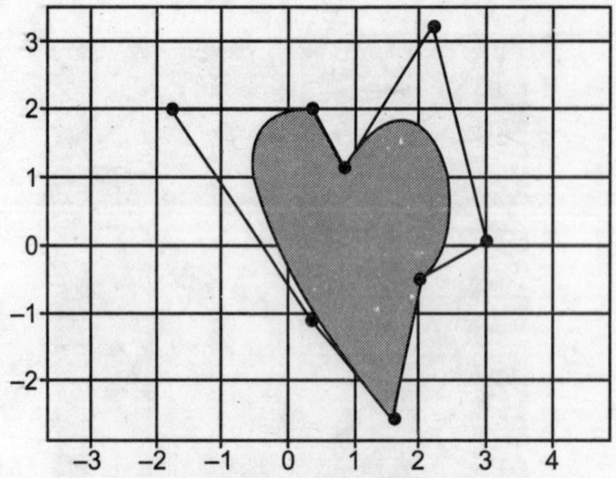

Path Patch

5.6.11 Three-Dimensional Plotting

The mplot3d toolkit has support for simple 3d graphs including surface, wireframe, scatter, and bar charts.

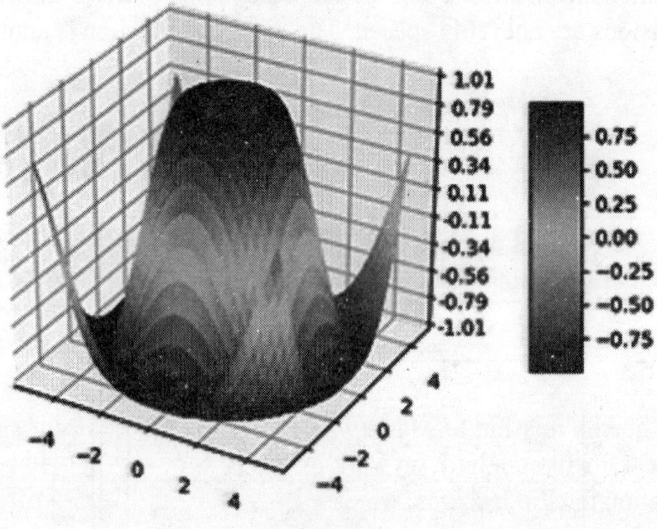

Surface3d

5.6.12 Streamplot

The **Streamplot()** function plots the streamlines of a vector field. In addition to simply plotting the streamlines, it allows you to map the colors and/or line widths of streamlines to a separate parameter, such as the speed or local intensity of the vector field.

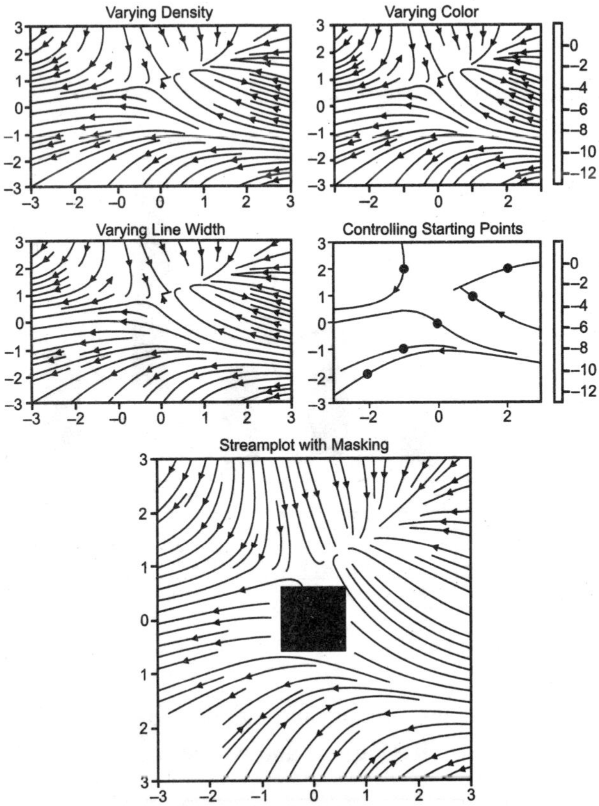

Streamplot with various plotting options.

This feature complements the quiver() function for plotting vector fields. Thanks to Tom Flannaghan and Tony Yu for adding the streamplot function.

5.6.13 Ellipses

In support of the Phoenix mission to Mars (which used Matplotlib to display ground tracking of spacecraft), Michael Droettboom built on work by Charlie Moad to provide an extremely accurate 8-spline approximation to elliptical arcs, which are insensitive to zoom level.

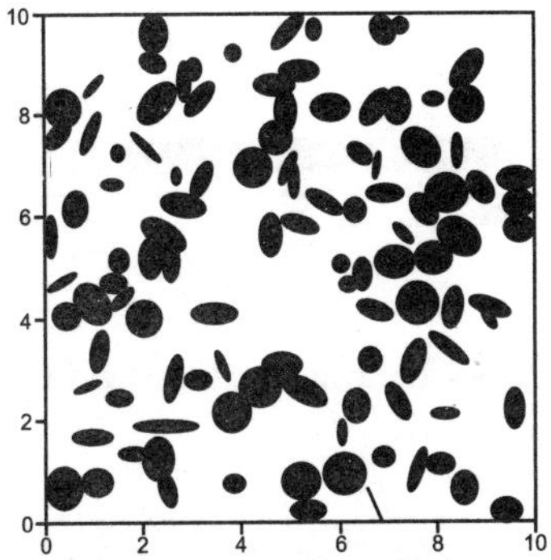

Ellipse Demo

5.6.14 Tables

The **table()** function adds a text table to an axes.

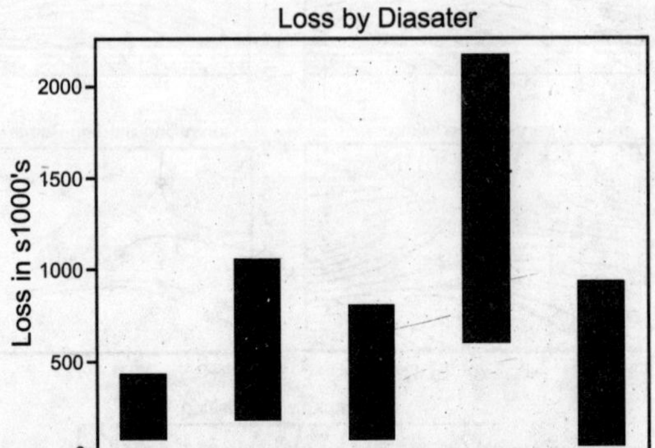

	Freeze	Wind	Flood	Quake	Hall
100 year	431.5	1049.4	799.6	2149.8	917.9
50 year	292.2	717.8	456.4	1368.5	865.6
20 year	213.8	636.0	305.7	1175.2	796.0
10 year	124.6	555.4	153.2	677.2	192.5
5 year	66.4	174.3	75.1	577.9	32.0

5.6.15 GUI widgets

Matplotlib[4] has basic GUI widgets that are independent of the graphical user interface you are using, allowing you to write cross GUI figures and widgets.

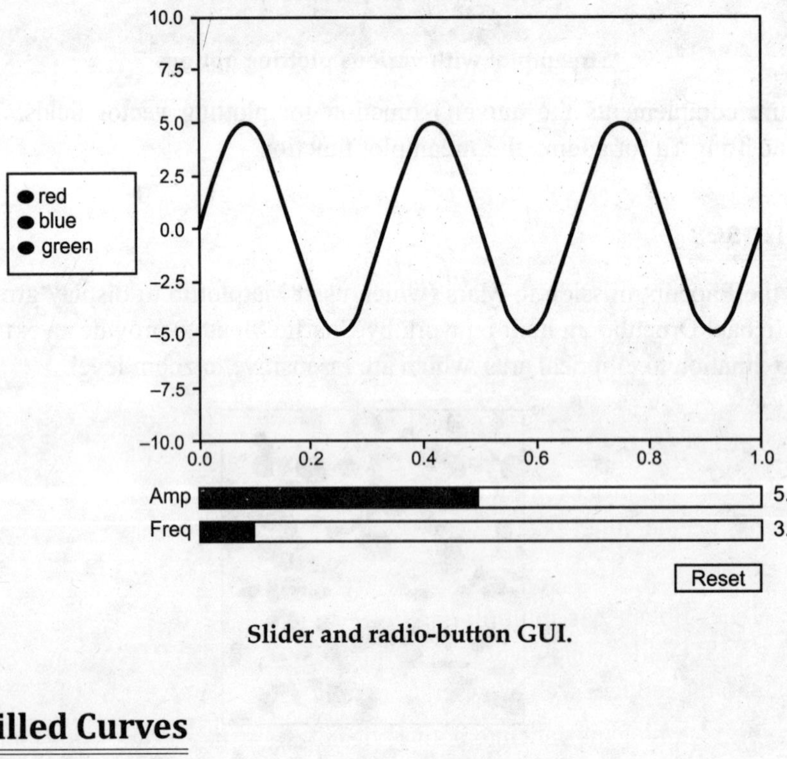

Slider and radio-button GUI.

5.6.16 Filled Curves

The **fill()** function lets you plot filled curves and polygons:

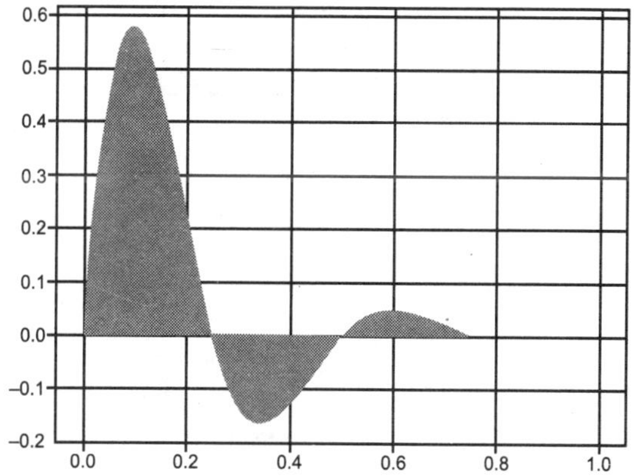

Fill

5.6.17 Date Handling

You can plot timeseries data with major and minor ticks and custom tick formatters for both.

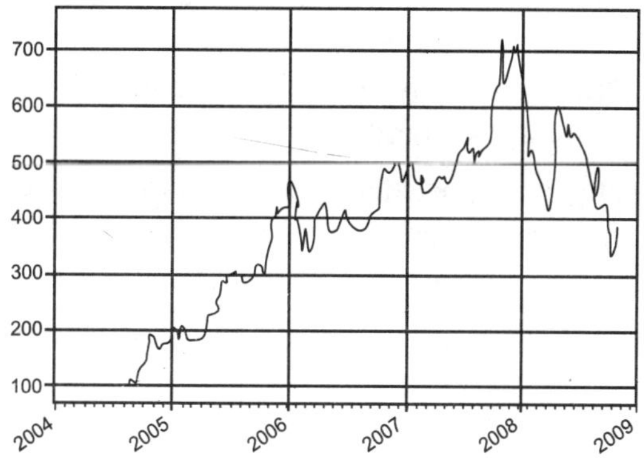

Date

5.7 INTRODUCTION TO BOKEH

Bokeh is a Python library for interactive visualization that targets web browsers for representation. This is the core difference between Bokeh and other visualization libraries. Look at the snapshot below, which explains the process flow of how Bokeh helps to present data to a web browser. Literally Bokeh has been defined as "the way the lens renders out-of-focus points of light".

As you can see, Bokeh has multiple language bindings (Python, R, lua and Julia). These bindings produce a JSON file, which works as an input for BokehJS (a Javascript library), which in turn presents data to the modern web browsers.

Bokeh can produce elegant and interactive visualization like D3.js with high-performance interactivity over very large or streaming datasets. Bokeh can help anyone who would like to quickly and easily create interactive plots, dashboards, and data applications.

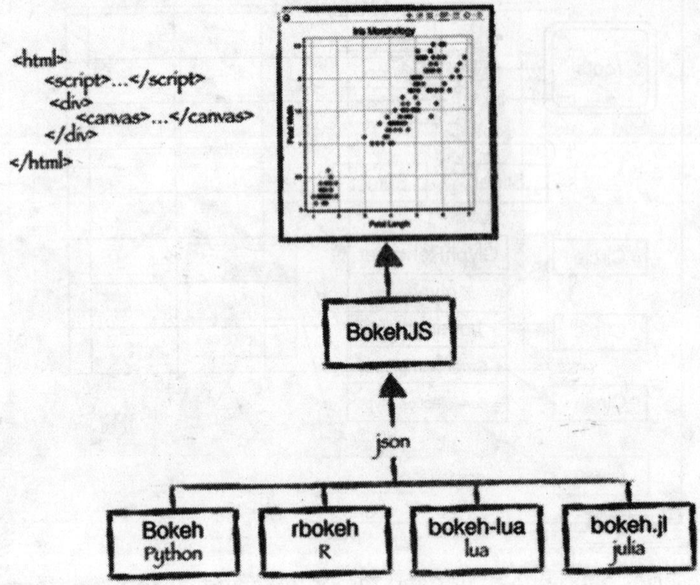

Luckily, many new Python data visualization libraries have been created in the past few years to close the gap. matplotlib has emerged as the main data visualization library, but there are also libraries such as vispy, bokeh, seaborn, pygal, folium, and networkx that either build on matplotlib or have functionality that it doesn't support.

Bokeh is a Python interactive visualization library that targets modern web browsers for presentation. Bokeh provides elegant, concise construction of novel graphics with high-performance interactivity over very large or streaming datasets in a quick and easy way.

To offer both simplicity and the powerful and flexible features needed for advanced customizations, Bokeh exposes two interface levels to users:

1. a low-level bokeh.models interface that provides the most flexibility to application developers.
2. an higher-level bokeh.plotting interface centered around composing visual glyphs.

5.7.1 A Low Level Bokeh Model

This interface provides different Bokeh models.One of the central design principals of Bokeh is that, regardless of how the plot creation code is spelled in Python (or other languages), the result is an object graph that encompasses all the visual and data aspects of the scene. Furthermore, this scene graph is to be serialized, and it is this serialized graph that the client library BokehJS uses to render the plot. The low-level objects that comprise a Bokeh scene graph are called Models.

These models are accumulated into Document instances, which can be serialized and sent to clients (typically browsers) for display or use there.

As a concrete example, consider a column layout with Slider and Select widgets, and a plot with some tools, an axis and grid, and a glyph renderer for circles. A simplified representation oh this document might look like the figure 5.5:

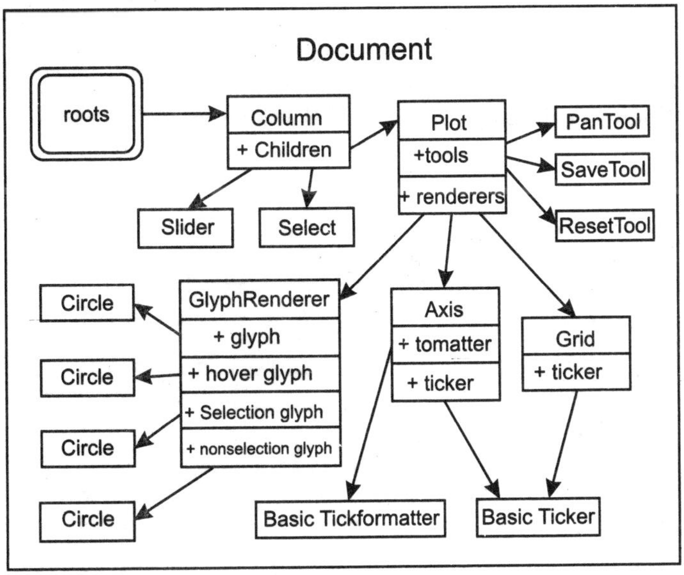

A Bokeh Document collects of Bokeh Models (e.g. plots, tools, glyphs, etc.) so that can be serialized as a single collection.

All of the rectangular boxes above are Bokeh models.This reference links in the sidebar document all built-in Bokeh models, together with their property attributes, as well as a JSON prototype illustrating what a serialized version of the model looks like.

5.7.2 An Higher-Level Bokeh Plotting Interface

This provides the facility to create a new Figure for plotting.Figure objects have many glyph methods that can be used to draw vectorized graphical glyphs:

```
annular_wedge()     hbar()                  ray()
annulus()           image()                 rect()
arc()               image_rgba()            segment()
asterisk()          image_url()             square()
bezier()            inverted_triangle()     square_cross()
circle()            line()                  square_x()
circle_cross()      multi_line()            step()
circle_x()          oval()                  text()
cross()             patch()                 triangle()
diamond()           patches()               vbar()
diamond_cross()     quad()                  wedge()
ellipse()           quadratic()             x()
```

5.7.3 Quick Installation

There are multiple ways to install Bokeh, and we recommend the easiest one, which is to use the Anaconda Python distribution and enter this command at a Bash or

Windows command prompt:

```
conda install bokeh
```

This installs all the dependencies that Bokeh needs. Anaconda minimizes installation effort on all platforms and configurations, including Windows, and also installs the examples into the examples/ subdirectory of your Anaconda or Miniconda installation directory.

If you are confident that you have installed all needed dependencies, such as NumPy, you may instead use pip at the command line:

pip install bokeh

Note : The pip method does not install the examples. Clone the Git repository and look in the examples/ directory of the checkout to see examples.

We will have to install Panda also.

5.7.4 Installation Instructions for Pandas

The easiest way[7] for the majority of users to install pandas is to install it as part of the Anaconda distribution, a cross platform distribution for data analysis and scientific computing. This is the recommended installation method for most users.

Instructions for installing from source, PyPI, various Linux distributions, or a development version are also provided. Pandas support is for Python version 2.7, 3.4, 3.5, and 3.6

Installing pandas

Installing pandas with Anaconda

Installing pandas and the rest of the NumPy and SciPy stack can be a little difficult for inexperienced users. The simplest way to install not only pandas, but Python and the most popular packages that make up the SciPystack (IPython, NumPy, Matplotlib, ...) is with Anaconda, a cross-platform (Linux, Mac OS X, Windows) Python distribution for data analytics and scientific computing.

After running a simple installer, the user will have access to pandas and the rest of the SciPy stack without needing to install anything else, and without needing to wait for any software to be compiled.

5.7.5 Getting Started : Visualization with Bokeh

Bokeh offers both powerful and flexible features which imparts simplicity and highly advanced customization. It provides multiple visualization interfaces to the user as shown below:

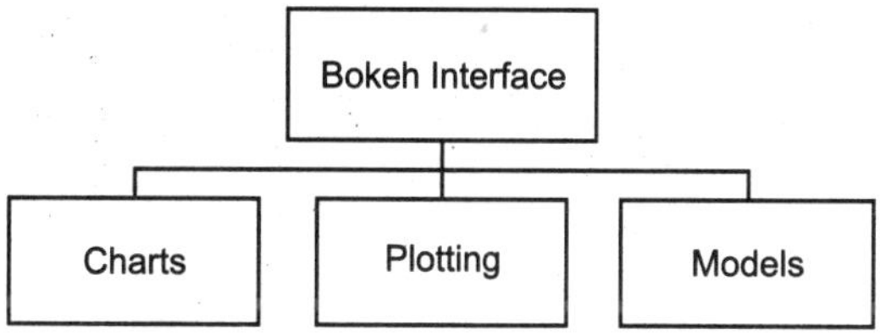

1. **Charts:** a high-level interface that is used to build complex statistical plots as quickly and in a simplistic manner.
2. **Plotting:** an intermediate-level interface that is centered around composing visual glyphs.
3. **Models:** a low-level interface that provides the maximum flexibility to application developers.

(*a*) Charts

As mentioned above, it is a high level interface used to present information in standard visualization form. These forms include box plot, bar chart, area plot, heat map, donut chart and many others. You can generate these plots just by passing data frames, numpy arrays and dictionaries.

Let's look at the common methodology to create a chart:

1. Import the library and functions/ methods
2. Prepare the data
3. Set the output mode (Notebook, Web Browser or Server)
4. Create chart with styling option (if required)
5. Visualize the chart

To understand these steps better, let me demonstrate these steps using example below:

Example: 5.2 (*a*) Charts: Create a bar chart and visualize it on web browser using Bokeh

We will follow above listed steps to create a chart:

Enter following line by line in your interpreter :

```
#Import library
from bokeh.charts import Bar, output_file, show #use output_
notebook to visualize it in notebook
# prepare data (dummy data)
data = {"y": [1, 2, 3, 4, 5]}
# Output to Line.HTML
output_file("lines.html", title="line plot example") #put output_
notebook() for notebook
# create a new line chat with a title and axis labels
p = Bar(data, title="Line Chart Example", xlabel='x',
ylabel='values', width=400, height=400)
# show the results
show(p)
```

Following shall be output:

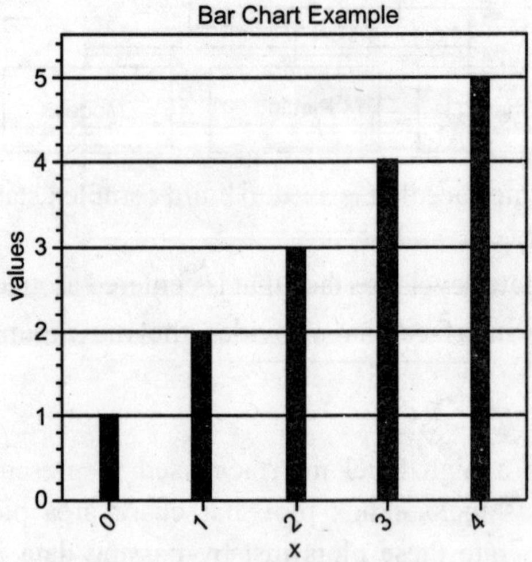

In the chart above, you can see the tools at the top (zoom, resize, reset, wheel zoom) and these tools allows you to interact with chart. You can also look at the multiple chart options (legend, xlabel, ylabel, xgrid, width, height and many other.

Example: 5.2 (*b*) Chart : Compare the distribution of sepal length and petal length of IRIS data set using Box plot on notebook

To create this visualization, firstly, you will have to import the iris data set using sklearn library. Then, follow the steps as discussed above to visualize chart in ipython notebook.

Enter following line by line in your interpreter :

```
#IRIS Data Set
from sklearn.datasets import load_iris
import pandas as pd
iris = load_iris()
df=pd.DataFrame(iris.data)
df.columns=['petal_width','petal_length','sepal_width','sepal_
length']
#Import library
from bokeh.charts import BoxPlot, output_notebook, show
data=df[['petal_length','sepal_length']]
# Output to Notebook
output_notebook()
# create a new line chat with a title and axis labels
p = BoxPlot(data, width=400, height=400)
# show the results
show(p)
```

Following shall be output:

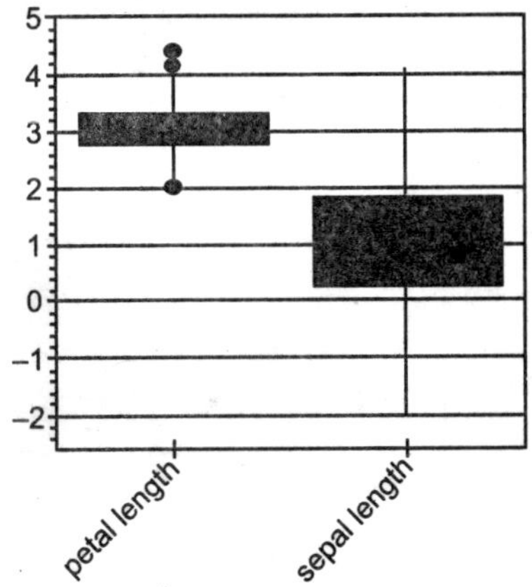

Example: 5.3 Chart : Bar Chart Simple

Enter following line by line in your interpreter(don't bother about line numbers) :

```
from bokeh.io import show, output_file
from bokeh.models import ColumnDataSource
from bokeh.palettes import Spectral6
from bokeh.plotting import figure
from bokeh.transform import factor_cmap

output_file("bar_colormapped.html")

fruits = ['Apples', 'Pears', 'Nectarines', 'Plums', 'Grapes', 'Strawberries']
counts = [5, 3, 4, 2, 4, 6]

source = ColumnDataSource(data=dict(fruits=fruits, counts=counts))

p = figure(x_range=fruits, plot_height=350, toolbar_location=None, title="Frui
p.vbar(x='fruits', top='counts', width=0.9, source=source, legend="fruits",
       line_color='white', fill_color=factor_cmap('fruits', palette=Spectral6,

p.xgrid.grid_line_color = None
p.y_range.start = 0
p.y_range.end = 9
p.legend.orientation = "horizontal"
p.legend.location = "top_center"

show(p)
```

Following shall be the output:

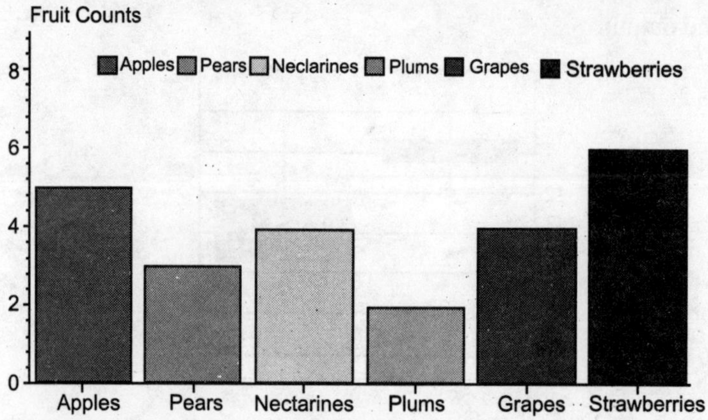

Example: 5.4 Chart : Nested Bar Colormapped.

Enter following line by line in your interpreter :

```
from bokeh.io import show, output_file
from bokeh.models import ColumnDataSource, FactorRange
from bokeh.plotting import figure
from bokeh.transform import factor_cmap
output_file("bar_nested_colormapped.html")
fruits = ['Apples', 'Pears', 'Nectarines', 'Plums', 'Grapes',
'Strawberries']
years = ['2015', '2016', '2017']
data = {'fruits' : fruits,
        '2015'   : [2, 1, 4, 3, 2, 4],
        '2016'   : [5, 3, 3, 2, 4, 6],
        '2017'   : [3, 2, 4, 4, 5, 3]}
palette = ["#c9d9d3", "#718dbf", "#e84d60"]
# this creates [ ("Apples", "2015"), ("Apples", "2016"),
("Apples", "2017"), ("Pears", "2015), ... ]
x = [ (fruit, year) for fruit in fruits for year in years ]
counts = sum(zip(data['2015'], data['2016'], data['2017']), ())
# like an hstack
source = ColumnDataSource(data=dict(x=x, counts=counts))
p = figure(x_range=FactorRange(*x), plot_height=350, title="Fruit
Counts by Year",
           toolbar_location=None, tools="")
p.vbar(x='x', top='counts', width=0.9, source=source, line_
color="white",
```

```
        fill_color=factor_cmap('x', palette=palette, factors=years,
start=1, end=2))
   p.y_range.start = 0
   p.x_range.range_padding = 0.1
   p.xaxis.major_label_orientation = 1
   p.xgrid.grid_line_color = None
   show(p)
```

Following shall be output:

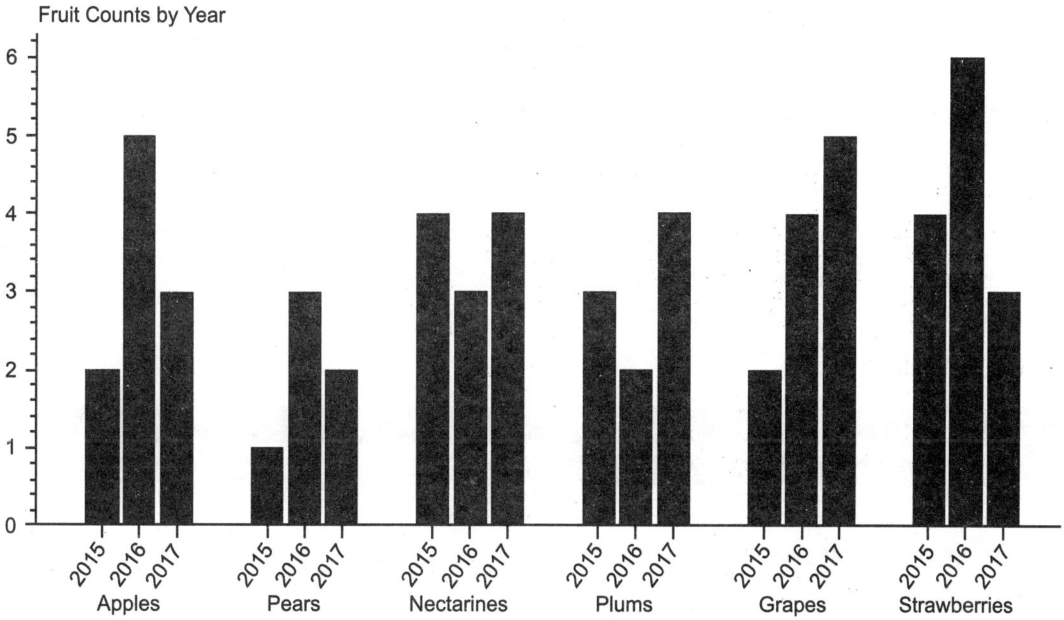

(*b*) Plotting

Plotting is an intermediate-level interface that is centered around composing visual glyphs. Here, you create a visualization by combining various visual elements (dot, circles, line, patch & many others) and tools (hover tool, zoom, Save, reset and others). Bokeh plots created using the bokeh.plotting interface comes with a default set of tools and visual styles.

For plotting, follow the below steps:

1. Import library, methods or functions
2. Select the output mode (notebook, web browser, server)
3. Activate a figure (similar like matplotlib)
4. Perform subsequent plotting operations, it will affect the generated figure.
5. Visualize it

To understand these steps better, let me demonstrate these steps using examples below:

Example 5.5 Create a line plot

Let's begin with some examples.

Plotting data in basic Python lists as a line plot including zoom, pan, save, and other tools is simple and straightforward:

Enter following line by line in your interpreter :

```
from bokeh.plotting import figure, output_file,show
# prepare some data
x = [1, 2, 3, 4, 5]
y = [5, 7, 3, 4, 6]
# output to static HTML file
output_file("lines.html")
# create a new plot with a title and axis labels
p = figure(title="simple line example", x_axis_label='x', y_axis_
label='y')
# add a line renderer with legend and line thickness
p.line(x, y, legend="Temp.", line_width=2)
# show the results
show(p)
```

Following shall be output:

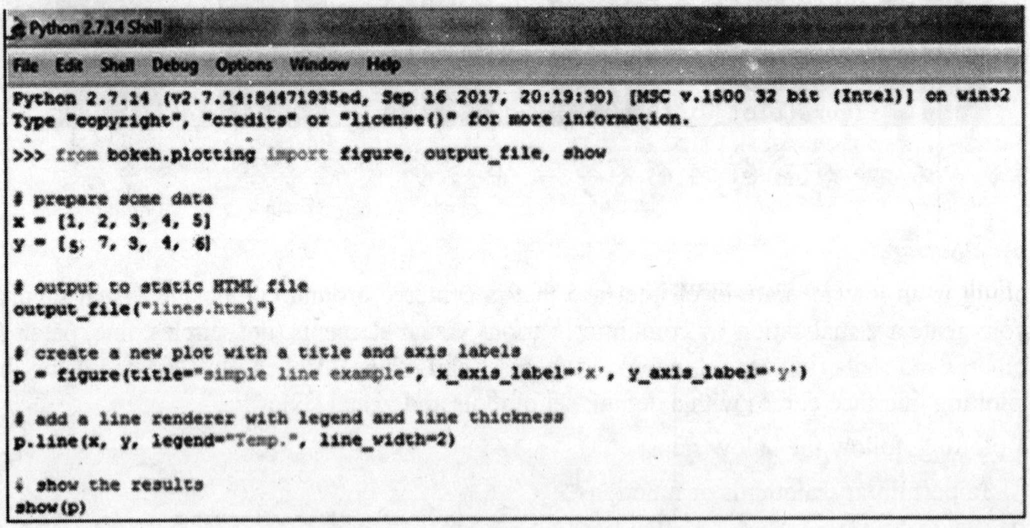

When you execute this script, you will see that a new output file “lines.html” is created, and that a browser automatically opens a new tab to display it. (For presentation purposes we have included the plot output directly inline in this document.)

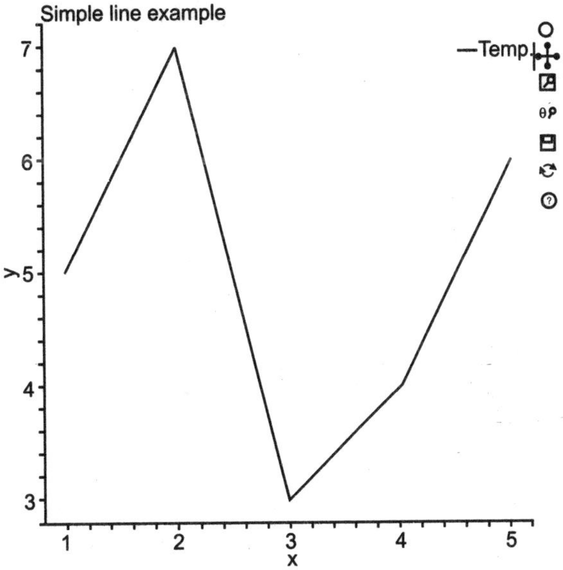

Example 5.6. Plot : Create a scatter square mark on XY frame of notebook

Enter following line by line in your interpreter :

```
from bokeh.plotting import figure, output_notebook, show

# output to notebook
output_notebook()
p = figure(plot_width=400, plot_height=400)
# add square with a size, color, and alpha
p.square([2, 5, 6, 4], [2, 3, 2, 1, 2], size=20, color="navy")
# show the results
show(p)
```

Following shall be the output:

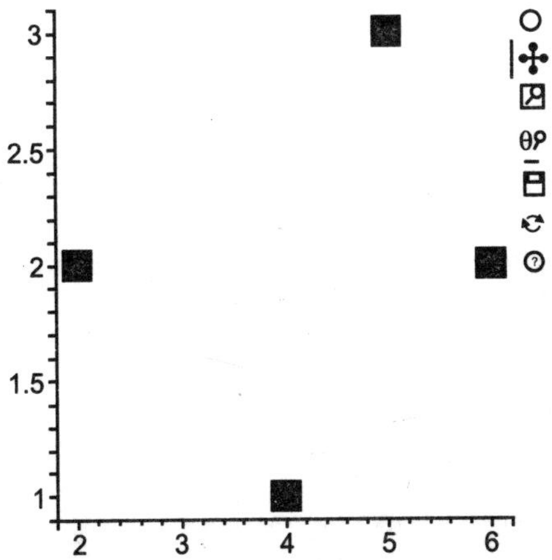

Similarly, you can create various other plots like line, wedges & arc, ovals, images, patches and many others.

Example 5.7 Plot : Combine two visual elements in a plot

Enter following line by line in your interpreter :

```
from bokeh.plotting import figure, output_notebook, show
# output to notebook
output_notebook()
p = figure(plot_width=400, plot_height=400)
# add square with a size, color, and alpha
p.square([2, 5, 6, 4], [2, 3, 2, 1, 2], size=20, color="navy")
p.line([1, 2, 3, 4, 5], [1, 2, 2, 4, 5], line_width=2) #added a
line plot to existing figure
# show the results
show(p)
```

Following shall be the output:

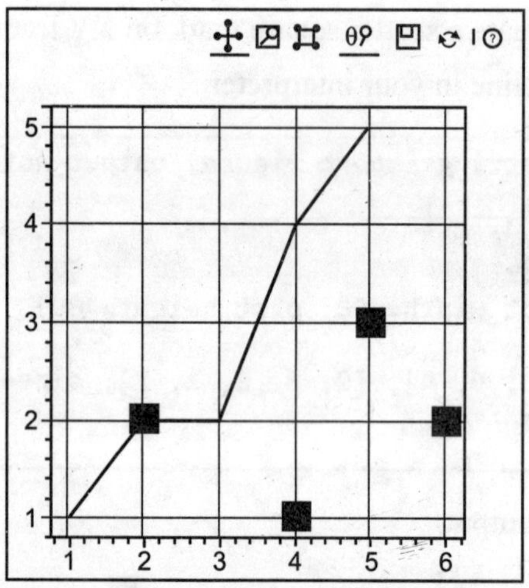

Example 5.8 Plot : Add a hover tool and axis labels to above plot

Enter following line by line in your interpreter :

```
from bokeh.plotting import figure, output_notebook, show
from bokeh.models import HoverTool, BoxSelectTool #For enabling
tools
# output to notebook
output_notebook()
#Add tools
TOOLS = [BoxSelectTool(), HoverTool()]
p = figure(plot_width=400, plot_height=400, tools=TOOLS)
# add a square with a size, color, and alpha
p.square([2, 5, 6, 4], [2, 3, 2, 1, 2], size=20, color="navy",
alpha=0.5)
```

```
#Visual Elements
p.xaxis.axis_label = "X-axis"
p.yaxis.axis_label = "Y-axis"
# show the results
show(p)
```

Following shall be the output:

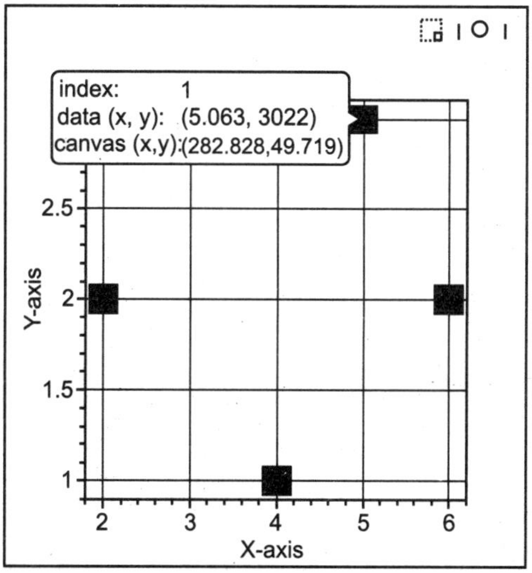

The basic steps to creating plots with the bokeh.plotting interface

The following are the basic steps to creating plots with the bokeh.plotting interface are:

1. Prepare some data (in this case plain python lists).
2. Tell Bokeh where to generate output (in this case using output_file(), with the filename "lines.html").
3. Call figure() to create a plot with some overall options like title, tools and axes labels.
4. Add renderers (in this case, Figure.line) for our data, with visual customizations like colors, legends and widths to the plot.
5. Ask Bokeh to show() or save() the results.

Steps three and four can be repeated to create more than one plot, as shown in some of the examples below.

Example 5.8 Plot :Creating More than one plot

Enter following line by line in your interpreter :

```
from bokeh.plotting import figure, output_file, show
# prepare some data
x = [0.1, 0.5, 1.0, 1.5, 2.0, 2.5, 3.0]
y0 = [i**2 for i in x]
y1 = [10**i for i in x]
y2 = [10**(i**2) for i in x]
# output to static HTML file
```

```
output_file("log_lines.html")
# create a new plot
p = figure(
    tools="pan,box_zoom,reset,save",
    y_axis_type="log", y_range=[0.001, 10**11], title="log axis example",
    x_axis_label='sections', y_axis_label='particles'
)
# add some renderers
p.line(x, x, legend="y=x")
p.circle(x, x, legend="y=x", fill_color="white", size=8)
p.line(x, y0, legend="y=x^2", line_width=3)
p.line(x, y1, legend="y=10^x", line_color="red")
p.circle(x, y1, legend="y=10^x", fill_color="red", line_color="red", size=6)
p.line(x, y2, legend="y=10^x^2", line_color="orange", line_dash="4 4")
# show the results
show(p)
```

Example 5.9 : Customising Output

The bokeh.plotting interface is also quite handy if we need to customize the output a bit more by adding more data series, glyphs, logarithmic axis, and so on. It's also possible to easily combine multiple glyphs together on one plot as shown below:

Enter following line by line in your interpreter :

```
from bokeh.plotting import figure, output_file, show
# prepare some data
x = [0.1, 0.5, 1.0, 1.5, 2.0, 2.5, 3.0]
y0 = [i**2 for i in x]
y1 = [10**i for i in x]
y2 = [10**(i**2) for i in x]

# output to static HTML file
output_file("log_lines.html")

# create a new plot
p = figure(
    tools="pan,box_zoom,reset,save",
    y_axis_type="log", y_range=[0.001, 10**11], title="Example Log Axis ",
    x_axis_label='Sections', y_axis_label='Particles'
)

# add some renderers
p.line(x, x, legend="y=x")
p.circle(x, x, legend="y=x", fill_color="green", size=8)
p.line(x, y0, legend="y=x^2", line_width=3)
p.line(x, y1, legend="y=10^x", line_color="black")
p.circle(x, y1, legend="y=10^x", fill_color="red", line_color="red", size=6)
p.line(x, y2, legend="y=10^x^2", line_color="orange", line_dash="4 4")

# show the results
show(p)
```

The following shall be output:

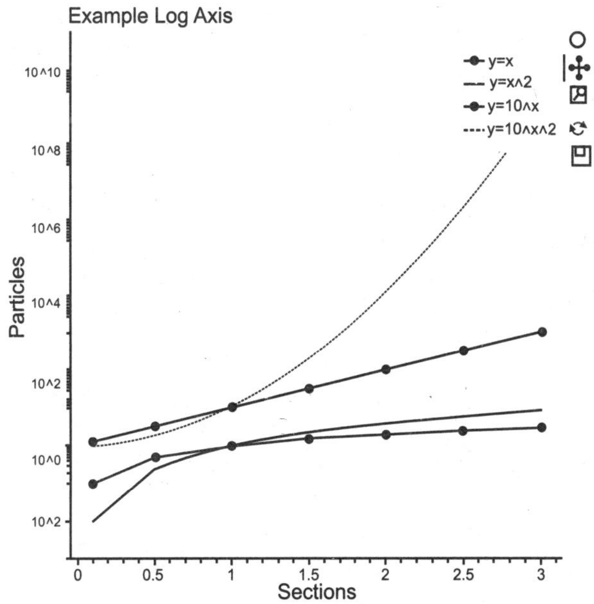

Example 5.10 : plotting on Bokeh server

To start plotting on Bokeh server, I have executed the command bokeh-server to initialize it followed by the commands used for visualization.

Prior to plotting visualization to Bokeh server, you need to run it.

If you are using a conda package, you can use run command bokeh-server from any directory using command. Else, python ./bokeh-server command should work in general.

There are multiple benefits of Plotting visualization on Bokeh server:

1. Plots can be published to larger audience
2. Visualize large data set interactively
3. Streaming data to automatically updating plots
4. Building dashboards and apps

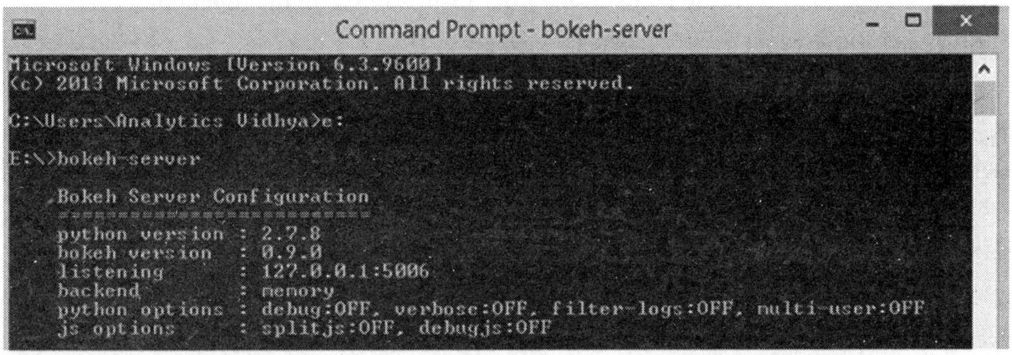

Example 5.11 : Adding Line Renderer

Enter following line by line in your interpreter :

```
p = fighure(plot_width = 600, plot_height = 600
# add a line renderer
p.line([7, 2, 3, 4, 6], [6, 4, 2, 4, 5], line_width = 4
|
```

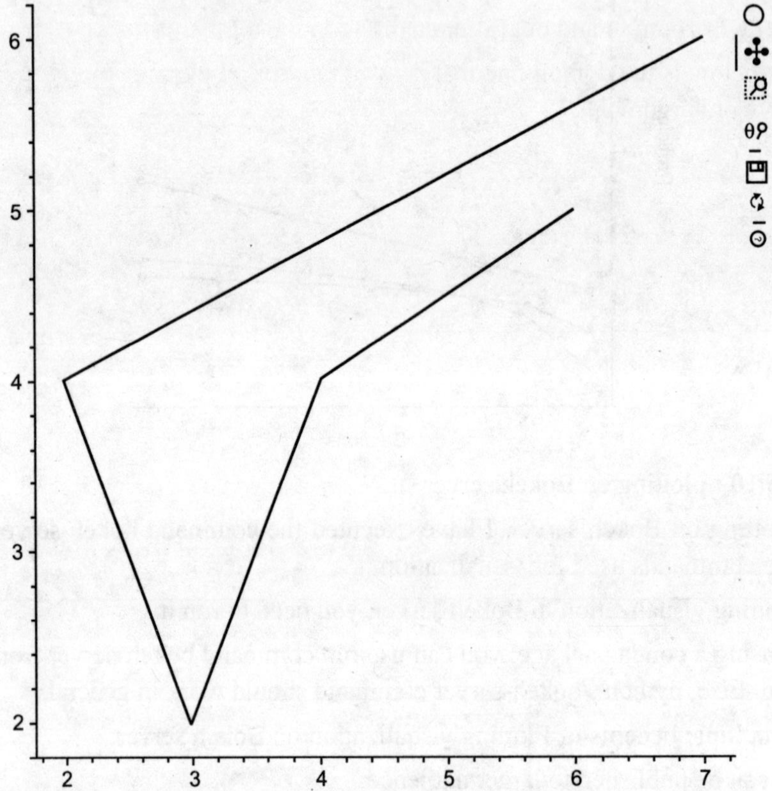

Example 5.12 : Using Figure Function

Here is a simple first example. First we'll import the figure function from bokeh.plotting, which will let us create all sorts of interesting plots easily. We also import the show and ouptut_notebook functions from bokeh.io — these let us display our results inline in the notebook.

```
from bokeh.plotting import figure
from bokeh.io import output_notebook, show
```

Next, we'll tell Bokeh to display its plots directly into the notebook. This will cause all of the Javascript and data to be embedded directly into the HTML of the notebook itself. (Bokeh can output straight to HTML files, or use a server, which we'll look at later.)

```
output_notebook()
```

BokehJS 0.12.7 successfully loaded.

Next, we'll import NumPy and create some simple data.

```
from numpy import cos, linspace
x = linspace(-6, 6, 100)
```

```
y = cos(x)
```

Now we'll call Bokeh's figure functtion to create a plot p. Then we call the circle() method of the plot to render a red circle at each of the points in x and y.

We can immediately interact with the plot:

click-drag will pan the plot around.

mousewheel will zoom in and out (after enabling in the toolbar)

The toolbar below is the default one that is available for all plots. It can be configured further via the tools keyword argument.

```
p = figure(width=500, height=500)
p.circle(x, y, size=7, color="firebrick", alpha=0.5)
show(p)
```

Enter following line by line in your interpreter :

```
from numpy import cos, linspace
x = linspace (-6, 6, 100)
y = cos (x)
p = fighure (width = 500, height = 500)
p.circle(x, y, size = 7, color = "firebrick", alpha = 0.5
show(p) |
```

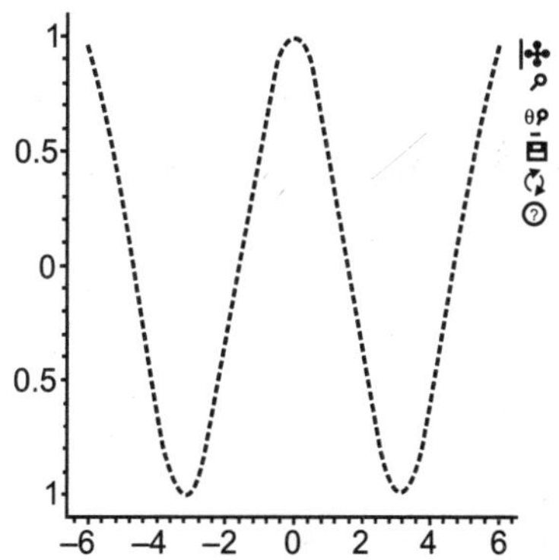

Example 5.13 Bar Plot Example

Bokeh's core display model relies on composing graphical primitives which are bound to data series. This is similar in spirit to Protovis and D3, and different than most other Python plotting libraries.

A slightly more sophisticated example demonstrates this idea.

Bokeh ships with a small set of interesting "sample data" in the bokeh.sampledata package. We'll load up some historical automobile mileage data, which is returned as a Pandas DataFrame.

Enter following line by line in your interpreter :

```
from bokeh.sampledata.autompg import autompg
```

```
grouped = autompg.groupby(“yr”)
mpg = grouped[“mpg”]
avg = mpg.mean()
std = mpg.std()
years = list(grouped.groups.keys())
american = autompg[autompg[“origin”]==1]
japanese = autompg[autompg[“origin”]==3]
```

For each year, we want to plot the distribution of MPG within that year.

```
p = figure(title=”MPG by Year (Japan and US)”)
p.vbar(x=years, bottom=avg-std, top=avg+std, width=0.8,
  fill_alpha=0.2, line_color=None, legend=”MPG 1 stddev”)
p.circle(x=japanese[“yr”], y=japanese[“mpg”], size=10,
alpha=0.5,
  color=”red”, legend=”Japanese”)
p.triangle(x=american[“yr”], y=american[“mpg”], size=10,
alpha=0.3,
    color=”blue”, legend=”American”)
p.legend.location = “top_left”
show(p)
```

Enter following line by line in your interpreter :

```
from bokeh.sampledata.autompg import autompg

grouped = autompg.groupby("yr")
mpg = grouped["mpg"]
avg = mpg.mean()
std = mpg.std()
years = list(grouped.groups.keys())
american = autompg[autompg["origin"]==1]
japanese = autompg[autompg["origin"]==3]
p = figure(title="MPG by Year (Japan and US)")

p.vbar(x=years, bottom=avg-std, top=avg+std, width=0.8,
       fill_alpha=0.2, line_color=None, legend="MPG 1 stddev")

p.circle(x=japanese["yr"], y=japanese["mpg"], size=10, alpha=0.5,
         color="red", legend="Japanese")

p.triangle(x=american["yr"], y=american["mpg"], size=10, alpha=0.3,
           color="blue", legend="American")

p.legend.location = "top_left"
show(p)
```

The following shall be the output:

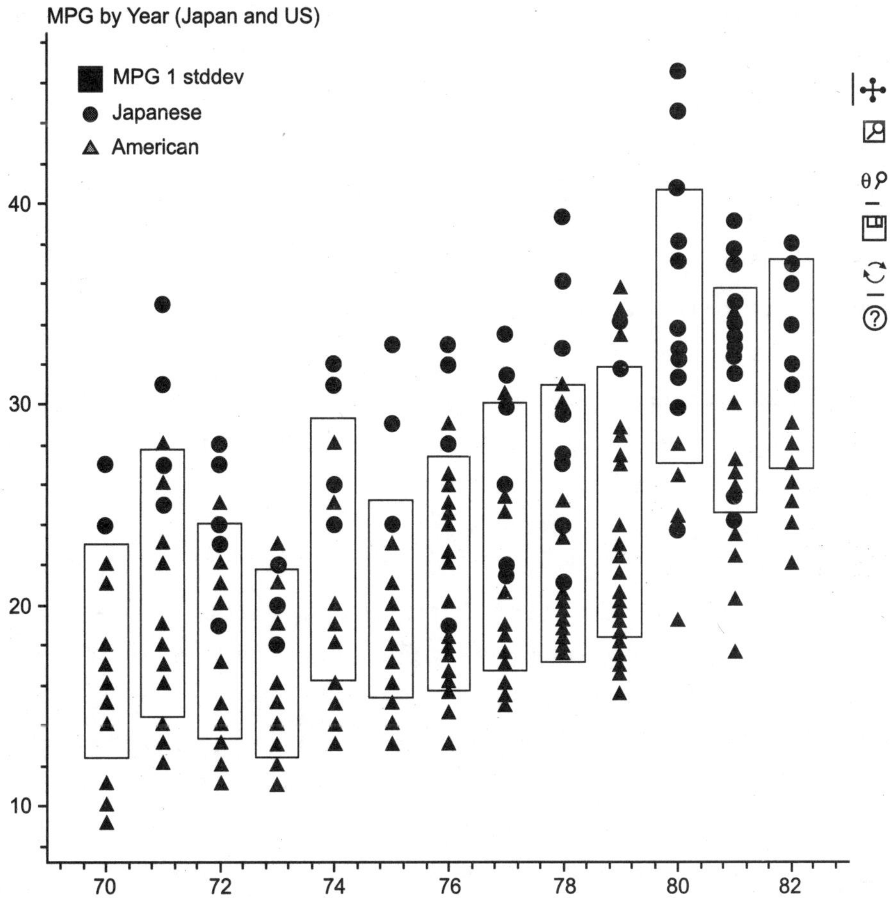

Example 5.14: Histogram example

Enter following code to generate a Histogram

```
import numpy as np
import scipy.special
from bokeh.layouts import gridplot
from bokeh.plotting import figure, show, output_file
p1 = figure(title="Normal Distribution (μ=0, σ=0.5)",tools="save",
  background_fill_color="#E8DDCB")
mu, sigma = 0, 0.5
measured = np.random.normal(mu, sigma, 1000)
hist, edges = np.histogram(measured, density=True, bins=50)
x = np.linspace(-2, 2, 1000)
pdf = 1/(sigma * np.sqrt(2*np.pi)) * np.exp(-(x-mu)**2 /
(2*sigma**2))
```

```
   cdf = (1+scipy.special.erf((x-mu)/np.sqrt(2*sigma**2)))/2
   p1.quad(top=hist, bottom=0, left=edges[:-1], right=edges[1:],
     fill_color="#036564", line_color="#033649")
   p1.line(x, pdf, line_color="#D95B43", line_width=8, alpha=0.7,
legend="PDF")
   p1.line(x, cdf, line_color="white", line_width=2, alpha=0.7,
legend="CDF")
   p1.legend.location = "center_right"
   p1.legend.background_fill_color = "darkgrey"
   p1.xaxis.axis_label = 'x'
   p1.yaxis.axis_label = 'Pr(x)'
   p2 = figure(title="Log Normal Distribution (μ=0, σ=0.5)",
tools="save",
     background_fill_color="#E8DDCB")
   mu, sigma = 0, 0.5
   measured = np.random.lognormal(mu, sigma, 1000)
   hist, edges = np.histogram(measured, density=True, bins=50)
   x = np.linspace(0.0001, 8.0, 1000)
   pdf = 1/(x* sigma * np.sqrt(2*np.pi)) * np.exp(-(np.log(x)-
mu)**2 / (2*sigma**2))
   cdf=(1+scipy.special.erf((np.log(x)-mu)/(np.sqrt(2)*sigma)))/2
   p2.quad(top=hist, bottom=0, left=edges[:-1], right=edges[1:],
     fill_color="#036564", line_color="#033649")
   p2.line(x, pdf, line_color="#D95B43", line_width=8, alpha=0.7,
legend="PDF")
   p2.line(x, cdf, line_color="white", line_width=2, alpha=0.7,
legend="CDF")
   p2.legend.location = "center_right"
   p2.legend.background_fill_color = "darkgrey"
   p2.xaxis.axis_label = 'x'
   p2.yaxis.axis_label = 'Pr(x)'
   p3 = figure(title="Gamma Distribution (k=1, θ=2)", tools="save",
     background_fill_color="#E8DDCB")
   k, theta = 1.0, 2.0
   measured = np.random.gamma(k, theta, 1000)
   hist, edges = np.histogram(measured, density=True, bins=50)
   x = np.linspace(0.0001, 20.0, 1000)
```

```
pdf = x**(k-1) * np.exp(-x/theta) / (theta**k * scipy.special.
gamma(k))
cdf = scipy.special.gammainc(k, x/theta) / scipy.special.
gamma(k)
p3.quad(top=hist, bottom=0, left=edges[:-1], right=edges[1:],
  fill_color="#036564", line_color="#033649")
p3.line(x, pdf, line_color="#D95B43", line_width=8, alpha=0.7,
legend="PDF")
p3.line(x, cdf, line_color="black", line_width=2, alpha=0.7,
legend="CDF")
p3.legend.location = "center_right"
p3.legend.background_fill_color = "orange"
p3.xaxis.axis_label = 'x'
p3.yaxis.axis_label = 'Pr(x)'
p4 = figure(title="Weibull Distribution (λ=1, k=1.25)",
tools="save",
  background_fill_color="#E8DDCB")
lam, k = 1, 1.25
measured = lam*(-np.log(np.random.uniform(0, 1, 1000)))**(1/k)
hist, edges = np.histogram(measured, density=True, bins=50)
x = np.linspace(0.0001, 8, 1000)
pdf = (k/lam)*(x/lam)**(k-1) * np.exp(-(x/lam)**k)
cdf = 1 - np.exp(-(x/lam)**k)
p4.quad(top=hist, bottom=0, left=edges[:-1], right=edges[1:],
fill_color="#036564", line_color="#033649")
  p4.line(x, pdf, line_color="#D95B43", line_width=8, alpha=0.7,
legend="PDF")
p4.line(x, cdf, line_color="white", line_width=2, alpha=0.7,
legend="CDF")
p4.legend.location = "center_right"
p4.legend.background_fill_color = "darkgrey"
p4.xaxis.axis_label = 'x'
p4.yaxis.axis_label = 'Pr(x)'
output_file('histogram.html', title="histogram.py example")
show(gridplot(p1,p2,p3,p4, ncols=2, plot_width=400, plot_
height=400, toolbar_location=None))
```

The following is the result:

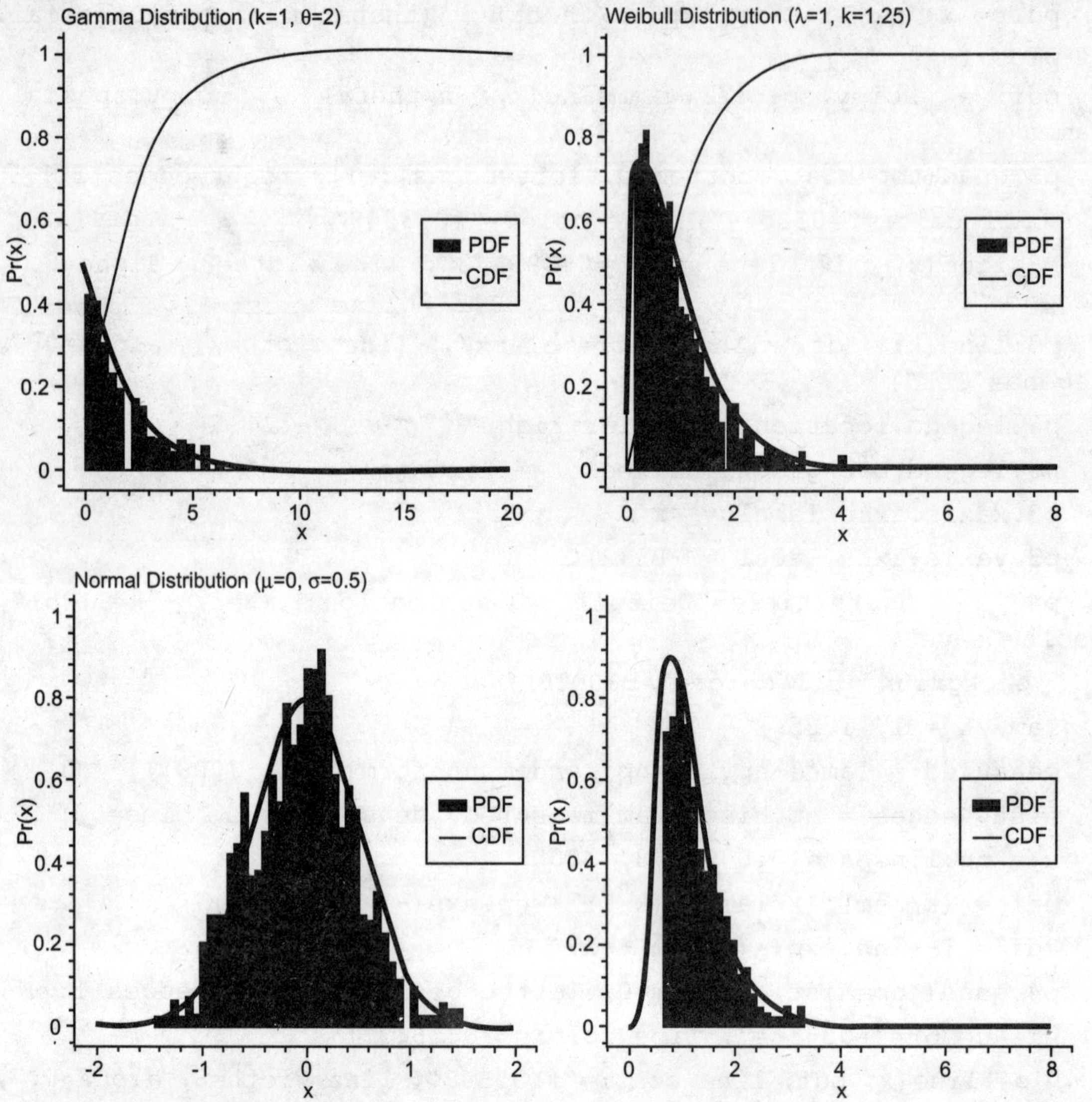

Example 5.14 Slider Curves (Cosine or sine)

Enter following code to generate a dynamic slider curve:

```
import numpy as np
from bokeh.layouts import row, widgetbox
from bokeh.models import CustomJS, Slider
from bokeh.plotting import figure, output_file, show, ColumnDataSource
x = np.linspace(0, 10, 500)
y = np.sin(x)
source = ColumnDataSource(data=dict(x=x, y=y))
```

```
plot = figure(y_range=(-10, 10), plot_width=400, plot_height=400)
plot.line('x', 'y', source=source, line_width=3, line_alpha=0.6)
callback = CustomJS(args=dict(source=source), code="""
  var data = source.data;
  var A = amp.value;
  var k = freq.value;
  var phi = phase.value;
  var B = offset.value;
  x = data['x']
  y = data['y']
  for (i = 0; i < x.length; i++) {
    y[i] = B + A*Math.sin(k*x[i]+phi);
  }
  source.change.emit();
""")
amp_slider = Slider(start=0.1, end=10, value=1, step=.1,
    title="Amplitude", callback=callback)
callback.args["amp"] = amp_slider
freq_slider = Slider(start=0.1, end=10, value=1, step=.1,
    title="Frequency", callback=callback)
callback.args["freq"] = freq_slider
phase_slider = Slider(start=0, end=6.4, value=0, step=.1,
    title="Phase", callback=callback)
callback.args["phase"] = phase_slider
offset_slider = Slider(start=-5, end=5, value=0, step=.1,
    title="Offset", callback=callback)
callback.args["offset"] = offset_slider
layout = row(
  plot,
  widgetbox(amp_slider, freq_slider, phase_slider, offset_
slider),
)
output_file("slider.html", title="slider.py example")
show(layout)
```

The following shall be the output:

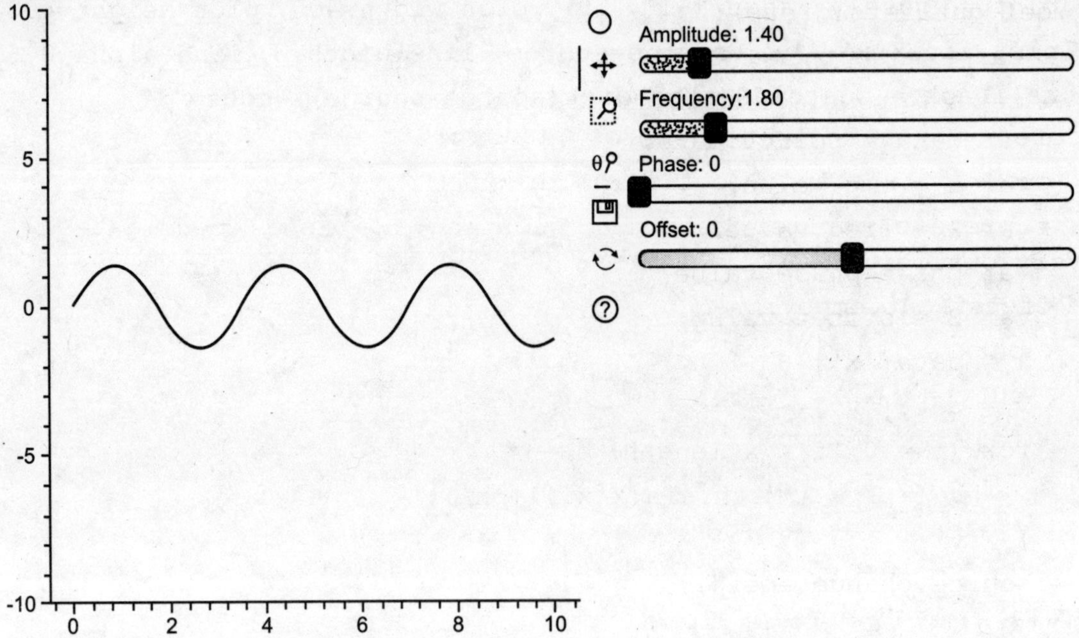

Example 5.16 : Box Plot Example

Enter following code to generate a dynamic slider curve:

```
import numpy as np
import pandas as pd
from bokeh.plotting import figure, show, output_file
# generate some synthetic time series for six different categories
cats = list("abcdef")
yy = np.random.randn(2000)
g = np.random.choice(cats, 2000)
for i, l in enumerate(cats):
  yy[g == l] += i // 2
df = pd.DataFrame(dict(score=yy, group=g))
# find the quartiles and IQR for each category
groups = df.groupby('group')
q1 = groups.quantile(q=0.25)
q2 = groups.quantile(q=0.5)
q3 = groups.quantile(q=0.75)
iqr = q3 - q1
upper = q3 + 1.5*iqr
lower = q1 - 1.5*iqr
# find the outliers for each category
```

```
def outliers(group):
  cat = group.name
  return group[(group.score > upper.loc[cat]['score']) | (group.
score < lower.loc[cat]['score'])]['score']
out = groups.apply(outliers).dropna()
# prepare outlier data for plotting, we need coordinates for
every outlier.
if not out.empty:
  outx = []
  outy = []
  for cat in cats:
    # only add outliers if they exist
    if not out.loc[cat].empty:
      for value in out[cat]:
        outx.append(cat)
        outy.append(value)
p = figure(tools="save", background_fill_color="#EFE8E2",
title="", x_range=cats)
# if no outliers, shrink lengths of stems to be no longer than
the minimums or maximums
qmin = groups.quantile(q=0.00)
qmax = groups.quantile(q=1.00)
upper.score = [min([x,y]) for (x,y) in zip(list(qmax.
loc[:,'score']),upper.score)]
lower.score = [max([x,y]) for (x,y) in zip(list(qmin.
loc[:,'score']),lower.score)]
# stems
p.segment(cats, upper.score, cats, q3.score, line_color="black")
p.segment(cats, lower.score, cats, q1.score, line_color="black")
# boxes
p.vbar(cats, 0.7, q2.score, q3.score, fill_color="#E08E79", line_
color="black")
p.vbar(cats, 0.7, q1.score, q2.score, fill_color="#3B8686", line_
color="black")
# whiskers (almost-0 height rects simpler than segments)
p.rect(cats, lower.score, 0.2, 0.01, line_color="black")
p.rect(cats, upper.score, 0.2, 0.01, line_color="black")
```

```
# outliers
if not out.empty:
  p.circle(outx, outy, size=6, color="#F38630", fill_alpha=0.6)
p.xgrid.grid_line_color = None
p.ygrid.grid_line_color = "white"
p.grid.grid_line_width = 2
p.xaxis.major_label_text_font_size="12pt"
output_file("boxplot.html", title="boxplot.py example")
show(p)
```

The following shall be the output Box

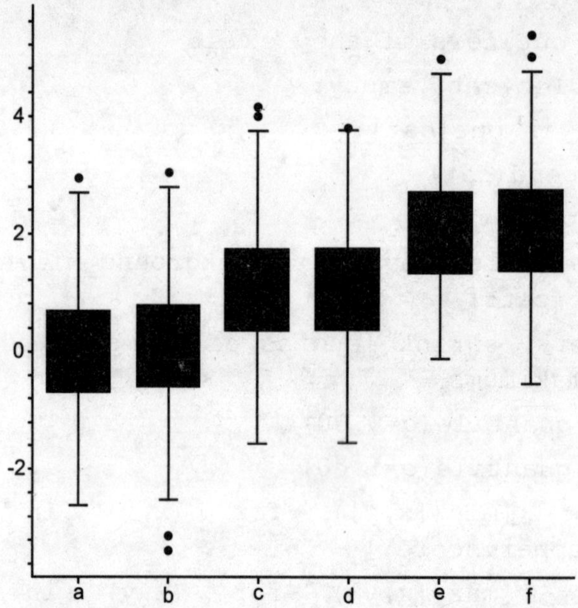

Example 5.16 : Legend Example

Enter following code to generate Legens on Sinusoidal curves:

```
import numpy as np
from bokeh.layouts import gridplot
from bokeh.plotting import figure, show, output_file
x = np.linspace(0, 4*np.pi, 100)
y = np.sin(x)
TOOLS = "pan,wheel_zoom,box_zoom,reset,save,box_select"
p1 = figure(title="Legend Example", tools=TOOLS)
p1.circle(x,   y, legend="sin(x)")
p1.circle(x, 2*y, legend="2*sin(x)", color="orange")
```

```
p1.circle(x, 3*y, legend="3*sin(x)", color="green")
p2 = figure(title="Another Legend Example", tools=TOOLS)
p2.circle(x, y, legend="sin(x)")
p2.line(x, y, legend="sin(x)")
p2.line(x, 2*y, legend="2*sin(x)", line_dash=(4, 4), line_
color="orange", line_width=2)
p2.square(x, 3*y, legend="3*sin(x)", fill_color=None, line_
color="green")
p2.line(x, 3*y, legend="3*sin(x)", line_color="green")
output_file("legend.html", title="legend.py example")
show(gridplot(p1, p2, ncols=2, plot_width=400, plot_height=400))
# open a browser
```

The following shall be the output:

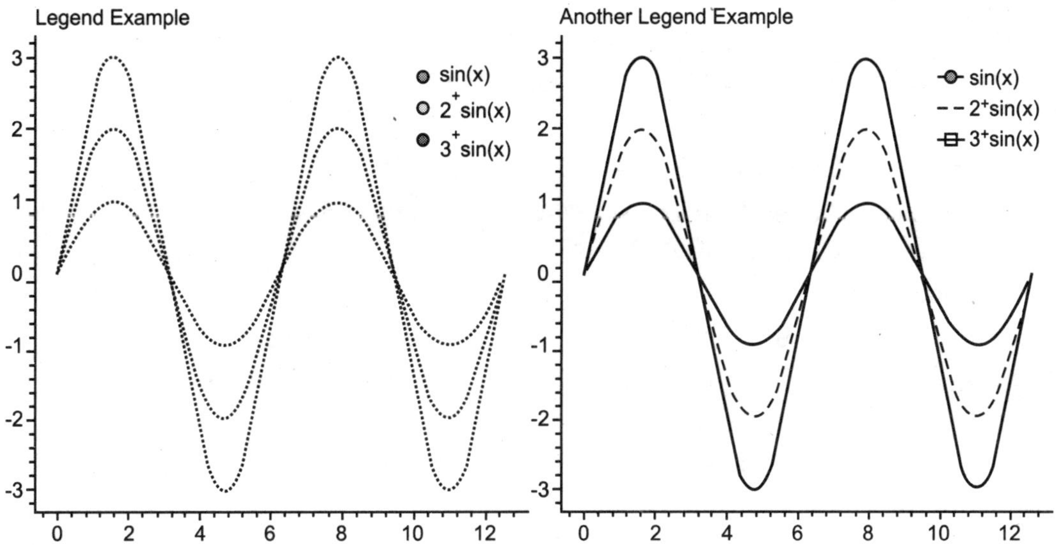

Example 5.18 : Example of Drawing Periodic Table

Enter following code line by line:

```
from bokeh.io import output_file, show
from bokeh.models import ColumnDataSource, HoverTool
from bokeh.plotting import figure
from bokeh.sampledata.periodic_table import elements
from bokeh.transform import dodge, factor_cmap
output_file("periodic.html")
periods = ["I", "II", "III", "IV", "V", "VI", "VII"]
groups = [str(x) for x in range(1, 19)]
df = elements.copy()
```

```
df["atomic mass"] = df["atomic mass"].astype(str)
df["group"] = df["group"].astype(str)
df["period"] = [periods[x-1] for x in df.period]
df = df[df.group != "-"]
df = df[df.symbol != "Lr"]
df = df[df.symbol != "Lu"]
cmap = {
  "alkali metal"         : "#a6cee3",
  "alkaline earth metal" : "#1f78b4",
  "metal"                : "#d93b43",
  "halogen"              : "#999d9a",
  "metalloid"            : "#e08d49",
  "noble gas"            : "#eaeaea",
  "nonmetal"             : "#f1d4Af",
  "transition metal"     : "#599d7A",
}
source = ColumnDataSource(df)
p = figure(title="Periodic Table (omitting LA and AC Series)", plot_width=1000, plot_height=450,
    tools="", toolbar_location=None,
    x_range=groups, y_range=list(reversed(periods)))
p.rect("group", "period", 0.95, 0.95, source=source, fill_alpha=0.6, legend="metal",
    color=factor_cmap('metal', palette=list(cmap.values()), factors=list(cmap.keys())))
text_props = {"source": source, "text_align": "left", "text_baseline": "middle"}
x = dodge("group", -0.4, range=p.x_range)
r = p.text(x=x, y="period", text="symbol", **text_props)
r.glyph.text_font_style="bold"
r = p.text(x=x, y=dodge("period", 0.3, range=p.y_range), text="atomic number", **text_props)
r.glyph.text_font_size="8pt"
r = p.text(x=x, y=dodge("period", -0.35, range=p.y_range), text="name", **text_props)
r.glyph.text_font_size="5pt"
r = p.text(x=x, y=dodge("period", -0.2, range=p.y_range),
```

```
text="atomic mass", **text_props)
  r.glyph.text_font_size="5pt"
  p.text(x=["3", "3"], y=["VI", "VII"], text=["LA", "AC"], text_
align="center", text_baseline="middle")
  p.add_tools(HoverTool(tooltips = [
    ("Name", "@name"),
    ("Atomic number", "@{atomic number}"),
    ("Atomic mass", "@{atomic mass}"),
    ("Type", "@metal"),
    ("CPK color", "$color[hex, swatch]:CPK"),
    ("Electronic configuration", "@{electronic configuration}"),
  ]))
  p.outline_line_color = None
  p.grid.grid_line_color = None
  p.axis.axis_line_color = None
  p.axis.major_tick_line_color = None
  p.axis.major_label_standoff = 0
  p.legend.orientation = "horizontal"
  p.legend.location ="top_center"
  show(p)
```

The following output shall be generated.

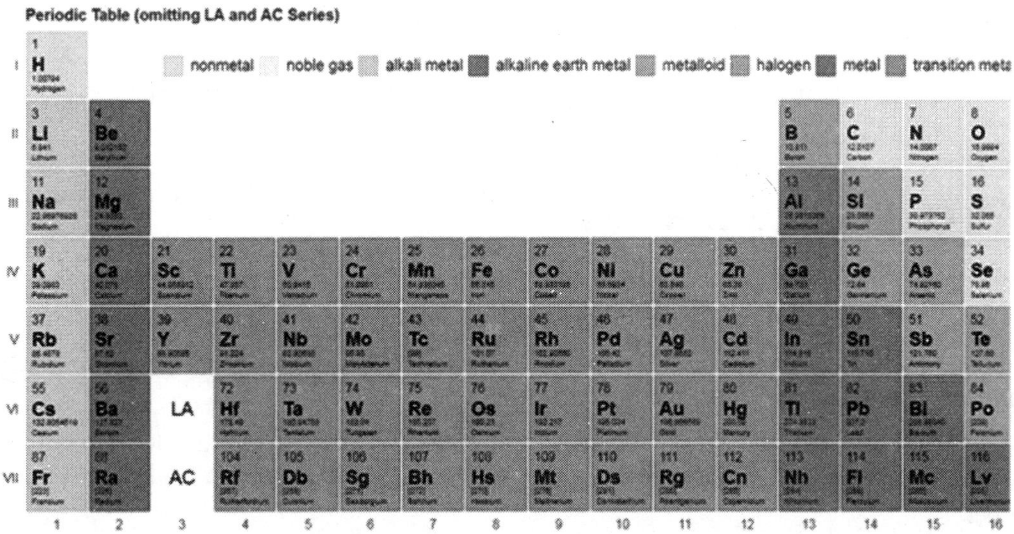

5.7.7 What does Bokeh offer to a data scientist ?

I started my data science journey as a BI professional and then worked my way through

For predictive modeling, data science and machine learning programmer has the alternatives of using tools like.

1. QlikView & Tableau for data visualization and
2. SAS & Python for predictive analytics & data science.

With Bokeh, you can continue to work in Python ecosystem, but still create these prototypes quickly. Bokeh is officially supported (and continuously tested) on CPython versions 2.7 and 3.5+ only. Other Python versions may function, possibly in limited capacity. In particular, converting NumPy arrays to lists may be useful with other versions. However, this guidance is only provided as-is, in case it happens to be useful, and does not imply any level of official support for other Python versions. All issues opened related to unsupported Python versions will be closed as invalid.

For basic usage, have the following libraries installed:

- NumPy
- Six
- Tornado >= 4.0
- DateUtil
- Jinja2
- Requests
- PyYaml

5.7.8 Benefits of Bokeh

1. Bokeh allows you to build complex statistical plots quickly and through simple commands
2. Bokeh provides you output in various medium like html, notebook and server
3. We can also embed Bokeh visualization to flask and django app
4. Bokeh can transform visualization written in other libraries like matplotlib, seaborn, ggplot
5. Bokeh has flexibility for applying interaction, layouts and different styling option to visualization

5.7.9 Challenges with Bokeh

Like with any upcoming open source library, Bokeh is undergoing a lot of development. So, the code you write today may not be entirely reusable in future.

It has relatively less visualization options, when compared to D3.js. Hence, it is unlikely in near future that it will challenge D3.js for its crown.

Given the benefits and the challenges, it is currently ideal to rapidly develop prototypes. However, if you want to create something for production environment, D3.js might still be your best bet.

5.7.10 Python Applications Area

Python is known for its general purpose nature that makes it applicable in almost each domain of software development. Python as a whole can be used in any sphere of development.

Here, we are specifing applications areas where python can be applied.

1. **Web Applications:** We can use Python to develop web applications. It provides libraries to handle internet protocols such as HTML and XML, JSON, Email processing, request, beautifulSoup, Feedparser etc. It also provides Frameworks such as Django, Pyramid, Flask etc to design and delelop web based applications. Some important developments are: PythonWikiEngines, Pocoo, PythonBlogSoftware etc.
2. **Desktop GUI Applications:** Python provides Tk GUI library to develop user interface in python based application. Some other useful toolkits wxWidgets, Kivy, pyqt that are useable on several platforms. The Kivy is popular for writing multitouch applications.
3. **Software Development:** Python is helpful for software development process. It works as a support language and can be used for build control and management, testing etc.
4. **Scientific and Numeric:** Python is popular and widely used in scientific and numeric computing. Some useful library and package are SciPy, Pandas, IPython etc. SciPy is group of packages of engineering, science and mathematics.
5. **Business Applications:** Python is used to build Bussiness applications like ERP and e-commerce systems. Tryton is a high level application platform.
6. **Console Based Application:** We can use Python to develop console based applications. For example: IPython.
7. **Audio or Video based Applications:** Python is awesome to perform multiple tasks and can be used to develop multimedia applications. Some of real applications are: TimPlayer, cplay etc.
8. **3D CAD Applications:** To create CAD application Fandango is a real application which provides full features of CAD.
9. **Enterprise Applications:** Python can be used to create applications which can be used within an Enterprise or an Organization. Some real time applications are: OpenErp, Tryton, Picalo etc.
10. **Applications for Images:** Using Python several application can be developed for image. Applications developed are: VPython, Gogh, imgSeek etc.

    There are several such applications which can be developed using Python

References

1. Python for Data Science – Tutorial for Beginners #1 – Python Basics Written by Tomi Mester on September 18, 2017
2. A Complete Tutorial to Learn Data Science with Python from Scratch by KUNAL JAIN , JANUARY 14, 2016
3. Python Matplotlib Tutorial – Data Visualizations In Python With Matplotlib by Aayushi Johari Aug 8, 2017

4. Documentation for Matplotlib version 2.1.2.vide .https://matplotlib.org/index.html
5. Tutorial on Interactive Data Visualization using Bokeh (in Python) by SUNIL RAY , AUGUST 28, 2015
6. Bokeh Reference Guide ,Bokeh's official site
7. pandas 0.22.0 documentation at https://pandas.pydata.org/pandas-docs/stable/index.html
9. Interactive Data Visualization using Bokeh (in Python) , SUNIL RAY , AUGUST 28, 2015

Chapter 6

RECENT TRENDS IN DATA SCIENCE

☞ Learning Objectives and Outcomes

In this unit we will learn about

- ☞ Recent trends in various data collection and analysis techniques,
- ☞ Various visualization techniques,
- ☞ Application development methods used in data science

6.1 RECENT TRENDS IN VARIOUS DATA COLLECTION AND ANALYSIS TECHNIQUES

Artificial intelligence, immersive experiences, digital twins, event-thinking and continuous adaptive security create a foundation for the next generation of digital business models and ecosystems. Gartner's Top 10 Strategic Technology Trends for 2018[1] gives a good overview of many of the top trends for 2018. As businesses and services aim more for the "connected world," the overlapping of the physical and digital layers around us will probably gain more relevance. Gartner, Inc. is an American research and advisory firm providing information technology related insight for IT and other business leaders located across the world. Its headquarters are in Stamford, Connecticut, United States. It was known as Gartner Group, Inc until 2000, when it was then changed to Gartner. The company was founded in 1979 by Gideon Gartner. These are discussed here in detail.

6.1.0 Intelligent Digital Mesh

Gartner calls the entwining of people, devices, content and services the intelligent digital mesh. It's enabled by digital models, business platforms and a rich, intelligent set of services to support digital business.[2]

Intelligent: How AI is seeping into virtually every technology and with a defined, well-scoped focus can allow more dynamic, flexible and potentially autonomous systems.

Digital: Blending the virtual and real worlds to create an immersive digitally enhanced and connected environment.

Mesh: The connections between an expanding set of people, business, devices, content and services to deliver digital outcomes.

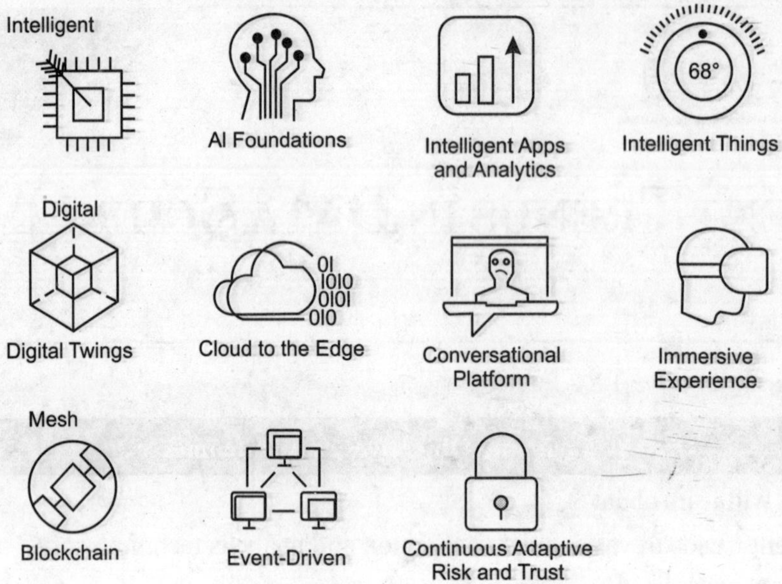

Fig. 6.1: Intelligent Digital Mesh

6.1.1 Artificial Intelligence (AI)

The widespread adoption of Artificial Intelligence into all scientific and business systems and decision-making applications. According to Gartner, 59 percent of organizations are still building their enterprise AI strategies while the remaining 41 percent of the organizations have already made the plunge.

Artificial intelligence is classified into two parts,

1. General AI and
2. Narrow AI.

General AI refers to making machines intelligent in a wide array of activities that involve thinking and reasoning. Narrow AI, on the other hand, involves the use of artificial intelligence for a very specific task. For instance, general AI would mean an algorithm that is capable of playing all kinds of board game while narrow AI will limit the range of machine capabilities to a specific game like chess or scrabble. Currently, only narrow AI is within the reach of developers and researchers. General AI is just a dream of researchers and perception among the masses that will take a lot of time for the human race to achieve

Machine learning is the ability of a computer system to learn from the environment and improve itself from experience without the need for any explicit programming. Machine learning focuses on enabling algorithms to learn from the data provided, gather insights and make predictions on previously unanalyzed data using the information gathered. Machine learning can be performed using multiple approaches. The three basic models of machine learning are supervised, unsupervised and reinforcement learning.

In case of supervised learning, labelled data is used to help machines recognize characteristics and use them for future data. For instance, if you want to classify pictures of cats and dogs then you can feed the data of a few labelled pictures and then the machine will classify all the remaining pictures for you. On the other hand, in unsupervised learning, we simply put unlabeled data and let machine understand the characteristics and classify it. Reinforcement machine learning algorithms interact with the environment by producing actions and then analyze errors or rewards. For example, to understand a game of chess an ML algorithm will not analyze individual moves but will study the game as a whole.

6.1.2 Intelligent Apps and Analytics (Smart Apps)

SmartApps are applications that allow users to tap into the capabilities of their devices to automate their lives. Most SmartApps are installed by the user via the SmartThings mobile client application.

Smart applications incorporate data-driven, actionable insights into the user experience. Insights are delivered in context as features in applications that enable users to more efficiently complete a desired task or action. They often take the form of recommendations, estimates, and suggested next actions. Smart applications can be consumer-facing or employee-facing. In some cases, the "user" is not a human, but a machine or system. In these cases, smart applications automate business and operational processes based on data-driven insights.

For example, retail smart applications make product recommendations based on analysis of customer buying behaviour while logistics applications provide data-driven estimates of delivery times of goods and products. Healthcare smart applications offer possible patient diagnosis and treatment recommendations to clinicians based on analyses of patient and research data.

No matter how effective your data science capabilities, data-driven insights hold no value if they can't be operationalized and acted upon. Smart applications surface insights in context to users and systems, so they can take corresponding actions.

The next several years will witness a steady rise in AI-driven apps and services. All managed software platforms like the ERP are currently on a race for AI integration in their existing systems for enhanced performance and value addition. This trend includes the use of digital assistants and virtual services.

6.1.3 Intelligent of Things (IoT)

Intelligent things use AI and machine learning to interact in a more intelligent way with people and surroundings. Some intelligent things wouldn't exist without AI, but others are existing things (i.e., a camera) that AI makes intelligent (i.e., a smart camera.) These things operate semiautonomously or autonomously in an unsupervised environment for a set amount of time to complete a particular task. Examples include a self-directing vacuum or autonomous farming vehicle. As the technology develops, AI and machine learning will increasingly appear in a variety of objects ranging from smart healthcare equipment to autonomous harvesting robots for farms.

As intelligent things proliferate, expect a shift from stand-alone intelligent things to a swarm of collaborative intelligent things. In this model, multiple devices will work together, either independently or with human input. The leading edge of this area is being used by the military, which is studying the use of drone swarms to attack or defend military targets. It's evident in the consumer world in the opening example showcased at CES, the consumer electronics event.

The Intelligent Things are semi-robotic, smarter versions of regular gadgets and equipments to make our lives easy. They will continue to expand at ever greater rates and in all parts of our lives.

6.1.4 Digital Twins

Digital Twins will bring together the connected world of sensors and humans. This technology trend will further the case of mechanized asset management.

In the context of IoT, digital twins are linked to real-world objects and offer information on the state of the counterparts, respond to changes, improve operations and add value. The idea of behind a digital twin is to harness the data and use algorithms for making reasonable projections about the future. For instance, with digital twins around, a Formula 1 race will no longer be just about praying for luck, hiring the bravest driver, or building the fastest car. Today, a car racing in Monaco is beaming data from the umpteen sensors wired on the car. And an analyst sitting in London will be able to study the data collected, analyze it, and relay optimal racing strategies back to the driver. This, the analyst does using a sophisticated computer model – the digital twin.

We have started seeing the major applications of Digital Twins in the following sectors.

1. **Manufacturing:** Digital Twin is poised to change the current face of manufacturing sector. Digital Twins have a significant impact on the way products are designed manufactured and maintained. It makes manufacturing more efficient and optimized while reducing the throughput times.
2. **Automobile:** Digital Twins can be used in the automobile sector for creating the virtual model of a connected vehicle. It captures the behavioral and operational data of the vehicle and helps in analyzing the overall vehicle performance as well as the connected features. It also helps in delivering a truly personalized/ customized service for the customers.
3. **Retail:** Appealing customer experience is key in the retail sector. Digital twin implementation can play a key role in augmenting the retail customer experience by creating virtual twins for customers and modeling fashions for them on it. Digital Twins also helps in better instore planning, security implementation and energy management in an optimized manner.
4. **Healthcare:** Digital Twins along with data from IoT can play a key role in the health care sector from cost savings to patient monitoring, preventative maintenance and providing personalized health care.
5. **Smart Cities:** The smart city planning and implementation with Digital Twins and IoT data helps enhancing economic development, efficient management of resources, reduction of ecological foot print and increase the overall quality of a citizen's life. The digital twin model can help city planners and policymakers in the smart city planning by gaining the insights from various sensor networks and intelligent systems. The data from the digital twins help them in arriving at informed decisions regarding the future as well.
6. **Industrial IoT:** Industrial firms with digital twin implementation can now monitor, track and control industrial systems digitally. Apart from the operational data, the digital twins capture environmental data such as location, configuration, financial models etc. which helps in predicting the future operations and anomalies

6.1.5 Cloud to the Edge: Edge Computing

Edge Computing describes a computing topology in which information processing and content collection and delivery are placed closer to the sources of this information. Such technology is directly related to the Internet of Things will expand with far-reaching implication on "sources of information.

In the context of IoT, 'edge' refers to the computing infrastructure that exists close to the sources of data, for example, industrial machines (e.g. wind turbine, magnetic resonance (MR) scanner, undersea blowout preventers), industrial controllers such as SCADA and Integrated Building Management Systems (IBMS) systems, and time series databases aggregating data from a variety of equipment and sensors. These devices typically reside away from the centralize computing available in the cloud. SCADA is remotr controlled IBMS and IBMS is automation systems for control of machinery and services in large building complexes.

Wikipedia defines Edge Computing as "pushing the frontier of computing applications, data, and services away from centralized nodes to the logical extremes of a network. It enables analytics and data gathering to occur at the source of the data. This approach requires leveraging resources that may not be continuously connected to a network such as laptops, smartphones, tablets and sensors."

According the multinational Company GE of USA "The role of edge computing to date has mostly been used to ingest, store, filter, and send data to cloud systems. We are at a point in time, however, where these computing systems are packing more compute, storage, and analytic power to consume and act on the data at the machine location. This capability will be more than valuable to industrial organizations—it will be indispensable."

While there are many outcomes that it can enable for industrial organizations, the Edge Computing Consortium identifies the following:

1. Predictive maintenance
2. Reducing costs
3. Security assurance
4. Product-to-service extension (new revenue streams)
5. Energy Efficiency Management
6. Lower energy consumption
7. Lower maintenance costs
8. Higher reliability
9. Smart manufacturing
10. Increased customer demands mean product service life is dramatically reduced
11. Customization of production modes
12. Small-quantity and multi-batch modes are beginning to replace high-volume manufacturing
13. Flexible device replacement
14. Flexible adjustments to production plan
15. Rapid deployment of new processes and models

6.1.6 Intelligent Platforms : Conversational Platforms

Conversational platforms will drive a paradigm shift in which the burden of translating intent shifts from user to computer. These systems are capable of simple answers "How's the weather?" or more complicated interactions "book a reservation at the Italian restaurant on Parker Ave." These platforms will continue to evolve to even more complex actions, such as collecting oral testimony from crime witnesses and acting on that information by creating a sketch of the suspect's face based on the testimony. The challenge that conversational platforms face is that users must communicate in a very structured way, and this is often a frustrating experience. A primary differentiator among conversational platforms will be the robustness of their conversational models and the API and event models used to access, invoke and orchestrate third-party services to deliver complex outcomes.

Intelligent Platforms business provides industrial software, control systems and embedded computing platforms to optimize their customers' assets and equipment. Their goal is to help customers grow the profitability of their businesses through high-performance solutions facilitated by the Industrial Internet.

The conversational platform pushes machine intelligence up a notch, where human expectations from digital systems will significantly rise. These systems, however, are expected to deliver results based on the event models and APIs they are fed with.

6.1.7 Immersive Experience

Augmented reality (AR), virtual reality (VR) and mixed reality are changing the way that people perceive and interact with the digital world. Combined with conversational platforms, a fundamental shift in the user experience to an invisible and immersive experience will emerge. Application vendors, system software vendors and development platform vendors will all compete to deliver this model.

The Immersive Experience related to augmented reality (AR) and virtual reality (VR) is already changing the world around us. The human-machine interaction will improve as research breakthroughs in AR and VR come about.

Augmented Reality is an enhanced version of reality where live direct or indirect views of physical real-world environments are augmented with superimposed computer-generated images over a user's view of the real-world, thus enhancing one's current perception of reality.Unlike virtual reality, which requires you to inhabit an entirely virtual environment, augmented reality uses your existing natural environment and simply overlays virtual information on top of it. As both virtual and real worlds harmoniously coexist, users of augmented reality experience a new and improved natural world where virtual information is used as a tool to provide assistance in everyday activities.

In most augmented reality applications, a user will see both synthetic and natural light. This is done by overlaying projected images on top of a pair of see-through goggles or glasses, which allow the images and interactive virtual objects to layer on top of the user's view of the real world. Augmented Reality devices are often self-contained, meaning that unlike the Oculus Rift or HTC Vive VR headsets, they are completely untethered and do not need a cable or desktop computer to function.

Over the next five years the focus will be on mixed reality, which is emerging as the immersive experience of choice, where the user interacts with digital and real-world objects while maintaining a presence in the physical world. Mixed reality exists along a spectrum and includes head-mounted displays (HMD) for AR or VR, as well as smartphone- and tablet-based AR. Given the ubiquity of mobile devices, Apple's release of ARkit and iPhone X, Google's Tango and ARCore, and the availability of cross-platform AR software development kits such as Wikitude, we expect the battles for smartphone-based AR and MR to heat up in 2018.

6.1.8 Blockchain

Blockchain will become a much more important technology for businesses across the globe. Very simply put, Blockchain enables un-trusted parties to engage in transactions. Blockchain holds promise for many industry sectors like the finance, healthcare, and content delivery. This technology is still maturing.

A blockchain,[2] originally block chain, is a continuously growing list of records, called blocks, which are linked and secured using cryptography. Each block typically contains a cryptographic hash of the previous block, a timestamp and transaction data. By design, a blockchain is inherently resistant to modification of the data. It is "an open, distributed ledger that can record transactions between two parties efficiently and in a verifiable and permanent way". For use as a distributed ledger, a blockchain is typically managed by a peer-to-peer network collectively adhering to a protocol for validating new blocks. Once recorded, the data in any given block cannot be altered retroactively without the alteration of all subsequent blocks, which requires collusion of the network majority.

Blockchain is a shared, distributed, decentralized and tokenized ledger that removes business friction by being independent of individual applications or participants. It allows untrusted parties to exchange commercial transactions. The technology holds the promise to change industries, and although the conversation often surrounds financial opportunities, blockchain has many potential applications in government, healthcare, content distribution, supply chain and more. However, many blockchain technologies are immature and unproven, and are largely unregulated.

A practical approach to blockchain demands a clear understanding of the business opportunity, the capabilities and limitations of blockchain, a trust architecture and the necessary implementation skills. Before embarking on a distributed-ledger project, ensure your team has the cryptographic skills to understand what is and isn't possible. Identify the integration points with existing infrastructures, and monitor the platform evolution and maturation. Use extreme caution when interacting with vendors, and ensure you are clearly identifying how the term "blockchain" is being used.

Blockchains are secure by design and are an example of a distributed computing system with high Byzantine fault tolerance. Decentralized consensus has therefore been achieved with a blockchain. This makes blockchains potentially suitable for the recording of events, medical records, and other records management activities, such as identity management,transaction processing, documenting provenance, food traceability or voting.

Blockchain was invented by Satoshi Nakamoto in 2008 for use in the cryptocurrency bitcoin, as its public transaction ledger.

6.1.9 Event Driven Techs

This trend is expected to bring about some revolutionary changes to joint stakeholders in businesses.

"Some business events or combinations of events constitute business moments — a detected situation that calls for some specific business action. The most consequential business moments are those that have implications for multiple parties, such as separate applications, lines of business or partners."

Digital businesses rely on the ability to sense and be ready to exploit new digital business moments. Business events reflect the discovery of notable states or state changes, such as completion of a purchase order. Some business events or combinations of events constitute business moments — a detected situation that calls for some specific business action. The most consequential business moments are those that have implications for multiple parties, such as separate applications, lines of business or partners.

With the advent of AI, the IoT, and other technologies, business events can be detected more quickly and analyzed in greater detail. Enterprises should embrace "event thinking" as part of a digital business strategy. By 2020, event-sourced, real-time situational awareness will be a required characteristic for 80% of digital business solutions, and 80% of new business ecosystems will require support for event processing.

6.1.10 Security : Continuous Adaptive Risk and Trust Assessment (CARTA)

In an ever more complex security environment of digital businesses, a sophisticated tech strategy known as "Continuous Adaptive Risk and Trust Assessment" (CARTA) will enable better decision making with adaptive responses to digital business. The basic premise of CARTA is trust.

Digital business creates a complex, evolving security environment. The use of increasingly sophisticated tools increases the threat potential. CARTA allows for real-time, risk and trust-based decision making with adaptive responses to security-enable digital business. Traditional security techniques using ownership and control rather than trust will not work in the digital world. Infrastructure and perimeter protection won't ensure accurate detection and can't protect against behind-the-perimeter insider attacks. This requires embracing people-centric security and empowering developers to take responsibility for security measures. Integrating security into your DevOps efforts to deliver a continuous "DevSecOps" process and exploring deception technologies (e.g., adaptive honeypots) to catch bad guys that have penetrated your network are two of the new techniques that should be explored to make CARTA a reality.

6.2 VARIOUS BIG DATA VISUALIZATION TOOLS

To make highly informed decisions quickly, organizational leaders need to be able to access and interpret data in real-time. Information, and the ability to decipher and act on it swiftly, has become a competitive differentiator. To identify new business opportunities ahead of the market, business leaders require the ability to access, evaluate, comprehend, and act on data faster and more effectively than ever before.

Effective graphics take advantage of pre-attentive processing and attributes and the relative strength of these attributes. For example, since humans can more easily process differences in line length than surface area, it may be more effective to use a bar chart (which takes advantage of line length to show comparison) rather than pie charts (which use surface area to show comparison).

A quick survey of the Big Data tools marketplace reveals the presence of big names including Microsoft, SAP, IBM and SAS. But there are plenty of specialist software vendors offering leading bog data visualization tools, and these include Tableau Software, Qlik and TIBCO Software. Leading data visualization products include those offered by:

1. **Google Chart:** Google is an obvious benchmark and well known for the user-friendliness offered by its products and Google chart is not an exception. It is one of the easiest tools for visualizing huge data sets. Google chart holds a wide range of chart gallery, from a simple line graph to complex hierarchical tree-like structure and you can use any of them that fits your requirement.
2. **Tableau:** Tableau desktop is an amazing data visualisation tool (SaaS) for manipulating big data and it's available to everyone. It has two other variants "Tableau Server" and cloud-based "Tableau Online" which are dedicatedly designed for big data related organizations.

   You don't have to be a coder to use this tool. This tool is very handy and provides lightning fast speed. The canvas or dashboard is user-friendly and 'drag and drop' compatible, therefore, it creates a homely atmosphere in any working environment. You can connect all your data from as little as a spreadsheet to as big as Hadoop, painlessly, and analyse deeply. Tableau Desktop is free for students and instructors, otherwise, Tableau desktop charges \$999 and \$1999 for personal and professional editions respectively for 1 year with support

   Tableau is often regarded as the grand master of data visualization software and for good reason. Tableau has a very large customer base of 57,000+ accounts across many industries due to its simplicity of use and ability to produce interactive visualizations far beyond those provided by general BI solutions. It is particularly well suited to handling the huge and very fast-changing datasets which are used in Big Data operations, including artificial intelligence and machine learning applications, thanks to integration with a large number of advanced database solutions including Hadoop, Amazon AWS, My SQL, SAP and Teradata. Extensive research and testing has gone into enabling Tableau to create graphics and visualizations as efficiently as possible, and to make them easy for humans to understand.
3. **Qlikview:** Qlik is one of the major players in the data analytics space with their Qlikview tool which is also one of the biggest competitors of Tableau. Qlikview boasts over 40,000 customers spanning across over 100 countries. Qlik is particularly known for its highly customizable setup and a host of features that help create the visualizations much faster. However, the available options could mean there would be a learning curve to get accustomed with the tool so as to use it to its full potential.

Apart from its data visualization prowess, Qlikview also offers analytics, business intelligence and enterprise reporting features. The clean and clutter-free user experience is one of the notable aspects of Qlikview. Qliksense is a sister package of Qlikview which is often used alongside the former to aid in data exploration and discovery. Another advantage of using Qlikview is the strong community of users and resources which will help you get starte Qlik with their Qlikview tool is the other major player in this space and Tableau's biggest competitor. The vendor has over 40,000 customer accounts across over 100 countries, and those that use it frequently cite its highly customizable setup and wide feature range as a key advantage. This however can mean that it takes more time to get to grips with and use it to its full potential. In addition to its data visualization capabilities Qlikview offers powerful business intelligence, analytics and enterprise reporting capabilities and I particularly like the clean and clutter-free user interface. Qlikview is commonly used alongside its sister package, Qliksense, which handles data exploration and discovery. There is also a strong community and there are plenty of third-party resources available online to help new users understand how to integrate it in their projects.

4. **Datawrapper:** Datawrapper is a data visualization tool that's gaining popularity fast, especially among media companies which use it for presenting statistics and creating charts. It has an easy to navigate user interface where you can easily upload a csv file to create maps, charts and visualizations that can be quickly added to reports. Although the tool is primarily aimed at journalists, it's flexibility should accommodate a host of applications apart from media usage.

   Datawrapper is increasingly becoming a popular choice, particularly among media organizations which frequently use it to create charts and present statistics. It has a simple, clear interface that makes it very easy to upload csv data and create straightforward charts, and also maps, that can quickly be embedded into reports.

5. **Oracle Visual Analyzer:** Introduced in 2015, this web-based tool within the Oracle Business Intelligence Cloud Service claimed a spot at the Magic Quadrant Business Intelligence and Analytics Platform report by Gartner. Interactive visuals and highly advanced analysis clubbed with a customizable dashboard are some of the key features of Oracle Visual Analyzer. Being highly scalable, this data visualization tool is very suitable for enterprises with large-scale deployments where deep insights and well curated reports are essential. he challenges of Big Data Visualization

6. **FusionCharts:** This is a very widely-used, JavaScript-based charting and visualization package that has established itself as one of the leaders in the paid-for market. It can produce 90 different chart types and integrates with a large number of platforms and frameworks giving a great deal of flexibility. One feature that has helped make FusionCharts very popular is that rather than having to start each new visualization from scratch, users can pick from a range of "live" example templates, simply plugging in their own data sources as needed.

7. **Highcharts:** Like FusionCharts this also requires a licence for commercial use, although it can be used freely as a trial, non-commercial or for personal use. Its website claims that it is used by 72 of the world's 100 largest companies and it is often chosen when a fast and

flexible solution must be rolled out, with a minimum need for specialist data visualization training before it can be put to work. A key to its success has been its focus on cross-browser support, meaning anyone can view and run its interactive visualizations, which is not always true with newer platforms.

8. **Microsoft Power BI:** Power BI is considered one of the best data visualization tools by industry experts and is being used across industries like finance, sales to operations. For basic requirements, the tool can even be used for free as it lets you analyze up to 1GB of data per user account without a paid subscription.

   Microsoft Power BI is a suite of business analytics tools from Microsoft primarily meant for analyzing data and sharing the insights. It enables you to explore and dig insights out of your data via any device you use – desktops, tablets or smartphones. It helps you derive quick answers from the data and also can connect to on-premises data sources for real time mapping and analysis.

   Your data source or format won't be a limitation with Power BI as it lets you connect hundreds of sources such as streaming data, data on cloud services, excel spreadsheets and most other data file formats.

9. **Plotly:** Plotly enables more complex and sophisticated visualizations, thanks to its integration with analytics-oriented programming languages such as Python, R and Matlab. It is built on top of the open source d3.js visualization libraries for JavaScript, but this commercial package (with a free non-commercial licence available) adds layers of user-friendliness and support as well as inbuilt support for APIs such as Salesforce.

10. **Sisense:** Sisense provides a full stack analytics platform but its visualization capabilities provide a simple-to-use drag and drop interface which allow charts and more complex graphics, as well as interactive visualizations, to be created with a minimum of hassle. It enables multiple sources of data to be gathered into one easily accessed repositories where it can be queried through dashboards instantaneously, even across Big Data-sized sets. Dashboards can then be shared across organizations ensuring even non technically-minded staff can find the answers they need to their problems.

6.2.1 Importance of Big Data Visualization

The amount of data created by corporations around the world is growing every year, and thanks to innovations such as the Internet of Things this growth shows no sign of abating. The problem for businesses is that this data is only useful if valuable insights can be extracted from it and acted upon.

To do that decision makers need to be able to access, evaluate, comprehend and act on data in near real-time, and Big Data visualization promises a way to be able to do just that. Big Data visualization is not the only way for decision makers to analyze data, but Big Data visualization techniques offer a fast and effective way to:

1. **Review large amounts of data** – data presented in graphical form enables decision makers to take in large amounts of data and gain an understanding of what it means very quickly – far more quickly than poring over spreadsheets or analyzing numerical tables.

2. **Spot trends** – time-sequence data often captures trends, but spotting trends hidden in data is notoriously hard to do – especially when the sources are diverse and the quantity of data is large. But the use of appropriate Big Data visualization techniques can make it easy to spot these trends, and in business terms a trend that is spotted early is an opportunity that can be acted upon.
3. **Identify correlations and unexpected relationships** – One of the huge strengths of Big Data visualization is that enables users to explore data sets – not to find answers specific questions, but to discover what unexpected insights the data can reveal. This can be done by adding or removing data sets, changing scales, removing outliers, and changing visualization types. Identifying previously unsuspected patterns and relationships in data can provide businesses with a huge competitive advantage.
4. **Present the data to others** – An oft-overlooked feature of Big Data visualization is that it provides a highly effective way to communicate any insights that it surfaces to others. That's because it can convey meaning very quickly and in a way that it is easy to understand: precisely what is needed in both internal and external business presentations.

6.2.2 Key Issues Big Data Visualization

Big Data visualization can be an extremely powerful business capability, but before an organization can take advantage of it some key issues need to be addressed. These include:

1. **Availability of visualization specialists:** Many Big Data visualization tools are designed to be easy enough for anyone in an organization to use, often suggesting appropriate Big Data visualization examples for the data sets under analysis. But to get the most out of some tools it may be necessary to employ a specialist in big data visualization techniques who can select the best data sets and visualization styles to ensure the data is exploited to the maximum.
2. **Visualization hardware resources:** Under the hood, Big Data visualization is essentially a computing task, and the ability to carry out this task quickly – to enable organizations to make decisions in a timely manner using real-time data – may require powerful computer hardware, fast storage systems, or even a move to cloud. That means Big Data visualization initiatives are as much an IT project as a management project.
3. **Data quality:** The insights that can be drawn from Big Data visualization are only as accurate as the data that is being visualized: if it is inaccurate or out of date then the value of any insights is questionable. That means people and processes need to be put in place to manage corporate data, metadata, data sources, and any transformations or data cleaning that are performed before storage.

6.2.3 Benefits of Data Visualization Tools

Every bit of data carries a story with it and these data visualization tools are the gateway to fathom the story it tries to tell us. It helps us to understand about the current statistics and the future trends of the market.

Data visualization tools and techniques offer executives and other knowledge workers new approaches to dramatically improve their ability to grasp information hiding in their data.

According to Brian Gentile, the Senior Vice President and General Manager, TIBCO Analytics Product Group, at TIBCO Software Inc., following are the top five benefits that data visualization offers to decision makers and their organizations.

1. **Absorb information in new and more constructive ways.**

   Researchers at the University of Pennsylvania School of Medicine have determined that the human retina can transmit data at roughly 10 million bits per second – about the same rate as an Ethernet connection. But most business intelligence reports that are compiled for senior management are typically populated with static tables and charts that fail to make information vivid for those who view it.

   By comparison, data visualization enables users to receive vast amounts of information regarding operational and business conditions. Data visualization allows decision makers to see connections between multi-dimensional data sets and provides new ways to interpret data through the use of heat maps, fever charts, and other rich graphical representations.

   Organizations that use visual data discovery are more likely to find the information they need when they need it and do so more productively than other companies.

2. **Visualize relationships and patterns between operational and business activities.**

   One of the key benefits of data visualization is how it enables users to more effectively see connections as they are occurring between operating conditions and business performance. In today's highly competitive business environment, finding these correlations among the data has never been more important.

   For example, suppose an executive team for an electronics retailer is viewing monthly customer data. The team is presented with a bar chart that shows that the company's net promoter score (NPS; willingness among customers to recommend a company or its products/services) has dipped by five points over the past month in the Midwestern United States. The data suggest to senior leadership that there's a problem with customer satisfaction in this territory, but don't provide any insights about why NPS scores have tumbled.

   By providing a multi-faceted view of business and operating dynamics, data visualization permits the senior leadership team to see that first-contact resolution rates in a Midwest customer call center have recently taken a nosedive, dramatically impacting customer satisfaction.

   The ability to make these types of correlations allows the executives to identify the root cause of the problem and act quickly to resolve it.

3. **Identify and act on emerging trends faster.**

   The volume of data that companies are able to gather about customers and market conditions can provide business leaders with insights into new revenue and business opportunities, presuming they can spot the opportunities in the mountain of data. Using data visualization, decision makers are able to grasp shifts in customer behaviors and market conditions across multiple data sets much more quickly.

For example, business leaders for a supermarket chain can use data visualization to see that not only are customers spending more in its stores as macro-economic conditions improve, but they are increasingly interested in purchasing ready-made foods.

A deeper dive into customer sentiment and other data reveals an emerging opportunity for the company to launch a catering service to customers who are entertaining more frequently and spending more across related food and beverage categories. Insights like this enable the company to act on this new business opportunity ahead of its rivals.

4. **Manipulate and interact directly with data.**

One of the greatest strengths of data visualization is how it brings actionable insights to the surface. Unlike one-dimensional tables and charts that can only be viewed, data visualization tools enable users to interact with data.

For example, an Excel spreadsheet or a canned report can inform a regional business leader for an automotive company that sales for its sedans are down for a particular month. However, the report won't inform the executive why sales of the sedans are down or whether certain styles or colors are performing better than others. Moreover, the information in the report could be days or weeks old, skewing the accuracy of the data and current sales trends.

By using real-time data visualization and predictive analytics, the executive can view up-to-date sales figures and see why certain sedans are underperforming and the reasons that sales are lagging – for example, discounts offered by competitors.

The executive can then determine the most effective actions to take based on analytical models she's able to develop herself. For example, she might launch a 10-day sales promotion for specific dealerships that are targeted at the most likely buyers with a price that undercuts the competition yet generates acceptable profit margins.

5. **Foster a new business language.**

Another advantage of using data visualization is its ability to tell a story through data.

Consider, for example, business leaders for a consumer packaged goods company who track key performance indicators such as EBITDA and net profit margin. They can gather only part of the story about current business conditions using a static bar chart. The chart might show that the company generated 2 percent revenue growth for the past month, but it doesn't reveal which categories are growing fastest or shrinking, or the reasons why.

A heat map could illustrate which product groups are performing well or underperforming, and allow business leaders to drill down into the data to determine the factors that are shaping sales. The data might reveal that pet-care products are underperforming, but that higher-income customers represent the majority of sales. These insights could be used to target promotions to this customer segment to increase conversion rates and revenue growth for this category.

6.3 VISUALIZING BIG DATA

Big data brings new challenges to visualization because of the speed, size and diversity of data that must be taken into account. The cardinality of the columns you are trying to visualize should also be considered. As already learnt in unit 1 of this book, one of the most common definitions of big data is data that is of such volume, variety and velocity that an organization must move beyond its comfort zone technologically to derive intelligence for effective decisions.

- Volume refers to the size of the data.
- Variety describes whether the data is structured, semistructured or unstructured.
- Velocity is the speed at which data pours in and how frequently it changes.

Building upon basic graphing and visualization techniques, SAS Visual Analytics has taken an innovative approach to addressing the challenges associated with visualizing big data. Using innovative, in-memory capabilities combined with SAS Analytics and data discovery, SAS provides new techniques based on core fundamentals of data analysis and the presentation of results. Handling Large Data Volumes

6.3.1 Autocharting Capability In SAS Visual Analytics

When working with massive amounts of data, it can be difficult to immediately grasp what visual might be the best to use. The autocharting capability in SAS Visual Analytics takes a look at the data you wish to examine and then, based on the amount of data and the type of data, it presents the most appropriate visualization. This helps business analysts and nontechnical users easily visualize their data. They can build hierarchies on the fly, interactively explore data and display the data in different ways to answer specific questions or solve new problems without having to rely on constant assistance from IT to provide changing views of information. Data volume can become an issue because traditional architectures and software may not be able to process huge amounts of data in a timely manner, thus requiring you to make compromises and aggregate the details you want to visualize. Even the most common descriptive statistics calculations can become complicated when you are dealing with big data and don't want to be restricted by column limits, storage constraints and limited support for different data types.

The SAS in-memory platform solves these issues by speeding up the task of data exploration, and a visual interface displays the results in an easy-to-understand visualization. For example, what if you have a billion rows in a data set and want to create a scatter plot on two measures? It would be impossible to see so many data points. And the application creating the visual may not be able to plot a billion points in a timely or effective manner. One potential solution is to use binning (the grouping together of data) on both axes so that you can effectively visualize the big data.

Box plots are another example of how the volume of data can affect the visual being shown. A box plot is a graphical display of five statistics (the minimum, lower quartile, median, upper quartile and maximum) that summarize the distribution of a set of data. The lower quartile (25th percentile) is represented by the lower edge of the box, and the upper quartile (75th percentile) is represented by the upper edge of the box. The median (50th percentile) is represented by a central line that divides the box into sections. Extreme values are represented by whiskers that extend out from the edges of the box. Usually, these display well when using big data (see Figure 6.2). Often, box plots are used to understand the outliers in the data. Generally speaking, the number of outliers in the data can be represented by 1 percent to 5 percent of the data. With traditionally sized data sets, viewing this proportion of the data is not necessarily hard to do. However, when you are working with massive amounts of data, viewing 1 percent to 5 percent of the data is challenging. For example, if you were working with a billion rows of data, the outliers would represent 10 million data points. If you bin the results and show a box plot with whiskers (Figure 6.2), you can view the distribution of the data and see the outliers – all calculated quickly on big data.

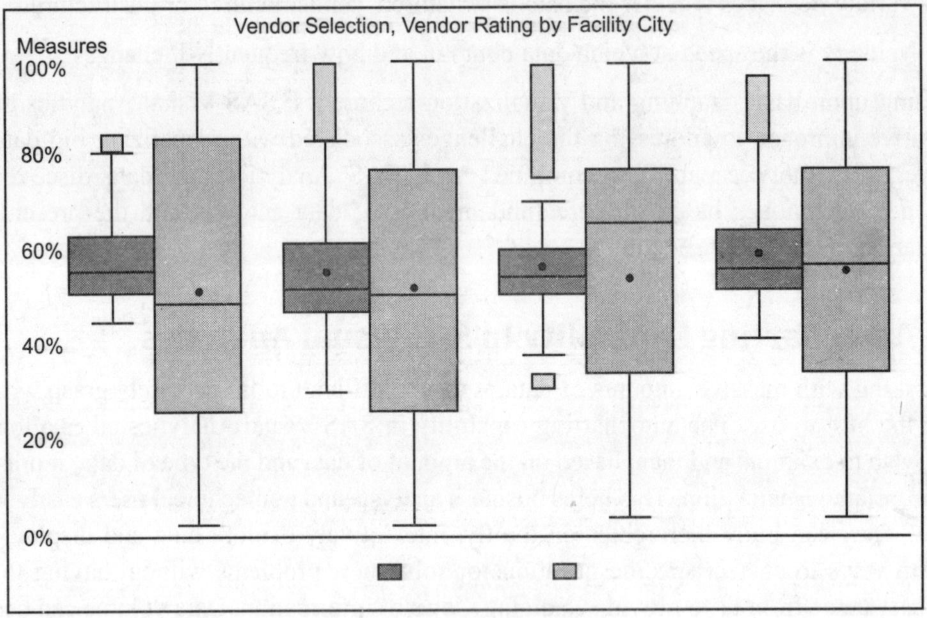

Fig. 6.2: This box plot compares the distribution of data points within a category.

6.3.2 Visualizing Semistructured and Unstructured Data Using Word Clouds and Network Diagrams

The variety of big data brings challenges because semistructured and unstructured data require new visualization techniques. A word cloud visual (where the size of the word represents its frequency within a body of text) can be used on unstructured data as a way to display high- or low-frequency words (see Figure 6.3). SAS Visual Analytics takes the concept of word clouds a step further by taking advantage of taxonomies and ontologies to make associations. Words are then organized into topics based on how the words are used. SAS Visual Analytics word clouds can display the hot topics of the day gleaned from such text analysis. Users can drill down by clicking on an individual topic to see exactly what words or phrases comprise that topic.

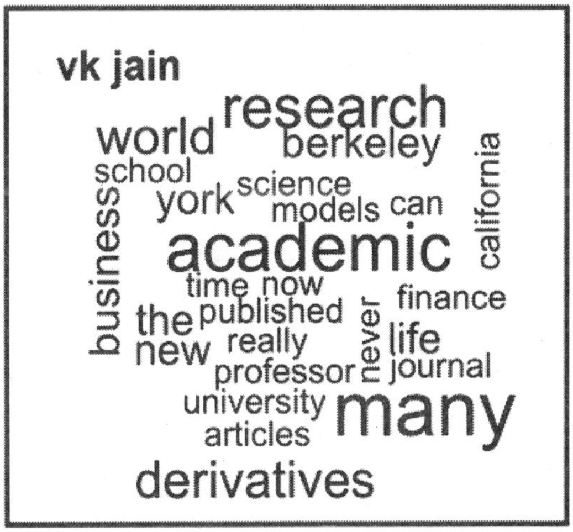

Fig. 6.3: SAS Visual Analytics Word Clouds for Ready Reference

For example, you could use the topic cloud to categorize customer comments on Twitter about your products or services and then click on a topic to drill down to see the actual comments. Another visualization technique that can be used for semi-structured or unstructured data is the network diagram. Network diagrams view relationships in terms of nodes (representing individual actors within the network) and ties (which represent relationships between the individuals, such as friendship, kinship, organizations, business relationships, etc.). These networks are often depicted in a diagram where nodes are represented as points and ties are represented as lines.

Network diagrams can be used in many applications and disciplines. For example, businesses analyze social networks to understand their interactions with customers, while counterintelligence and law enforcement might map a clandestine or covert organization such as an espionage ring, an organized crime family or a street gang. You can also superimpose the network diagram on a map, for example, to show the relationship or product sales across geographic areas (see Figure 6.4)

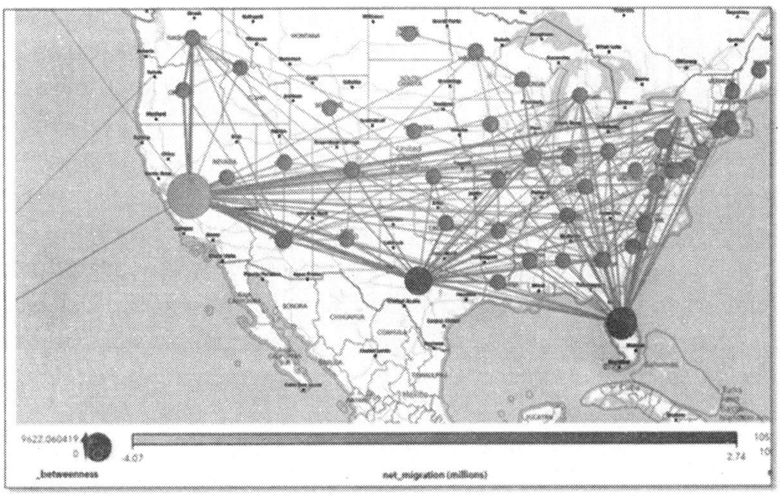

Fig. 6.4: Network diagrams explore relationships within a data set, including connections across geographic areas.

6.3.3 Visualization With Correlation Matrices

Velocity is all about the speed at which data is coming into the organization. The ability to access and process varying velocities of data quickly is critical. A correlation matrix combines big data and fast response times to quickly identify which variables are related. It also shows how strong the relationships are between variables. SAS Visual Analytics makes it easy to assess the relationships. Simply select a group of variables and drop them into a visualization pane. The intelligent autocharting function displays a color-coded correlation matrix that quickly identifies strong and weak relationships between the variables. Darker boxes indicate a stronger correlation; lighter boxes indicate a weaker correlation If you hover over a box, a summary of the relationship is shown.

The Role of Memory in Vision While that's an overview of how we process visual information, let's discuss the vital role of memory in our vision. There are two types of memory that come into play when we process visual information. Long-term memory Working memory Long-term Memory This type of memory is what makes us always expect the units to be marked off on the X and Y axes of a chart, or the date range selector at the top of a dashboard. This type of memory is formed by past interactions and experiences. It needs to be considered when designing the layout of a dashboard or visualization. There should be good reason to go contrary to long-term memory when deciding the basic structure of a dashboard or visualization. A discussion of long-term memory is out of the scope of this white paper. Instead, we'll focus on the other type - working memory. Working Memory When we look at a line chart, or notice a number in a dashboard, we use our working memory to store just the information we need at the moment. This type of memory breaks the entire visual into small chunks of information, in a process appropriately called 'chunking.' Surprisingly, for all the complexity of our brain, our working memory can hold only about 3 chunks of information at any given time. When perceiving a complex visual, we're constantly replacing the 3 available slots in our working memory. This is why when designing a visual or a dashboard, one of our goals is to limit the number of prominent chunks of information that we want the user to notice, and pack as much information as possible into each chunk. While we want to avoid information overload, a sound understanding of this concept can help us direct the attention of the viewer in a natural way. Next, Let's discuss working memory in depth. Just as any language has alphabets, which are combined to form words, the language of data visualization consists of certain basic building blocks called preattentive attributes.

6.4 PREATTENTIVE ATTRIBUTES

Colin Ware[3], terms the basic building blocks of the visualization process as 'Preattentive attributes.' These attributes are what immediately catch our eye when we look at a visualization. They can be perceived in less than 10 milliseconds, even before we make a conscious effort to notice them. Here's a list of the preattentive attributes:

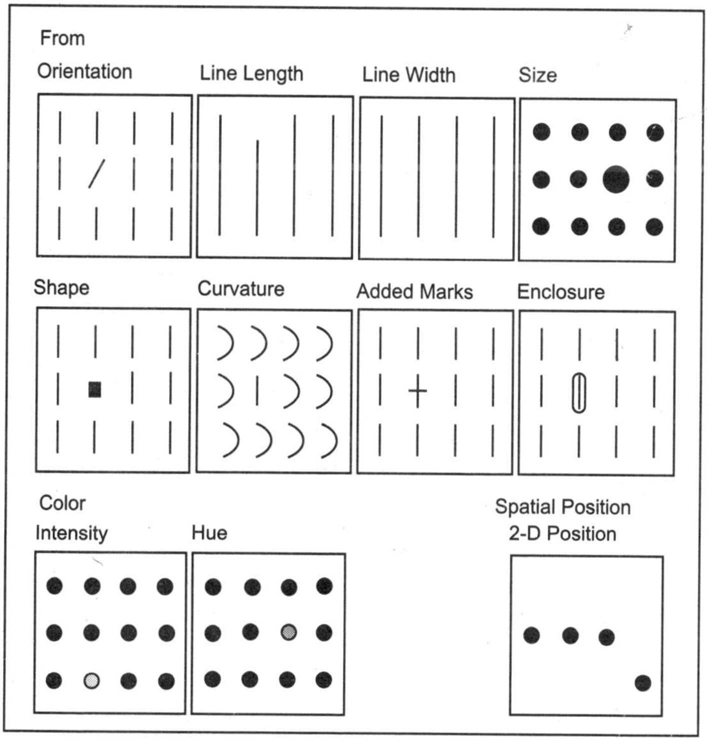

Fig. 6.5: Preattentive Attributes : Basic building blocks of the visualization process

These attributes come into play when we analyze any visualization. Of this list, only Position, and Length can used to perceive quantitative data with precision. The other attributes are useful for perceiving other types of data such as categorical, or relational data. For example, both the pie chart and the bar chart below show the same data. But you can't easily tell from the pie chart which is the biggest pie. That's more clearly visible in the bar chart as it calls on the preattentive attribute of length.

Considering preattentive attributes can help when deciding which chart type to use for our data. While preattentive attributes are what we immediately identify in a visual, they aren't the only things we notice. We go on to form patterns out of the preattentive attributes.

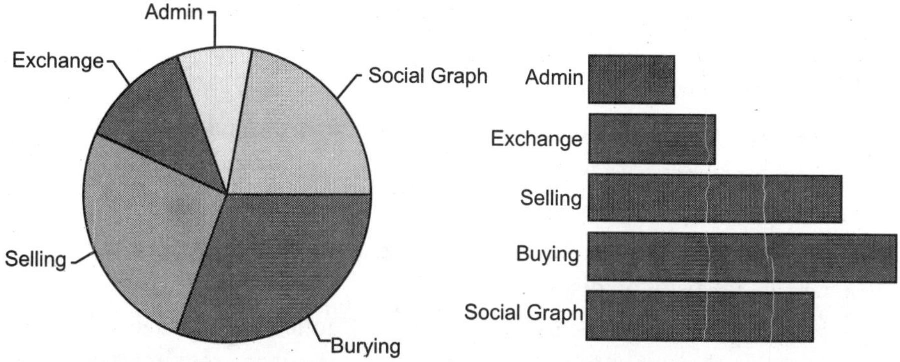

Fig. 6.6: Forming Analytical Patterns Out of Preattentive Attributes

If preattentive attributes are the alphabets of visual language, analytical patterns are the words we form using them. We immediately identify the preattentive attributes in a visualization. We then combine the preattentive attributes to seek out analytical patterns in the visual. Here are the basic analytical patterns that we identify when looking at a visual:

6.5 CHALLENGES OF BIG DATA VISUALIZATION

Scalability and dynamics are two major challenges in visual analytics. Table 6.1 shows the research status for static data and dynamic data according to the data size. For big dynamic data, solutions for type A problems or type B problems often do not work for A and B problems[4].

Table 6.1. The research status and challenge of visual analytics

Data Type	Samll, mid-sized	Big-sized
Static data	Well studied	Open issues type A
Dynamic data	Open issues type B	Highly challenging (A and B) >> A + B

Table 6.1. The research status and challenge of visual analytics

Visualization systems must contend with unstructured data forms such as graphs, tables, text, trees, and other metadata. Big data often has unstructured formats. Due to bandwidth limitations and power requirements, visualization should move closer to the data to extract meaningful information efficiently. Visualization software should be run in an in situ manner. Because of the big data size, the need for massive parallelization is a challenge in visualization. The challenge in parallel visualization algorithms is decomposing a problem into independent tasks that can be run concurrently.

Effective data visualization is a key part of the discovery process in the era of big data. For the challenges of high complexity and high dimensionality in big data, there are different dimensionality reduction methods. However, they may not always be applicable. The more dimensions are visualized effectively, the higher are the chances of recognizing potentially interesting patterns, correlations, or outliers.

There are also following problems for big data visualization[5]:

- Visual noise: Most of the objects in dataset are too relative to each other. Users cannot divide them as separate objects on the screen.
- Information loss: Reduction of visible data sets can be used, but leads to information loss.
- Large image perception: Data visualization methods are not only limited by aspect ratio and resolution of device, but also by physical perception limits.
- High rate of image change: Users observe data and cannot react to the number of data change or its intensity on display.
- High performance requirements: It can be hardly noticed in static visualization because of lower visualization speed requirements--high performance requirement.

Perceptual and interactive scalability are also challenges of big data visualization. Visualizing every data point can lead to over-plotting and may overwhelm users' perceptual and cognitive capacities; reducing the data through sampling or filtering can elide interesting structures or outliers. Querying large data stores can result in high latency, disrupting fluent interaction [13].

In Big Data applications, it is difficult to conduct data visualization because of the large size and high dimension of big data. Most of current Big Data visualization tools have poor performances in scalability, functionalities, and response time. Uncertainty can result in a great challenge to effective uncertainty-aware visualization and arise during a visual analytics process[5].

6.8 POTENTIAL SOLUTIONS

Following are the proposed solutions to some challenges or problems about visualization and big Following are the solutions [6]:

1. Meeting the need for speed: One possible solution is hardware. Increased memory and powerful parallel processing can be used. Another method is putting data in-memory but using a grid computing approach, where many machines are used.
2. Understanding the data: One solution is to have the proper domain expertise in place.
3. Addressing data quality: It is necessary to ensure the data is clean through the process of data governance or information management.
4. Displaying meaningful results: One way is to cluster data into a higher-level view where smaller groups of data are visible and the data can be effectively visualized.
5. Dealing with outliers: Possible solutions arc to rcmovc thc outliers from the data or create a separate chart for the outliers.

6.9 FUTURE PROGRESS OF BIG DATA VISUALIZATION

As for how visualization should be designed in the era of big data, visualization approaches should provide an overview first, then allow zooming and filtering, and provide deep details on demand[7]. Visualization can play an important role in using big data to get a complete view of customers. Relationships are an important aspect of many big data scenarios. Social networks are perhaps the most prominent example and are very difficult to understand in text or tabular format; however, visualization can make emerging network trends and patterns apparent. A cloud-based visualization method was proposed to visualize an inherence relationship of users on social network. The method can intuitionally present the users' social relationship based on the correlation matrix to represent a hierarchical relationship of user nodes of social network. In addition, the method uses Hadoop based on cloud for the distributed parallel processing of visualization, which helps expedite the big data of social network.

Big data visualization can be performed through a number of approaches such as more than one view per representation display, dynamical changes in number of factors, and filtering (dynamic query filters, star-field display, and tight coupling), etc. Several visualization methods were analyzed and classified[8] according to data criteria: (1) large data volume, (2) data variety, and (3) data dynamics.

1. **Treemap:** It is based on space-filling visualization of hierarchical data.

2. **Circle Packing:** It is a direct alternative to treemap. Besides the fact that as primitive shape it uses circles, which also can be included into circles from a higher hierarchy level.
3. **Sunburst:** It uses treemap visualization and is converted to polar coordinate system. The main difference is that the variable parameters are not width and height, but a radius and arc length.
4. **Parallel Coordinates:** It allows visual analysis to be extended with multiple data factors for different objects.
5. **Streamgraph:** It is a type of a stacked area graph that is displaced around a central axis resulting in flowing and organic shape.
6. **Circular Network Diagram:** Data object are placed around a circle and linked by curves based on the rate of their relativeness. The different line width or color saturation is usually used to measure object relativeness.

Table 6.2. Properties of visualization methods

Method name	large data volume	Data variety	Data dynamics
Treemap	+	–	–
Circle packing	+	–	–
Sunburst	+	–	+
Parallel coordinates	+	+	+
Streamgraph	+	–	+
Circular network diagram	+	+	–

6.2 and Table 6.3[8] show the classifications. 6.2 indicates which method can process large volume data, various data, and changing data with time. According to 6.3, visualization methods can be classified according to Big Data classes.

Table 6.3. Classification of visualization methods

Method name	Big data class
Treemap	Can be applied only to hierarchical data
Circle packing	Can be applied only to hierarchical data
Sunburst	Volume + Velocity
Parallel coordinates	Volume + Velocity + Variety
Streamgraph	Volume + Velocity
Circular network diagram	Volume + Variety

A lot of big data visualization tools run on the Hadoop platform.

Big data processing tools can process ZB (zettabytes) and PB (petabytes) data quite naturally, but they often cannot visualize ZB and PB data. At present, big data processing tools include Hadoop, High Performance Computing and Communications, Storm, Apache Drill, RapidMiner, and Pentaho BI. Data visualization tools include NodeBox, R, Weka, Gephi, Google Chart API, Flot, D3, and Visual.ly, etc. A big data visualization algorithm analysis integrated model based on RHadoop was proposed. The integrated model can process ZB and PB data and show valuable results via visualization. The model is suitable for the design of parallel algorithms for ZB and PB data

They analyze big data efficiently, but lack adequate visualization. Some software with the functions of visualization and interaction for visualizing data has been developed[9]:

1 **Pentaho:** It supports the spectrum of BI functions such as analysis, dashboard, enterprise-class reporting, and data mining.
2. **Flare:** An ActionScript library for creating data visualization that runs in Adobe Flash Player.
3. **Jasper Reports:** It has a novel software layer for generating reports from the big data storages.
4. **Dygraphs:** It is quick and elastic open source JavaScript charting collection that helps discover and understand opaque data sets.
5. **Datameer Analytics Solution and Cloudera:** Datameer and Cloudera have partnered to make it easier and faster to put Hadoop into production and help users to leverage the power of Hadoop.
6. **Platfora:** Platfora converts raw big data in Hadoop into interactive data processing engine. It has modular functionality of in-memory data engine.
7. **Many Eyes:** It is a visualization tool launched by IBM. Many Eyes is a public website where users can upload data and create interactive visualization.
8. **Tableau:** It is a business intelligence (BI) software tool that supports interactive and visual analysis of data. It has an in-memory data engine to accelerate visualization.

Tableau has three main products to process large-scale datasets, including Tableau Desktop, Tableau Sever, and Tableau Public. Tableau also embed Hadoop infrastructure. It uses Hive to structure queries and cache information for in-memory analytics. Caching helps reduce the latency of a Hadoop cluster. Therefore, it can provide an interactive mechanism between users and Big Data applications.

Interactive visual cluster analysis is the most intuitive way for discovering clustering patterns. The most challenging step is visualizing multidimensional data and allowing users to interactively explore the data and identify clustering structures. Optimized star-coordinate visualization models for effective interactive cluster exploration on big data were developed. The star-coordinate models are probably the most scalable technique for visualizing large datasets compared with other multidimensional visualization methods such as parallel coordinates and scatter-plot matrix[10]:

1. Parallel coordinates and scatter-plot matrix are often used for less than ten dimensions, while star coordinates can handle tens of dimensions.

2. The star-coordinate visualization can scale up to many points with the help of density-based representation.
3. Star-coordinate based cluster visualization does not try to calculate pairwise distances between records; it uses the property of the underlying mapping model to partially keep the distance relationship. This is very useful in processing big data.

Direct visualization of big data sources is often not possible or effective. Analytics plays a key role by helping reduce the size and complexity of big data. The visualization and analytics can be integrated so that they work best. IBM has embedded visualization capabilities into business analytics solutions. What makes this possible is the IBM Rapidly Adaptive Visualization Engine (RAVE).

RAVE and extensible visualization capabilities help use effective visualization that provides a better understanding of big data[11]. IBM products, such as IBM® InfoSphere® BigInsights™ and IBM SPSS® Analytic Catalyst, use visualization libraries and RAVE to enable interactive visualizations that can help gain great insight from big data. InfoSphere BigInsights is the software that helps analyze and discover business insights hidden in big data. SPSS Analytic Catalyst automates big data preparation, chooses proper analytics procedures, and display results via interactive visualization[11].

The use of immersive virtual reality (VR) platforms for scientific data visualization has been in the process of exploration including software and inexpensive commodity hardware. These potentially powerful and innovative tools for multi-dimensional data visualization can provide an easy path to collaborative data visualization. Immersion provides benefits beyond traditional "desktop" visualization tools: it results in a better perception of data scape geometry and more intuitive data understanding. Immersive visualization should become one of the foundations to explore the higher dimensionality and abstraction that are attendant with big data. The intrinsic human pattern recognition (or visual discovery) skills should be maximized through using emerging technologies associated with the immersive VR[12].

REFERENCES

1. Kasey Panetta in his article " Gartner Top 10 StrategicTechnology Trends for 2018" October 3, 2017
2. "Blockchains: The great chain of being sure about things". The Economist. 31 October 2015. Archived from the original on 3 July 2016. Retrieved 18 June 2016. The technology behind bitcoin lets people who do not know or trust each other build a dependable ledger. This has implications far beyond the crypto currency.
3. Colin Ware]Preattentive Attributes Used by Our Working Memory Colin Ware, Director of the Data Visualization Research Lab at the University of New Hampshire
4. Big Data and Visualization: Methods, Challenges and Technology Progress Lidong Wang, Guanghui Wang, Cheryl Ann Alexander, Digital Technologies. 2015, 1(1), 33-38
5. E.Y. Gorodov and V.V. Gubarev, Analytical Review of Data Visualization Methods in Application to Big Data, Journal of Electrical and Computer Engineering, 013, Article ID 969458, pp. 1-7.

6. SAS Institute Inc., Five big data challenges and how to overcome them with visual analytics, Report, 2013, pp. 1-2.
7. F. Shull, Getting an Intuition for Big Data, IEEE Software, July/August 2013, pp. 1-5.
8. E.Y. Gorodov and V.V. Gubarev, Analytical Review of Data Visualization Methods in Application to Big Data, Journal of Electrical and Computer Engineering, 013, Article ID 969458, pp. 1-7.
9. V. Sucharitha, S.R. Subash and P. Prakash , Visualization of Big Data: Its Tools and Challenges, International Journal of Applied Engineering Research, 9(18), 2014, pp. 5277-5290.
10. K. Chen, Optimizing star-coordinate visualization models for effective interactive cluster exploration on big data, Intelligent Data Analysis, 18, 2014, pp. 117-136.
11. T. A. Keahey, Using visualization to understand big data, Technical Report, IBM Corporation, 2013, pp. 1-16.
12. C. Donalek, S.G. Djorgovski, A. Cioc, A. Wang, J. Zhang, E. Lawler, S. Yeh, A. Mahabal, M. Graham, A. Drake, S. Davidoff, J.S. Norris, G. Longo, Immersive and Collaborative Data Visualization Using Virtual Reality Platforms, 2014 IEEE International Conference on Big Data, pp. 1-6.

ANNEXURE

R PROGRAMMING LANGUAGE & SOFTWARE ENVIRONMENT FOR STATISTICAL ANALYSIS AND GRAPHICS

1. INTRODUCTION TO R IS A PROGRAMMING LANGUAGE AND SOFTWARE ENVIRONMENT

R is a programming language and software environment for statistical analysis, graphics representation and reporting. The name is partly based on the (first) names of the first two R authors (Robert Gentleman and Ross Ihaka), and partly a play on the name of the Bell Labs language 'S' R can be regarded as an implementation of the S language which was developed at Bell Laboratories by Rick Becker, John Chambers and Allan Wilks, and also forms the basis of the S-Plus systems.

2. DOWNLOADING R FOR WINDOWS

Windows Installation You can download the Windows installer version of R from R-3.2.2 for Windows (32/64 bit) and save it in a local directory. As it is a Windows installer (.exe) with a name "R-version-win.exe". You can just double click and run the installer accepting the default settings. If your Windows is 32-bit version, it installs the 32-bit version. But if your windows is 64-bit, then it installs both the 32-bit and 64-bit versions. After installation you can locate the icon to run the Program in a directory structure "R\R3.2.2\bin\i386\Rgui.exe" under the Windows Program Files. Clicking this icon brings up the R-GUI which is the R console to do R Programming.

3. THE R ENVIRONMENT

R is an integrated suite of software facilities for data manipulation, calculation and graphical display. The following are the important features of R:

1. R is a well-developed, simple and effective programming language (called 'S') which includes conditionals, loops, user defined recursive functions and input and output facilities. R has an effective data handling and storage facility.
2. R provides a suite of operators for calculations on arrays, lists, vectors and matrices.

3. R provides a large, coherent and integrated collection of tools for data analysis
4. R provides graphical facilities for data analysis and display either directly at the computer or printing at the papers.
5. As a conclusion, R is world's most widely used statistics programming language. It's the # 1 choice of data scientists and supported by a vibrant and talented community of contributors. R is taught in universities and deployed in mission critical business applications.

4. R AND STATISTICS

Many people use R as a statistics system. We prefer to think of it of an environment within which many classical and modern statistical techniques have been implemented. A few of these are built into the base R environment, but many are supplied as packages. There are about 25 packages supplied with R (called "standard" and "recommended" packages) and many more are available through the CRAN family of Internet sites (via https://CRAN.R-project.org) and elsewhere

5. GETTING STARTED WITH R PROGRAMMING

5.1 Getting help with Functions and Features

R has an inbuilt help facility similar to the man facility of UNIX. To get more information on any specific named function, for example solve, the command is

```
> help(solve)
```

An alternative is

```
> ?solve
```

On most R installations help is available in HTML format by running

```
> help.start()
```

which will launch a Web browser that allows the help pages to be browsed with hyperlinks. On UNIX, subsequent help requests are sent to the HTML-based help system

R Console

```
> Help.start()
starting httpd help server ... done
If nothing happens, you should open
'http://127.0..1:15160/doc/html/index/html' yourself
>|
```

At beginning the R console shall look like :

```
R Console

R version 3.4.3 (2017-11-30)--Kite-Eating Tree--
Copyright (C) 2017 The R Foundation for Statistical Computing
Platform: 1386-w64-mingw32/1386 (32-bit)

R is free software and comes with ASSOLUTELY NO WARRANTY.
You are welcome to radistribute is under certain condition.
Type '11cense()'or '11cense()' for distribute details.

R is a collaborative project with many contributors.
Type 'contributors()'for more information and
'citation()' on how to cite R or R packages in publications.

Type 'demo()' for some demos, 'help()' for on-line help, or
'help.start()' for an HTML browser interface to help.
Type 'q() to quite R.
>|
```

It ends with a command prompt > after which you can enter command linewise. Aftereach line you have to press Enter key. To start learning programming for statistical experience, first clear the screen by using clear screen command from **Edit** menu of console and by clicking the **Clear Screen** option.

Interacting with R. Unlike languages like C, Fortran, or Java, R is an interactive programming langauge. This means that R works interactively, using a question-and-answer model:

1. Start R
2. Type a command and press Enter
3. R executes this command (often printing the result)
4. R then waits for more input
5. Type q() to exit

Here are some simple examples:

```
> 2 + 2
[1] 4
```

This means that you have asked R to add two constants 2 and two, and R has given the answer as [1] 4 . [1] indicates line # 1 and 4 is the answer.

```
> exp(-3) ## exponential function
[1] 0.04978707
> log(100, base = 10)
```

R Console

```
> 2+2
{1} 4
> exp(-3)##exponential function
{1} 0.04978707
> log (100, base # 10)
[1] 2
> log(100, base # 10)
{1} 3
> |
```

Enter following command

```
>Runif(10)
```

The last command generates ten random variables; the result (which is printed) is a vector of 10 numbers. exp(), log(), and runif() are functions.

R features very strong graphics capabilities. The simplest way to produce plots is to use the plot() function. We will learn more about graphics in a different tutorial.

Enter following at command prompt.

```
> plot(runif(10))
```

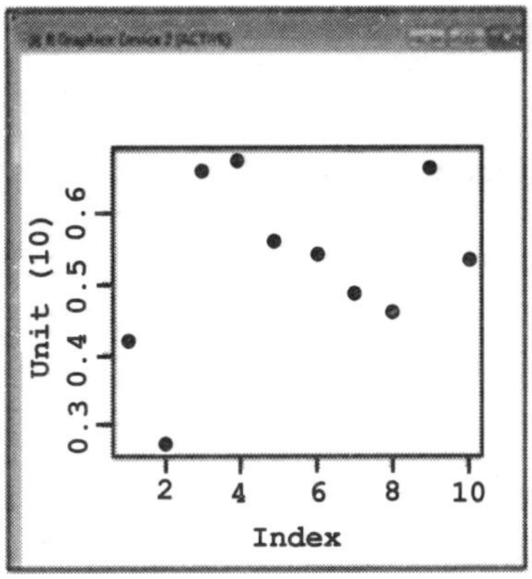

6. VARIABLES.

As in other programming languages, R has symbolic variables which can be assigned values. Assignment is done using the '<-' operator. The more C-like '=' also works (with some exceptions).

We can write

```
> x = 2   or
> x <- 2
```

Both have the same meaning

```
> x + x
[1] 4
> y = x + 3
```

```
> y
[1] 5
```

Entering strings

```
> s <- "this is a character string"
> s [1] "this is a character string"
```

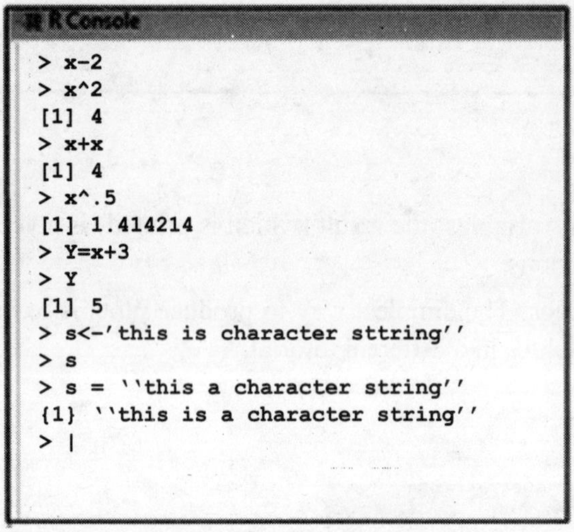

7. VECTORS AND ASSIGNMENT

R operates on named data structures. The simplest such structure is the numeric vector, which is a single entity consisting of an ordered collection of numbers. To set up a vector named x, say, consisting of five numbers, namely 10.4, 5.6, 3.1, 6.4 and 21.7, use the R command

```
> x <- c(10.4, 5.6, 3.1, 6.4, 21.7)
```

This is an assignment statement using the function c() which in this context can take an arbitrary number of vector arguments and whose value is a vector got by concatenating its arguments end to end.A number occurring by itself in an expression is taken as a vector of length one. Notice that the assignment operator ('<-'), which consists of the two characters "<" i.e. less Than and '-' ("minus") occurring strictly side-by-side and it 'points' to the object receiving the value of the expression. In most contexts the '=' operator can be used as an alternative.

Assignment can also be made using the function assign(). An equivalent way of making the same assignment as above is with:

```
>assign("x", c(10.4, 5.6, 3.1, 6.4, 21.7))
```

The usual operator, <-, can be thought of as a syntactic short-cut to this. Assignments can also be made in the other direction, using the obvious change in the assignment operator. So the same assignment could be made using

```
> c(10.4, 5.6, 3.1, 6.4, 21.7) -> x
```

The further assignment

```
> y <- c(x, 0, x)
```

would create a vector y with 11 entries consisting of two copies of x with a zero in the middle place.

8. VECTORIZED ARITHMETIC

The elementary data types in R are all vectors; even the scalar variables we defined above are stored as vectors of length one. The c(...) construct can be used to create vectors:

```
> weight <- c(60, 72, 57, 90, 95, 72)
> weight [1] 60 72 57 90 95 72
```

To generate a vector of regularly spaced numbers, use

```
> seq(0, 1, length = 11) [1] 0.0 0.1 0.2 0.3 0.4 0.5 0.6 0.7
0.8 0.9 1.0
> 1:10 [1] 1 2 3 4 5 6 7 8 9 10
```

The c() function can be used to combine vectors as well as scalars, e.g.,

```
> x <- seq(0, 1, length = 6)
> c(x, 1:10, 100) [1] 0.0 0.2 0.4 0.6 0.8 1.0 1.0 2.0 3.0 4.0
5.0 6.0 [1] 7.0 8.0 9.0 10.0 100.0
```

Common arithmetic operations (including +, -, *, /, ^) and mathematical functions (e.g. sin(), cos(), log()) work element-wise on vectors, and produce another vector:

```
> height <- c(1.75, 1.80, 1.65, 1.90, 1.74, 1.91)
> height^2 [1] 3.0625 3.2400 2.7225 3.6100 3.0276 3.6481
> bmi <- weight / height^2
> bmi [1] 19.59184 22.22222 20.93664 24.93075 31.37799 19.73630
> log(bmi) [1] 2.975113 3.101093 3.041501 3.216102 3.446107
2.982460
```

When two vectors are not of equal length, the shorter one is recycled. For example, The following adds 0 to all the odd elements and 2 to all the even elements of 1:**10:**

```
> 1:10 + c(0, 2) [1] 1 4 3 6 5 8 7 10 9 12
```

These simple vectorized arithmetic rules are among the most powerful design features of the R language.

9. GENERATING REGULAR SEQUENCES

R has a number of facilities for generating commonly used sequences of numbers. For example 1:10 is the vector c(1, 2, ..., 9, 10). The colon operator has high priority within an expression, so, for example 2*1:10 is the vector c(2, 4, ..., 8, 10).

```
> 1:10
[1] 1 2 3 4 5 6 7 8 9 10
> 10:1
{1} 10 9 8 7 6 5 4 3 2 1
> 2#1:10
[1] 2 4 6 8 10 12 14 16 18 20
> |
```

The function **seq()** is a more general facility for generating sequences. It has five arguments, only some of which may be specified in any one call. The first two arguments, if given, specify the beginning and end of the sequence, and if these are the only two arguments given the result is the same as the colon operator. That is **seq(2,10)** is the same vector as 2:10.

Arguments to seq(), and to many other R functions, can also be given in named form, in which case the order in which they appear is irrelevant. The first two arguments may be named from=value and to=value; thus seq(1,30), seq(from=1, to=30) and seq(to=30, from=1) are all the same as 1:30. The next two arguments to seq() may be named by=value and length=value, which specify a step size and a length for the sequence respectively. If neither of these is given, the default by=1 is assumed.

For example

```
> seq(-5, 5, by=.2) -> s3
```

generates in s3 the vector c(-5.0, -4.8, -4.6, ..., 4.6, 4.8, 5.0).

```
R Console
> seq(-5, 0 by#.2)->s3
>s3
[1]-5.0 - 4.8 - 4.6 - 4.4 - 4.2 - 4.0 - 3.8 - 3.6 -3.4 -3.2 -3.0 -2.8 -2.6 -2.4 -2.2
[16] -2.0 -1.8 -1.6 -1.4 -1.2 -1.0 -0.8 -0.8 -0.6 -0.4 -0.2 0.0 0.2 0.4 0.6 0.8
[31] 1.0 1.2 1.4 1.6 1.8 2.0 1.8 2.0 2.2 2.4 2.6 2.8 3.0 3.2 3.4 3.6 3.8
[46] 4.0 4.2 4.4 4.6 4.8 5.0
>|
```

Similarly

```
> s4 <- seq(length=51, from=-5, by=.2)
```

We can generate a series of square roots by a command like

```
>sqrt(5:10)
```

```
> sqrt (5)
[1] 2.236068
> sqrt (5:10)
[1] 2.236068 2.449490 2.645751 2.828427 3.000000 3.162278
>|
```

A related function is rep() which can be used for replicating an object in various complicated ways. The simplest form is

```
> s5 <- rep(x=5, times=5)
```

which will put five copies of x end-to-end in s5. Another useful version is > s6 <- rep(x, each=5) which repeats each element of x five times before moving on to the next.

```
> s5 <-req(x-5), times=5)
> 25
[1] 5 5 5 5 5
>|
```

10. SCALARS FROM VECTORS.

Many functions summarize a data vector by producing a scalar from a vector, e.g.,

```
> sum(weight)
[1] 446
> length(weight)
[1] 6
> avg.weight <- mean(weight)
> avg.weight
[1] 74.33333
```

Quantiles can be computed using the quantile() function. IQR() computes the inter-quartile range.

```
> xquants <- quantile(x)
> xquants
```

```
R Console
> x <-rnorm (100)
> xquants <-quantile (x)
> xquants
-2.35449065 -0.61522700 0.07212228 0.64554498 2.22899007
> xqunats [4] - xqunats [2]
        75
1.260772
> 1.260772
[1]quantile (x, probe -c(0.2, 0.4, 0.6, 0.8)
-0.7398870 -0.2850785 0.2325715 0.7730473
>|
```

11. SQL

SQL stands for structured query language. It is one of the most widely used languages for extracting data from databases in traditional data warehouses and big data technologies. In order to demonstrate the basics of SQL we will be working with examples. In order to focus on the language itself, we will be using SQL inside R. In terms of writing SQL code this is exactly as would be done in a database.

The core of SQL are three statements: SELECT, FROM and WHERE. The following examples make use of the most common use cases of SQL. Navigate to the folder **bda/part2/SQL_**

introduction and open the **SQL_introduction.Rproj** file. Then open the 01_select.R script. In order to write SQL code in R we need to install the **sqldf** package as demonstrated in the following code.

```
# Install the sqldf package
install.packages('sqldf')
# load the library
library('sqldf')
library(nycflights13)
# We will be working with the fligths dataset in order to
introduce SQL
# Let's take a look at the table
str(flights)
# Classes 'tbl_d', 'tbl' and 'data.frame': 336776 obs. of 16
variables:
# $ year      : int  2013 2013 2013 2013 2013 2013 2013 2013
2013 2013 ...
# $ month     : int  1 1 1 1 1 1 1 1 1 1 ...
# $ day       : int  1 1 1 1 1 1 1 1 1 1 ...
# $ dep_time : int  517 533 542 544 554 554 555 557 557 558 ...
# $ dep_delay: num  2 4 2 -1 -6 -4 -5 -3 -3 -2 ...
# $ arr_time : int  830 850 923 1004 812 740 913 709 838 753 ...
# $ arr_delay: num  11 20 33 -18 -25 12 19 -14 -8 8 ...
# $ carrier   : chr  "UA" "UA" "AA" "B6" ...
# $ tailnum   : chr  "N14228" "N24211" "N619AA" "N804JB" ...
# $ flight   : int 1545 1714 1141 725 461 1696 507 5708 79 301...
# $ origin    : chr  "EWR" "LGA" "JFK" "JFK" ...
# $ dest      : chr  "IAH" "IAH" "MIA" "BQN" ...
# $ air_time : num  227 227 160 183 116 150 158 53 140 138 ...
# $ distance : num  1400 1416 1089 1576 762 ...
# $ hour      : num  5 5 5 5 5 5 5 5 5 5 ...
# $ minute    : num  17 33 42 44 54 54 55 57 57 58 ...
The select statement is used to retrieve columns from tables
and do calculations on them. The simplest SELECT statement is
demonstrated in ej1. We can also create new variables as shown in
ej2.
### SELECT statement
ej1 = sqldf("
```

```
SELECT
  dep_time
  ,dep_delay
  ,arr_time
  ,carrier
  ,tailnum
  FROM
  flights
")
head(ej1)
  #     dep_time    dep_delay    arr_time    carrier tailnum
 # 1      517         2      830        UA           N14228
 # 2      533         4      850        UA           N24211
 # 3      542         2      923        AA           N619AA
 # 4      544        -1     1004        B6           N804JB
 # 5      554        -6      812        DL           N668DN
 # 6      554        -4      740        UA           N39463
# In R we can use SQL with the sqldf function. It works exactly
the same as in
a database
# The data.frame (in this case flights) represents the table we
are querying
and goes in the FROM statement
# We can also compute new variables in the select statement
using the syntax:
# old_variables as new_variable
ej2 = sqldf("
  SELECT
  arr_delay - dep_delay as gain,
  carrier
  FROM
  flights
")
ej2[1:5, ]
#    gain   carrier
```

```
# 1    9    UA
# 2   16    UA
# 3   31    AA
# 4  -17    B6
# 5  -19    DL
```

One of the most common used features of SQL is the group by statement. This allows to compute a numeric value for different groups of another variable. Open the script 02_group_by.R.

```
### GROUP BY
# Computing the average
ej3 = sqldf("
  SELECT
  avg(arr_delay) as mean_arr_delay,
  avg(dep_delay) as mean_dep_delay,
  carrier
  FROM
  flights
  GROUP BY
  carrier
")
         #    mean_arr_delay   mean_dep_delay carrier
       # 1      7.3796692       16.725769       9E
       # 2      0.3642909        8.586016       AA
       # 3     -9.9308886        5.804775       AS
       # 4      9.4579733       13.022522       B6
       # 5      1.6443409        9.264505       DL
       # 6     15.7964311       19.955390       EV
       # 7     21.9207048       20.215543       F9
       # 8     20.1159055       18.726075       FL
       # 9     -6.9152047        4.900585       HA
       # 10    10.7747334       10.552041       MQ
       # 11    11.9310345       12.586207       OO
       # 12     3.5580111       12.106073       UA
       # 13     2.1295951        3.782418       US
       # 14     1.7644644       12.869421       VX
       # 15     9.6491199       17.711744       WN
       # 16    15.5569853       18.996330       YV
```

12. CHARTS AND GRAPHS

The first approach to analyzing data is to visually analyze it. The objectives at doing this are normally finding relations between variables and univariate descriptions of the variables. We can divide these strategies as :

- Univariate analysis
- Multivariate analysis

12.1 Univariate Graphical Methods

Univariate is a statistical term. In practice, it means we want to analyze a variable independently from the rest of the data. The plots that allow to do this efficiently are –

13. BOX-PLOTS

Box-Plots are normally used to compare distributions. It is a great way to visually inspect if there are differences between distributions. We can see if there are differences between the price of diamonds for different cut.

```
   # We will be using the ggplot2 library for plotting
   library(ggplot2)
   data("diamonds")
   # We will be using the diamonds dataset to analyze distributions
of numeric variables
   head(diamonds)
 #   carat cut        color clarity depth table price   x    y    z
# 1  0.23  Ideal        E     SI2    61.5   55    326  3.95 3.98 2.43
# 2  0.21  Premium      E     SI1    59.8   61    326  3.89 3.84 2.31
# 3  0.23  Good         E     VS1    56.9   65    327  4.05 4.07 2.31
# 4  0.29  Premium      I     VS2    62.4   58    334  4.20 4.23 2.63
# 5  0.31  Good         J     SI2    63.3   58    335  4.34 4.35 2.75
# 6  0.24  Very Good    J    VVS2    62.8   57    336  3.94 3.96 2.48

   ### Box-Plots
   p = ggplot(diamonds, aes(x = cut, y = price, fill = cut)) +
     geom_box-plot() +
     theme_bw()
   print(p)
```

We can see in the plot there are differences in the distribution of diamonds price in different types of cut.

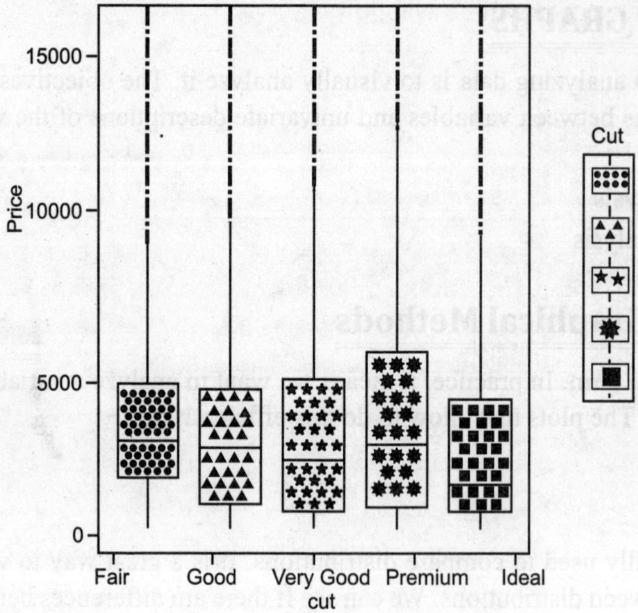

13. HISTOGRAMS

```
source('01_box_plots.R')
# We can plot histograms for each level of the cut factor
variable using
facet_grid
p = ggplot(diamonds, aes(x = price, fill = cut)) +
  geom_histogram() +
  facet_grid(cut ~ .) +
  theme_bw()
p
# the previous plot doesn't allow to visuallize correctly the
data because of
the differences in scale
# we can turn this off using the scales argument of facet_grid
p = ggplot(diamonds, aes(x = price, fill = cut)) +
  geom_histogram() +
  facet_grid(cut ~ ., scales = 'free') +
  theme_bw()
p
png('02_histogram_diamonds_cut.png')
print(p)
dev.off()
```

The output of the above code will be as follows –

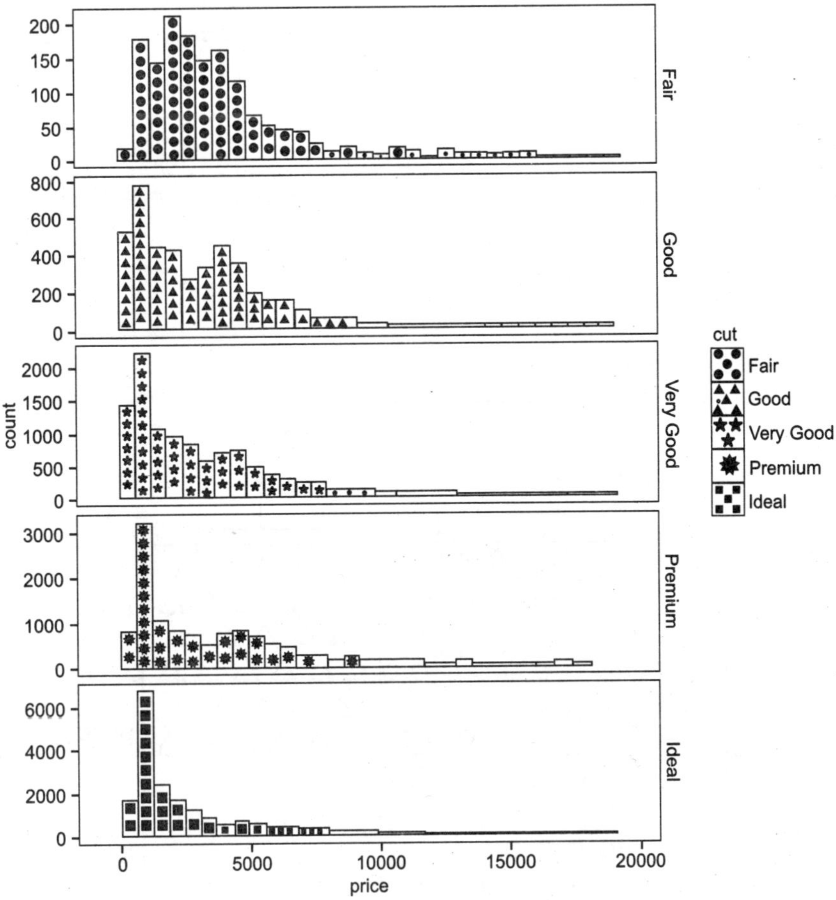

14. MULTIVARIATE GRAPHICAL METHODS

Multivariate graphical methods in exploratory data analysis have the objective of finding relationships among different variables. There are two ways to accomplish this that are commonly used: plotting a correlation matrix of numeric variables or simply plotting the raw data as a matrix of scatter plots.

In order to demonstrate this, we will use the diamonds dataset. To follow the code, open the script **bda/part2/charts/03_multivariate_analysis.R.**

```
library(ggplot2)
data(diamonds)
# Correlation matrix plots
keep_vars = c('carat', 'depth', 'price', 'table')
df = diamonds[, keep_vars]
# compute the correlation matrix
```

```
M_cor = cor(df)
     #          carat       depth        price       table
  # carat 1.00000000  0.02822431  0.9215913   0.1816175
  # depth 0.02822431  1.00000000  -0.0106474  -0.2957785
  # price 0.92159130  -0.01064740 1.0000000   0.1271339
  # table 0.18161755  -0.29577852 0.1271339   1.0000000
# plots
heat-map(M_cor)
```

The code will produce the following output –

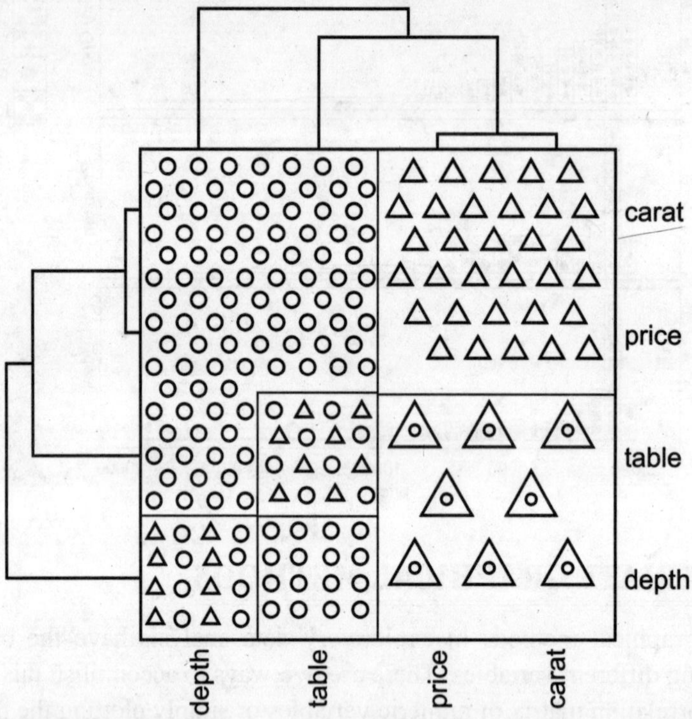

This is a summary, it tells us that there is a strong correlation between price and caret, and not much among the other variables.

A correlation matrix can be useful when we have a large number of variables in which case plotting the raw data would not be practical. As mentioned, it is possible to show the raw data also –

```
library(GGally)
ggpairs(df)
```

We can see in the plot that the results displayed in the heat-map are confirmed, there is a 0.922 correlation between the price and carat variables.

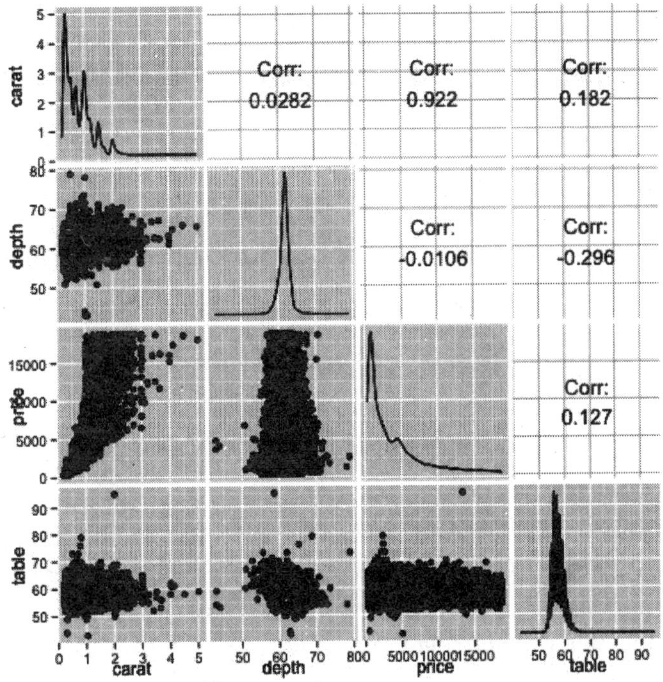

It is possible to visualize this relationship in the price-carat scatterplot located in the (3, 1) index of the scatterplot matrix.

A data sample is called **qualitative**, also known as **categorical**, if its values belong to a collection of known defined non-overlapping classes. Common examples include student letter grade (A, B, C, D or F), commercial bond rating (AAA, AAB, ...) and consumer clothing shoe sizes (1, 2, 3, ...).

The **frequency distribution** of a data variable is a summary of the data occurrence in a collection of non-overlapping categories.

Quantitative data, also known as **continuous** data, consists of numeric data that support arithmetic operations.

15. QUARTILE

There are several **quartiles** of an observation variable. The **first quartile**, or **lower quartile**, is the value that cuts off the first 25% of the data when it is sorted in ascending order. The **second quartile**, or **median**, is the value that cuts off the first 50%. The **third quartile**, or **upper quartile**, is the value that cuts off the first 75% Percentile

The nth **percentile** of an observation variable is the value that cuts off the first n percent of the data values when it is sorted in ascending order.

Interquartile Range

The **interquartile range** of an observation variable is the difference of its upper and lower quartiles. It is a measure of how far apart the middle portion of data spreads in value.

Interquartile Range = Upper Quartile – Lower Quartile

16. VARIANCE

The **variance** is a numerical measure of how the data values is dispersed around the mean. In particular, the **sample variance** is defined as:

$$s^2 = \frac{1}{n-1}\sum_{i=1}^{N}(x_i - \bar{x})^2$$

Similarly, the **population variance** is defined in terms of the population mean μ and population size N:

$$\sigma^2 = \frac{1}{N}\sum_{i=1}^{N}(x_i - \mu)^2$$

18. COVARIANCE

The **covariance** of two variables x and y in a data set measures how the two are linearly related. A positive covariance would indicate a positive linear relationship between the variables, and a negative covariance would indicate the opposite.

The **sample covariance** is defined in terms of the sample means as:

$$s_{xy} = \frac{1}{n-y}\sum_{i=1}^{N}(x_i - \bar{x})(y_i - \bar{y})$$

Similarly, the **population covariance** is defined in terms of the population mean μx, μy as:

$$\sigma_{xy} = \frac{1}{N}\sum_{i=1}^{N}(x_i - \bar{x})(y_i - \mu_y)$$

19. CORRELATION COEFFICIENT

The **correlation coefficient** of two variables in a data set equals to their covariance divided by the product of their individual standard deviations. It is a normalized measurement of how the two are linearly related.

Formally, the **sample correlation coefficient** is defined by the following formula, where s_x and s_y are the sample standard deviations, and s_{xy} is the sample covariance.

$$r_{xy} = \frac{s_{xy}}{\vartheta_x \vartheta_y}$$

Similarly, the **population correlation coefficient** is defined as follows, where σ_x and σ_y are the population standard deviations, and σ_{xy} is the population covariance.

$$\rho_{xy} = \text{``}\frac{\sigma_{xy}}{\sigma_x \sigma_y}$$

If the correlation coefficient is close to 1, it would indicate that the variables are positively linearly related and the scatter plot falls almost along a straight line with positive slope. For -1, it indicates that the variables are negatively linearly related and the scatter plot almost falls along a straight line with negative slope. And for zero, it would indicate a weak linear relationship between the variables.

20. SKEWNESS

The **skewness** of a data population is defined by the following formula, where μ2 and μ3 are the second and third central moments.

$$\gamma_1 = \mu_3/\mu_2^{3/2}$$

Intuitively, the skewness is a measure of symmetry. As a rule, negative skewness indicates that the mean of the data values is less than the median, and the data distribution is *left-skewed.* Positive skewness would indicate that the mean of the data values is larger than the median, and the data distribution is *right-skewed.*

21. KURTOSIS

The **kurtosis** of a univariate population is defined by the following formula, where μ_2 and μ_4 are respectively the second and fourth central moments.

$$\gamma_2 = \mu_4/\mu_2^{3/2} - 3$$

Intuitively, the *kurtosis* describes the *tail shape* of the data distribution. The normal distribution has zero kurtosis and thus the standard tail shape. It is said to be **mesokurtic**. Negative kurtosis would indicate a *thin-tailed* data distribution, and is said to be *platykurtic*. Positive kurtosis would indicate a *fat-tailed* distribution, and is said to be **leptokurtic**.

22. PROBABILITY DISTRIBUTIONS

A **probability distribution** describes how the values of a random variable is distributed. For example, the collection of all possible outcomes of a sequence of coin tossing is known to follow the binomial distribution. Whereas the means of sufficiently large samples of a data population are known to resemble the normal distribution. Since the characteristics of these theoretical distributions are well understood, they can be used to make statistical inferences on the entire data population as a whole.

In the following example, effort shall be to demonstrate how to compute a few well-known probability distributions that occurs frequently in statistical study.

1. Binomial Distribution
2. Poisson Distribution
3. Continuous Uniform Distribution
4. Exponential Distribution
5. Normal Distribution
6. Chi-squared Distribution
7. Student t Distribution

8. F Distribution
9. Binomial Distribution

23. BINOMIAL DISTRIBUTION

The **binomial distribution** is a discrete probability distribution. It describes the outcome of *n* independent trials in an experiment. Each trial is assumed to have only two outcomes, either success or failure. If the probability of a successful trial is *p*, then the probability of having *x* successful outcomes in an experiment of *n* independent trials is as follows.

$$f(x) = \binom{n}{x} p^x (1-p)^{(n-x)} \quad where\ x = 0, 1, 2, \ldots, n$$

Exercise 1: Suppose there are twelve multiple choice questions in an English class quiz. Each question has five possible answers, and only one of them is correct. Find the probability of having four or less correct answers if a student attempts to answer every question at random.

Solution: Since only one out of five possible answers is correct, the probability of answering a question correctly by random is 1/5=0.2. We can find the probability of having exactly 4 correct answers by random attempts as follows.

```
> dbinom(4, size=12, prob=0.2)
[1] 0.1329
```

To find the probability of having four or less correct answers by random attempts, we apply the function dbinom with x = 0,…,4.

```
> dbinom(0, size=12, prob=0.2) +
+ dbinom(1, size=12, prob=0.2) +
+ dbinom(2, size=12, prob=0.2) +
+ dbinom(3, size=12, prob=0.2) +
+ dbinom(4, size=12, prob=0.2)
[1] 0.9274
```

Alternatively, we can use the cumulative probability function for binomial distribution pbinom.

```
> pbinom(4, size=12, prob=0.2)
[1] 0.92744
```

Answer

The probability of four or less questions answered correctly by random in a twelve question multiple choice quiz is 92.7%.

24. POISSON DISTRIBUTION

The **Poisson distribution** is the probability distribution of independent event occurrences in an interval. If λ is the mean occurrence per interval, then the probability of having x occurrences within a given interval is:

$$f(x) = \frac{\lambda^x e^{-\lambda}}{x!} \quad \text{where } x = 0, 1, 2, 3, \ldots$$

Exercise 2: If there are twelve cars crossing a bridge per minute on average, find the probability of having seventeen or more cars crossing the bridge in a particular minute.

Solution: The probability of having *sixteen or less* cars crossing the bridge in a particular minute is given by the function ppois.

```
> ppois(16, lambda=12)    # lower tail
[1] 0.89871
```

Hence the probability of having seventeen or more cars crossing the bridge in a minute is in the upper tail of the probability density function.

```
> ppois(16, lambda=12, lower=FALSE)    # upper tail
[1] 0.10129
```

Answer

If there are twelve cars crossing a bridge per minute on average, the probability of having seventeen or more cars crossing the bridge in a particular minute is 10.1%.

25. CONTINUOUS UNIFORM DISTRIBUTION

The **continuous uniform distribution** is the probability distribution of random number selection from the continuous interval between a and b. Its density function is defined by the following.

$$f(x) = \begin{cases} \frac{1}{b-a} & \text{when } a \le x \le b \\ 0 & \text{when } x < a \text{ or } x > b \end{cases}$$

Here is a graph of the continuous uniform distribution with a = 1, b = 3.

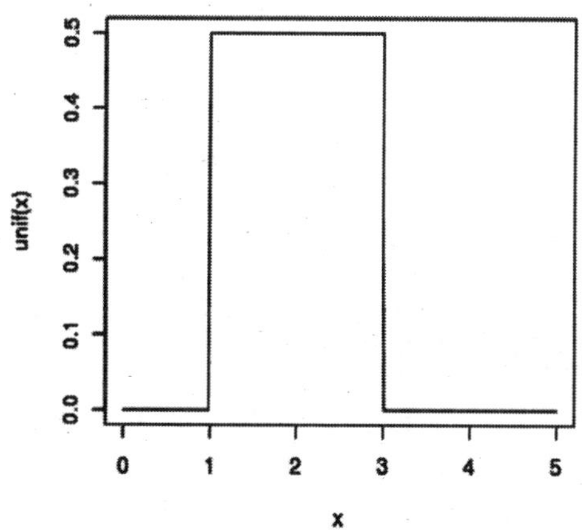

Exercise 3: Select ten random numbers between one and three.

Solution: We apply the generation function runif of the uniform distribution to generate ten random numbers between one and three.

```
> runif(10, min=1, max=3)
[1] 1.6121 1.2028 1.9306 2.4233 1.6874 1.1502 2.7068
[8] 1.4455 2.4122 2.2171
```

26. EXPONENTIAL DISTRIBUTION

The **exponential distribution** describes the arrival time of a randomly recurring independent event sequence. If μ is the mean waiting time for the next event recurrence, its probability density function is:

$$f(x) = \begin{cases} \frac{1}{\mu} e^{-x/\mu} & when\ a \geq 0 \\ 0 & when\ x < 0 \end{cases}$$

Here is a graph of the exponential distribution with μ = 1.

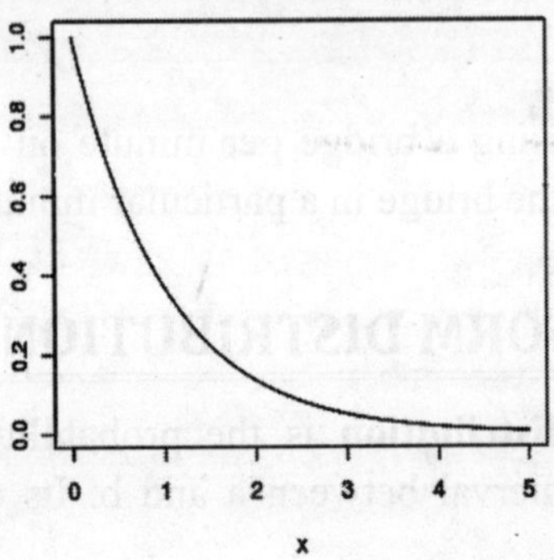

Exercise 4: Suppose the mean checkout time of a supermarket cashier is three minutes. Find the probability of a customer checkout being completed by the cashier in less than two minutes.

Solution: The checkout processing rate is equals to one divided by the mean checkout completion time. Hence the processing rate is 1/3 checkouts per minute. We then apply the function pexp of the exponential distribution with rate=1/3.

```
> pexp(2, rate=1/3)
[1] 0.48658
```

Answer

The probability of finishing a checkout in under two minutes by the cashier is 48.7%

27. NORMAL DISTRIBUTION

The **normal distribution** is defined by the following probability density function, where μ is the population mean and σ^2 is the variance.

$$f(x) = \frac{1}{\sigma\sqrt{2\pi}} e^{-(x-\mu)^2/2\sigma^2}$$

If a random variable X follows the normal distribution, then we write:

$$x \sim N(\mu, \sigma^2)$$

In particular, the normal distribution with $\mu = 0$ and $\sigma = 1$ is called the *standard normal distribution*, and is denoted as N(0,1). It can be graphed as follows.

In particular, the normal distribution with $\mu = 0$ and $\sigma = 1$ is called the *standard normal distribution*, and is denoted as $N(0,1)$. It can be graphed as follows.

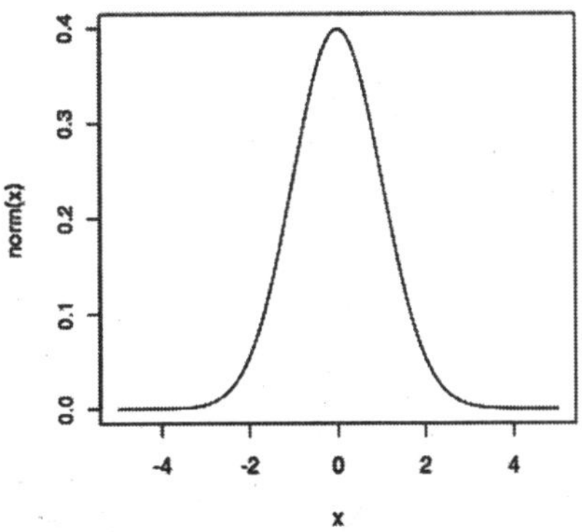

The normal distribution is important because of the **Central Limit Theorem**, which states that the population of all possible samples of size n from a population with mean μ and variance σ^2 approaches a normal distribution with mean μ and σ^2/n when n approaches infinity.

Exercise 5: Assume that the test scores of a college entrance exam fits a normal distribution. Furthermore, the mean test score is 72, and the standard deviation is 15.2. What is the percentage of students scoring 84 or more in the exam?

Solution: We apply the function pnorm of the normal distribution with mean 72 and standard deviation 15.2. Since we are looking for the percentage of students scoring higher than 84, we are interested in the *upper tail* of the normal distribution.

```
> pnorm(84, mean=72, sd=15.2, lower.tail=FALSE)
[1] 0.21492
```

Answer

The percentage of students scoring 84 or more in the college entrance exam is 21.5%.

28. CHI-SQUARED DISTRIBUTION

If $X_1, X_2, \ldots, X_m$ are m independent random variables having the standard normal distribution, then the following quantity follows a **Chi-Squared distribution** with *m degrees of freedom*. Its mean is m, and its variance is $2m$.

$$v = X_1^2 + X_2^2 + \ldots + X_m^2 \sim X_{(m)}^2$$

Here is a graph of the Chi-Squared distribution 7 degrees of freedom.

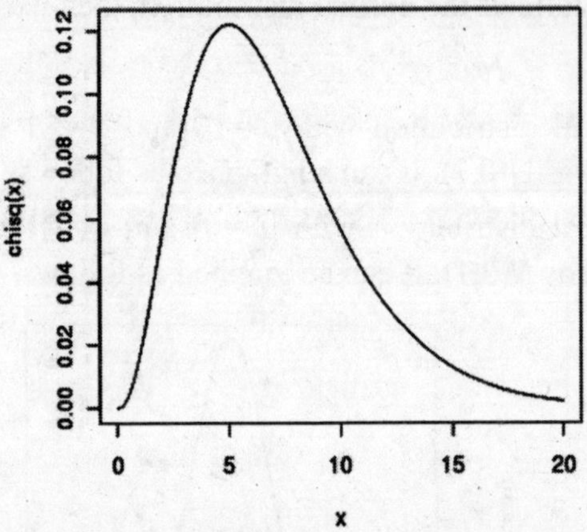

Exercise 6: Find the 95th percentile of the Chi-Squared distribution with 7 degrees of freedom.

Solution: We apply the quantile function qchisq of the Chi-Squared distribution against the decimal values 0.95.

```
> qchisq(.95, df=7)          # 7 degrees of freedom
[1] 14.067
```

Answer

The 95th percentile of the Chi-Squared distribution with 7 d egrees of freedom is 14.067.

29. STUDENT T DISTRIBUTION

Assume that a random variable Z has the standard normal distribution, and another random variable V has the Chi-Squared distribution with m degrees of freedom. Assume further that Z and V are independent, then the following quantity follows a Student t distribution with m degrees of freedom.

$$t = \frac{Z}{\sqrt{V/m}} \sim t_{(m)}$$

Here is a graph of the Student t distribution with 5 degrees of freedom.

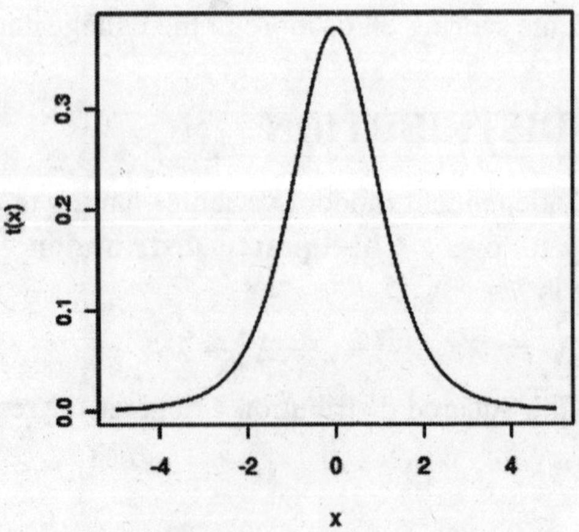

Exercise 7: Find the 2.5th and 97.5th percentiles of the Student t distribution with 5 degrees of freedom.

Solution: We apply the quantile function qt of the Student t distribution against the decimal values 0.025 and 0.975.

```
> qt(c(.025, .975), df=5)    # 5 degrees of freedom
[1] -2.5706  2.5706
```

Answer

The 2.5th and 97.5th percentiles of the Student t distribution with 5 degrees of freedom are -2.5706 and 2.5706 respectively.